THE TRIAL OF THE GENERALS

Also published as a companion to this book:

A Mass For Jesse James - A Journey through 1980's Ireland

Fintan O'Toole

THE TRIAL OF THE GENERALS

SELECTED JOURNALISM 1980 - 1990

COLM TÓIBÍN

Raven Arts Press/Dublin

The Trial of the Generals
is first published in 1990 by
The Raven Arts Press
P.O.Box 1430
Finglas
Dublin 11
Ireland

ISBN 1 85186 081 9

Designed by Rapid Productions, cover photo by Colm Henry,
printed and bound in Ireland by Colour Books Ltd., Baldoyle.

CONTENTS

For Andy Hinds

I.
DAYS OF MIRACLES AND WONDER

Ireland at the World Cup

Ireland v Holland

It was Thursday and everybody realised that if we lost tonight, it would be a nightmare.

On Sunday when Ireland played Egypt I had watched that extraordinary energy which comes from a crowd, I had seen it surge ten minutes before the end in a huge effort of voice and will. *Come on, Ireland, come on.* It grew desperate and then it petered out.

I watched the stadium clear after the match, and I walked into town with the others, nobody talking much, everyone keeping their disappointment to themselves with the prospect of a long, dull evening ahead, with not much chance of a drink until midnight. All the beautiful energy gone.

Just ten days before this we had travelled to the stadium in Cagliari, we had gone through the elaborate system of searching and counter-searching the police had organised. They made no distinction between us and the English fans; we were all hooligans to them. In the hour before the match, as we filled the terraces, however, the police relaxed, and began to laugh at the beat of the bodhrans which reverberated throughout the stadium.

Within ten minutes all our nightmares had come true: England scored, and the England fans went wild. We pointed at them and sang "You only sing when you're winning". Playing England was special: beating England would be more important than simply winning. If this was Holland or Egypt, it would be good to win as well, but not so terrible to lose.

So we were ready when our goal came in the second half. It was our turn to go ape, and they were stunned and silent, as we knew they would be. We had waited, we had sung our hearts out, and here it was. And from then on there was only the counting of seconds, the cheering and the singing, and the hope that we could hold it at a draw. "You're not singing any more," the Irish fans taunted the English fans, and it was true.

7

When the match was over, the Irish fans sang: "We know you don't believe us, but we're going to win the World Cup."

The Irish fans left the stadium in a state of elation and exhiliration, embracing the police, posing for photographs with members of the army, giving them caps and scarves to take home. Later, I saw a policeman carrying a large, inflated plastic shamrock.

Beating England that night in Cagliari, in Ireland's first World Cup match, what was it like? It was great, it was wonderful, even if it was only a draw.

And once more now in Palermo it wasn't going to be just about football, it wasn't going to be about speed or skill, tactics or training. Once more we were going to let our football team stand for our fate in some way. Restore our confidence, fill us with pride. Or, on the other hand, let us down, let us know that we're out of our league.

Ireland, so vulnerable now, so susceptible, so ready for heroes. Ireland, puzzled by the post-Christian universe, wounded by unemployment and emigration. Ireland suddenly had something to believe in. And this was our last chance tonight, this was it.

Like everybody else I lived in terror of walking back into Palermo later not knowing what to say to the person beside me, as it sunk in that we had conned ourselves by letting sport stand for more than it should, for letting the great myth-making capacities of a game have power over us.

It had been a strange week in Palermo. After the draw of Sunday in the Egypt match the Irish fans congregated in the bars along the Via Belmonte.

At midnight they started to drink, by one o'clock they had started to sing, by two there was several loud singing sessions going on, by three the police were trying to get everyone to go home, and by four they were succeeding.

But the songs were all melancholy and low-key. There was no real enthusiasm. It was as though everyone was slowly recovering from a hangover. And soccer wasn't mentioned. There were no songs and slogans from the game. People were singing to forget the game.

On Tuesday night Italy beat Czechoslovakia and the whole of Palermo, it seemed, got into their cars and drove even faster and crazier around the city than normal.

They honked their horns and waved flags, big carloads of them, children and all. It was as though they'd won the World Cup.

This was a display of unrestrained joy. After an hour or so, when the crowd thinned out, the real business of the night got underway.

Everybody was now young and carefully dressed, and victory in sport opened up possibilities of sex: sexual allure and sexual encounter. There was no display of crude nationalism here, this was about body heat.

Now on Thursday as we went out to the stadium for the Dutch game we had more important things on our minds. Losing, for example. After all the hope, not to join the countries that didn't get through the first round. We had to win, or draw. It was going to be hard, we could only hope and cheer.

Night was coming down and there was a great echo of voices against the sheer wall of the mountain in the background.

Long before the game started you could feel the tension, rising now as the teams came out, you could sense the enthusiasm and the fear. Now we had to do it. This was the big one.

Three fellows with foam cowboy hats came and sat in front of us. They were shouting slogans even before they sat down. Jack Charlton came on the pitch looking casual, cool, betraying nothing, unlike the fans who were now in a frenzy of roaring as the game began.

Even in the first few minutes, I felt the old fear. I could see the Dutch refinement and finesse and I could see that we didn't have these things; not just the team, but us, all of us cheering, all of us on the stands, we, too, lacked what our team lacked, and this was going to make us lose.

The Dutch goal came like an electric shock. Immediately the Irish fans shouted "Ireland, Ireland", because you had to do something, you couldn't just sit there. But all around me over the next ten minutes, people wore a glazed look, they stopped being a group and became individuals.

Despite regular outbursts of cheering and support, there was a subdued atmosphere. This couldn't be happening.

And Ireland's terrible weakness became more and more apparent the more they put the pressure on. Our team could move the ball up the field, but they couldn't score. Each time they tried and failed.

And now the Dutch still seemed capable of scoring again. There was fear that they would move up the field, like a clean, beautifully smooth engine and do it again. Once or twice, it nearly happened. The three guys with the foam cowboy hats sat there watching, stunned, not moving an inch. You couldn't dare to hope.

In the last five minutes of the first half there were two half-hearted near Irish goals. The Irish flag, which said Veni Vidi Vici, had started to sag. At half time the Dutch fans could keep waving their flags. They were going to win.

There was now a great deal at stake for Ireland, which had given itself so completely to this experience, which had let soccer and the World Cup become such a part of national consciousness.

The first ten minutes of the second half were amazing. There were five opportunities for an Irish goal.

All around me there was excitement and despair. It couldn't be done; we just didn't have the skill. Ireland, the land of missed opportunities. We shook our heads in despair and then started to cheer again.

Each time now they took the ball up the field we looked at each other, or nudged each other, or cheered louder, now it could be done, now, and then no, not now. We didn't have it in us. We were out of our league.

With 20 minutes to go the crowd roared Ireland, Ireland. The energy was fierce, concentrated, there was still a will to win.

And then the goal came and we cheered and roared, as though we had always known that this goal would come, as though it was ours all along. Everything changed. The three men in foam cowboy hats went crazy. We had it. The Dutch had flair and creativity; we had power, force and we had put it to good use. Ireland, Ireland.

Now it was a matter of time. There was still a feeling that one pass could do it, the Dutch could score again, but this soon gave way to relief and joy and the knowledge that now in the last minutes they were only playing, it was only a game, whereas up to now it had been as important as life itself.

"Are You Watching Jimmy Hill" the fans sang, as they had sung under similar circumstances at the England match. This World Cup, if you forgot about the Egypt match, was giving Ireland value for money.

At the press conference afterwards Jack Charlton said that the fans could give Palermo one of the best parties in its history. They did just that. The natives couldn't get over the two sides fraternising so freely and warmly, singing each other's songs, trying out each other's languages.

The Via Belmonte was overflowing with joy and beer. The songs now were not the morose songs sung on Sunday night, the songs were all about soccer, the songs were mixed with slogans. Fans moved from bar to bar.

As after the England match I hung around the streets with people I didn't know. There was a special warmth in Palermo on Thursday night, as there had been in Cagliari after the England match.

At half past three the bars were still serving sandwiches and the police were trying to stop the singing so the neighbours could get to sleep.

The plans for Genoa were already made. The Dutch were wearing Irish hats, and the Irish were Dutchmen in disguise.

Ireland was on the road again, on its way somewhere, detedmined to have a good time.

All the fear and terror of the match was over. At four o'clock in the morning the fans were still singing.

Ireland v. Romania

This was the week when the yuppies came out to play. This was the week when the boys with the big salaries flew out for the day to capture and take home a small slice of the World Cup experience, and promised, when we won, to fly out once more to Rome and maybe, with the help of God, to Naples.

This was the week when the Irish crowd in the square in Genoa chanted: "If you've been to three matches, clap your hands," as others, raw looking and just off the plane, explained that they had arrived without as much as outline planning permission from the missus, and they were going to stay until the bitter end, at least Rome, and maybe, and you'd never know, Naples. In the meantime, they were going to ring home.

This was the week when the accents of Malahide and Dun Laoghaire could be heard in the bars, when you could meet a travel agent and he could tell you that every single yuppie in Galway had come out on a plane that day and if the plane crashed, then there would be no more yuppies in Galway.

Fellas, he said, were prepared to make the ultimate sacrifice and give up the job just to be here, just for this great buzz, but most of them, on the other hand, were going back home straight after the match to take their place once more among the yuppies of Galway.

This was the week when fans coming to Italy brought their tennis racquets with them, and managed a game in their posh hotels in the afternoon before the match.

These are, after all, the days of miracles and wonder. Last Sunday night in Genoa, for example, and the next night were a cross between a classic Fellini film and a Fleadh Ceoil.

The Irish fans took to the fountains in the main square. They didn't just dive in, some wearing underpants, others fully clothed, they had themselves hoisted up into the upper reaches of the fountain where no man had yet set foot, and they raised the Irish flag and waved it and generally made a great show of themselves while the rest of us, landlubbers, waved from down below and desperately tried to get more drink from the bars around the square, who ran out of beer, and sold us bottles of wine instead, which we drank from the neck.

Everywhere you moved that night you met people you knew, people you had met from the long, hard World Cup trail. And everybody had a story to tell, they had slept in stations, or been incredibly lucky and booked a train ticket from Palermo to Genoa and slept all the way, or got stuck in Rome with the train strike and decided to go to the airport and fly up, to hell with the expense.

It was a night of shouting and drinking and stories. This was Ireland's lost generation having one of its last hurrahs. By the time the next games came round some of these guys would be married, settled in England, or Europe, too busy to take three weeks off to follow their team across Europe.

It was remarkable when people told their stories: of their battle to get from one island to another, then find accommodation and then secure tickets, and then have a ball, it was remarkable how organised they all were, how cool, how they seemed to have the world sussed.

This is the generation who left school here when there were no jobs in Ireland anymore, when you had to go off on your own to England, or Europe and find things out for yourself.

And all these new skills could now be put to good use in finding a place for the night. All the skills which an emigrant community knows so well could be put to good use now in finding tickets against all the odds. These guys had found jobs in foreign countries, places to live, now this world Cup thing was no problem to them.

Take the Irish fans in Palermo, for example. They took one look at the city and realised that the possibilities of having serious crack were low. And then word spread, as it only can in an emigrant community, that there was a place called Cefalu about fifty kilometres from the city with a good train service.

It was cheap, and it was used to tourists and their drinking habits, and this is where the Irish fans went, and this is where they assembled every night in the main square, to drink beer, sing their hearts out and mingle with the Italians and the Dutch and wave the Irish flag.

Anyone who went there said that it was mighty, the Italians and the Irish loved each other, and even the Dutch, God help them, tried to join in by singing "For He's A Jolly Good Fellow" every so often in between bouts of the Irish fans singing "The Wild Rover" and "There's Only One Schillaci".

12

The wild Irish. The blokes who found jobs for themselves in Ireland against all the odds, or left, but felt no bitterness in their hearts against the country they would come to know less and less about as the years went by. They still wanted to be part of it, and in Germany during the European Championships two years ago, they had nights beyond their belief, nights which will be fixed forever in their minds, nights when the complex fate of being Irish came into its own.

Now they were in Genoa on the night before the match, soon they would all travel to Rome clamouring for tickets.

There were problems about tickets here too and a shortage of places to stay, but there were still yuppies to jeer and more stories to tell. So many of them now had odd, black economy jobs that it was easy for them to take four weeks or five weeks off work without worry. Did I know how to get tickets for Rome, people kept asking, including the three Cork students who had driven from Cork to Palermo in a Commer van. No one, at this stage, was even thinking about Naples.

The first time I heard the word Naples was over lunch on the day of the Romania match. An Irishman with his family had driven down from his villa in Nice (if you don't mind) and they would all be driving back after the match. He wouldn't be able to go to Rome, he said, but Naples now, he grinned, he fancied a trip to Naples. What did anyone think of our chances? People laughed nervously. Let's win the Romanian match first.

There was a terrible optimism among the fans that evening, but as soon as the game started all our feelings that this would be a walk-over dissolved real, real fast. It was the old story: our bullish energy (so like ourselves in many ways, full of enthusiasm and force) and their finesse and sheer style. It was Irish set dancing versus classical ballet.

The man beside me, whom I now had come to know as we had shared the agonies of a number of matches, looked at me grimly. He didn't need to speak. His look said that this was dangerous, that these players had real class. Suddenly, I thought once more that we were going to lose. And that's when the match became really exciting.

The noise was growing louder and more forceful as the game went on.

A few times in the second half we nearly scored, we nearly did it, and the whole place held its breath, already making plans for Rome, but it didn't happen, and the clapping and shouting grew once more. We needed it. The man beside me looked at me a few more times:

that grave look, he was still worried and tense, but as the game came to an end it still seemed possible that we could do it.

But it could still elude us, as at some stage, here or in Rome, or in Naples, it would have to happen. That second when all that sleeping in stations, queueing for tickets and singing our hearts out, in one second it could go, and we would have to pack our bags. There was no score.

Naples, indeed.

Along the row of seats we got to know each other, and when the penalties began we stayed close together as though we were in a war trench rather than a football match. We glanced at each other in worry and terror as each kick was taken.

The drama of earlier was now gone, the heroism of the boys in green was not something that we could cheer for, or enjoy now. This was music for the solo cello, this was single combat, this was the death penalty, this was abject loneliness. This was agony.

How could you concentrate when so much was at stake? How could you risk being the man who lost the World Cup for Ireland?

When David O'Leary did it, the man beside me took a jump at me, and started to hit me wildly with the palm of his hand on the back. He buried his face in my shirt and started to sob.

I took a lift into town with the Cork students and their Commer van. We hooted our horn and waved our flag at the fans now trying to make it into town for the Italian match on television. One of those we passed, they said, owned one of the biggest shops in Cork.

It was, as Jack Charlton said it would be, a great party. The Italians, who had won their match too, took to the streets, like they were going to storm the Bastille. The police had to turn off the fountain in the main square for fear that someone would drown. Cars circled the city, waving flags, Italians shouting for joy. The Irish fans took over the bars, and toured the streets, bottles in their hands, and big, loud smiles on their faces.

It was as good, they said, as a night in Germany, as any of the nights in Cefalu. To see the Italians so happy, and the bars so full and the night so warm and the police so tolerant. And now to make plans for the next move - Rome. This was happiness and sheer bliss. And then the question, still nervous, do you think we'll make it to Naples?

And where to sleep? That night in Genoa many simply lay down on the ground and fell asleep where they were. There would be enough time for sleeping in beds, a whole lifetime. And in the morning they would set off for Rome.

We were outnumbered, that much was clear. But somehow, it wasn't important, we had come a long way.

The Italian fans were wonderful, their roars of support came in huge waves. But that didn't matter either - they had been doing this for years - it was in their blood. We had just started.

Before the match, we watched the dying, deeply exciting minutes of the Argentina-Yugoslavia match. It brought it all back: those moments of Irish agony in Genoa, and it made what we were about to face now more immediate, more dear, more full of excitement.

We came prepared not simply to be out-numbered but ready, as well, to be out-classed. Our rough and ready tactics would look blunt and crude against the expected display of subtlety and skill. We were ready to lose, the odds were against us.

But in the first ten minutes, our players took control. We were so proud in the stadium as they dominated the ball, put the fear of God into the supporters around us, who had been so cocky before the game. There were things we did which we had never done before. It was as though new skills as well as boundless energy had come our way. Maybe it was the Pope's blessing.

In other words me and the man beside me thought that we were going to win!

We couldn't believe it, but we thought it. We did not sit back, we sat forward, we never grew smug but remained tense and excited. We shouted our heads off whenever we could.

We thought it could be done. And a few times in the first half it nearly was done. Even if we didn't win, we said, in those few moments when you could say something, even if we didn't win, we put up a great display of courage under pressure.

But we still thought that it could be done.

When the Italians scored, we nearly died. We sat down forlorn while the Italians all around us jumped for joy. But we didn't think it was the end. We thought we were in with a chance, and this made the rest of the game so tense, so difficult to watch and so full of opportunities to hope, hope, hope.

We could have scored, too, that goal could have been ours. Our language in the stadium moved from the conditional perfect to the imperative mood. Could have, would have. Come on, come on.

The Italian fans, in their great delight, began to play, making human waves around the stadium, but we were too busy watching the game to enjoy this too much. Watching and waiting. It could happen. "Come on you boys in green", could be heard clearly now;

the supporters were still ready for it. The game was still fast. In the seventh minute of the second half we almost scored a goal. We were unlucky, as they had been lucky. The Italian fans in front of us even admitted that they had luck on their side. We needed luck.

It could happen at any moment, there was no slackening. Both sides wanted to win. Now, we had everything to lose because losing is lousy when it happens, no matter how great the odds.

The Italians were starting to dominate the second half. A free kick by Staunton was crucial, the man beside me said, but this was only because everything was crucial.

We could have scored. It could have been done. Now there were two corner throws. The Italians understood how close it was, and their cheering grew louder. Each pass now was crucial. We kept them under pressure. Please, come on score.

There were twenty minutes left. We were still in the game. It was hard not to keep thinking how easy a goal comes, how suddenly, what a shock it is when it happens, how suddenly everything changes. It could happen now, wait, now. Oh... We could still do it. We could beat the Italians.

There were seven minutes to go. We were outnumbered in the stadium and now it suddenly mattered. We looked around at them, they could shout us down, and they had beaten us. The man beside me still thought that it could be done. But I didn't.

We played so well, even to the end, right to the end.

We were, as Jackie Charlton said at the press conference afterwards, "disappointed and proud", because our team, as one of the Italian journalists said at the same conference, had "played like champions" and given one of the best teams in the world a run for their money and given us value for ours.

It was a great night for Ireland.

We were so close and we had come so far. If we had to lose, then this was the way to go. It was a great match.

The Sunday Independent, June/July 1990

II.
THE TRIAL OF
THE GENERALS

*Early in 1985, a group of Argentinian military personnel, including
General Galtieri who started the Falklands War, were put on trial
in Buenos Aires for their involvement in the torture and
disappearance of thousands of people.*

They always came at night like in the movies. Day after day new
witnesses tell of the sound of cars pulling up outside houses and
loud bangs at the door with voices shouting: "Open up, open up'. In
the last week of September 1976 they went after the Union of
Secondary School Students who had sought a lowering in transport
fares. Most of the kids they took in have never been seen since;
most of them are dead. The only information we have about them
comes from fellow prisoners who have survived.

Pablo Diaz survived. At four in the morning they came for him.
He was eighteen and had been involved in the campaign for cheaper
fares. His brother answered the door; the men said they were from
the army, although they wore no uniforms. They brought all the
family into the living room and made them lie face-down on the
floor; upstairs they found a list of names and demanded to know
who were the people on the list. Pablo Diaz's sister told them they
were the children she taught in primary school. They stole a camera,
some jewellery, some clothes. They took Pablo Diaz away with
them. For three months the family heard nothing of him.

In February 1977 the family got news of Pablo Diaz from an
anonymous caller and they went to see an army general who told
them that he had been arrested while distributing pamphlets in the
street. The mother said he had been taken from the house at four in
the morning. The general said no, that he was arrested while
distributing pamphlets in the street. The mother repeated that this
was not true. The general had nothing more to say.

"Our ages ranged between fourteen and eighteen", Pablo Diaz
told the court. "We had our eyes covered and our hands tied all the
time. But sometimes we could untie ourselves and try and look
around. There were an equal number of boys and girls. The only

17

clothes we wore were the rags of our underwear. Some of the girls were almost naked".

The torturers always wanted to know names of friends and associates from school who might know something about subversion. They told him they had a lie detector. "I told them it was okay, they could use it. I thought it was one of those things we saw in the movies where a dial moves when you tell a lie".

It wasn't a lie detector; it was an electric cattle prod. They stripped him and tied him down. They turned on the current and he could smell himself burning, it was like the smell of meat burning, he said. They used the prod on his genitals, his lips; they forced his mouth open and they used the prod on his gums.

When you are being tortured you clench your fists; one day they told him that when he was ready to give names he was to open his hands and they would turn off the current. That day the torture was so bad that he kept on clenching and unclenching his fists

They turned the current off and asked for names. He said he had no names. They asked him why he had unclenched his fists. They said he was just playing with them. "We're going to teach you", one of them said. He told another to go and get a wrench. When he brought the wrench they used it to pull out a nail from one of Pablo Diaz's feet. The pain was so excruciating that he kept asking them to kill him, just kill him.

For three months the members of the Union of Secondary School Students who had sought a travel concession were held. Their hands were tied behind their backs, the rope was attached to a noose around their necks so that if they tried to move their hands the noose would tighten. They were all blindfolded. They were tortured almost every day. For the first week they were given no food; after that rations were meagre. Pablo Diaz cried so much that his blindfold began to rot; his eyes became infected; he kept telling the guards that he was going blind, that if they could just take off the blindfold and put on a clean one he would be okay. They ignored him, however, and over the next couple of months his eyesight deteriorated until he was completely blind. Later a prison doctor washed his eyes with alcohol and slowly partial sight was restored.

The cells were damp and cold. Pablo Diaz tried to make contact with his fellow students and they tried to organise singing competitions to keep their spirits up but it was difficult as, in Pablo Diaz's words, "there had grown a relationship between the silence, the solitude and the torture". Through the wall he began to form a friendship with a girl named Claudia, who was later murdered like the rest of them. Slowly he fell in love with her, even though he had never seen her. He would tell her that when they got out that they would become *novios*, she would be his girlfriend. One day a guard took his blindfold off and let him into her cell. He told the court that she said to him: "thanks for the strength you have given me but please don't touch me. We can never have a relationship. Don't touch me because during the torture they raped me. They raped me in front and behind".

They told Pablo Diaz they were going to shoot him, they left his blindfold on and his hands tied, he could feel the gun against his head; others in the room to be shot too, were screaming, but he remained still. "It is just a second but this second will stay in my memory for ever. A soldier fired the gun and I stayed there waiting for the pain and blood to appear..." He heard voices but still wasn't sure whether he was alive or dead.

After three months in this concentration camp called Banfield, he was officially charged with distributing pamphlets in the street and held for four years. He was one of the few secondary school students detained in September 1976 who ever saw the light of day again.

These are the figures. In 1973 nineteen people disappeared in Argentina and are presumed murdered by the security forces; in 1974 the figure went up to fifty; in 1975 it rose to 359; in 1976 the generals took over from Isabel Peron, 3,850 people were detained and never seen again; the following year, 1977, the figure was 2,845; in 1978 it went down to 955; in 1979 to 1,701; in 1980 to seventy eight; in 1981 to twenty; in 1982 to twelve; in 1983 to nine. We are thus talking about the murder of between eight and nine thousand people. The figures come from CONADEP, the independent body which was set up to monitor the disappearances. The figures are backed up by names, dates, and details. Most observers believe that the figures are conservative; some believe that they are very conservative.

It is impossible to tell how many were detained during this period and later released. Most people here accept 100,000 as a conservative figure. It is believed that half of this number was beaten or tortured. I have been told by several journalists who worked here during 1976 and 1977 that if you were taken in by the army or the police you had roughly a one in ten chance of being murdered. If, however, you were detained by the navy you had only a one in ten chance of getting out alive.

The trial of the nine generals and admirals who ran this country between the coup in March 1976 and the elections in 1982 is now in

19

its fifth week. The accused, charged with gross infringements of human rights, include three former Presidents: Viola, Videla and Galtieri. If found guilty they will be publicly stripped of their rank and imprisoned for up to twenty-five years. They are not required to attend the trial and all except Videla, who refuses to recognise the court, have appointed lawyers to defend them. The state has appointed a lawyer to defend Videla.

The six judges are young, much younger than the defence team. Each judge spends a week as President of the court, and then hands over to another of the six. Only the President can ask the witnesses questions; all communication from the defence and the prosecution must come through him. Most of the questions from the defence are disallowed. Half of them have already been answered - the defence doesn't seem to listen - and the President immediately says: "That has already been answered, do you have another question?' The defence then attempts to suggest that the witness or the subject of the evidence is a member of a subversive organisation. The presiding judge makes clear that the witnesses are not on trial, the accused are on trial and such questions are always disallowed. The third type of questions are the most insidious and frightening. A man who told the court that his sister had been threatened was asked by the defence for his sister's address. A man who said his wife was too frightened to give evidence was asked for her name. On both occasions a shiver went through the court and the judge refused to allow the question to be answered.

It is easy to dismiss what happened in Argentina between 1976 and 1980 as another example of South American irrationality and cruelty, the world made flesh by the writings of Gabriel Garcia Marquez where the general spends the morning in the brothel, the mayor is on the make and the air is thick with mosquitos. It is easy to see torture with an electric cattle prod, detention without trial, sudden disappearances of people as part of the appalling metaphysics of South America, which will always be with us.

What happened in Argentina, however, was not metaphysical. What happened in Argentina was political. It belongs much more to contemporary European history than to the world of El Gaucho Martin Fierro. What happened in Argentina belongs to the scenario where the men in power perceive a threat from terrorism, real or imaginary, and instruct the security forces to defeat terrorism by any means at their disposal. The security forces comply.

What happened in Argentina arose from the peculiar rhetoric of Peronism, which is fierce in its nationalism and deeply radical in its tone, but can be easily misunderstood. Peronism contains the anger of Argentina in all its hazy contradictions. It is xenophobic, and unpredictable, but strangely conservative. It stands for both the trade unionist and once in power, the property holder. It is a deeply irrational political force and all the more powerful for that. During Peron's last period in power between 1973 and 1976, links were developed with Libya and the Arab world, much to the consternation of the United States. Two paramilitary groups, both maintaining shadowy links with Peronism, the Monteneros and ERP, also developed links with Libya. The generals took over power determined to rid Argentina of its radical political forces.

So far there has been no evidence that Viola, Videla, Galtieri or any of their colleagues made any effort to stop the army detaining, torturing and murdering members of the Peronist party, who were the main opposition, or trade unionists, members of left-wing groups, or friends, relatives and associates of any of these. Or just people they happened to find in places where they were looking for someone else. Or names that came from nowhere.

Bodies were found but there wasn't much publicity. Life continued as normal, as it did elsewhere in Europe under similar circumstances. Those who drew attention to what was happening were accused of offering aid to the subversives, of helping the Monteneros. When the armed forces came in the night and dragged off a member of the family, the family called the police, they tried to make statements in police stations, they hired lawyers and went to the courts; they applied over and over for *habeas corpus*; they believed the system was still working. Nobody knew what was happening and if people had been told they wouldn't have believed it.

It is easy to find the torturers, the prison staff, the police, army and navy personnel and there is enough definite evidence to lock hundreds of them up. Some of them are already serving sentences. But this trial, which may run for six months more, is not designed to deal with them. This trial is designed to get the nine top men who ran the place during these years, the men who, whether directly or indirectly, gave the orders. The politicians are on trial.

During these years there were between one hundred and two hundred secret centres for detention, torture and murder in the greater Buenos Aires area. This week we have been hearing about one of those, known to its inmates as El Club Atletico. We have been hearing in particular about the activities of two torturers:

Julian El Turco and Colores.

Witnesses come in groups to give evidence about how someone was detained, or about a single place of detention, or about how a group of people or an individual was tortured or murdered. So that you might get the mother first to tell how her daughter was dragged off in the night and then someone who was taken in on the same night and saw the daughter for the last time.

Everybody who was detained at El Club Atletico remembers Julian El Turco and Colores. Colores was so-called because he had fair hair and freckles. Evidence is given that he loved torturing prisoners; he enjoyed being in the room with the electric cattle prod. Julian El Turco, they remember, those who survive, was much bigger and stronger than Colores. Grasiella Trotte was three months pregnant when Julian El Turco and Colores started torturing her, holding the cattle prod on her vagina, on her breasts. Eventually she had to be sent to the infirmary. The only other patient there was a man whose skin had been burnt off, whose body was full of ulcers and sores, who screamed day and night, who screamed for his wife and his child. Julian El Turco came up one day to the infirmary and broke his jaw so he could no longer eat. No other evidence was given about him.

Sometimes it is difficult to see why a witness is being brought on at a certain time and where the witness's evidence is leading. We start one day in the third week with Ricardo Castro who tells how he saw the police take his girlfriend away as he approached her house. It is two days before the story is followed up by the court and we hear evidence from the girl's uncle, her father, her brother-in-law and we hear nothing more of the girl. Evidence is then given by a worker in the Bendix factory who was detained and later released, followed by the evidence from the relatives of four colleagues of his who were detained on the same night and never seen again.

Evidence is given from more relatives of people who were detained at that time and not seen again. Then a police doctor gives evidence of how he was called when thirty bodies had been recovered after an explosion in the Fatima area of Buenos Aires. He examined the bodies and found that all but two had been shot in the head before the explosion. Some were later identified as being the relatives of those who had given evidence. There is a rumour that a policeman involved is going to give evidence. He will be the second policeman directly involved in the detention centres to give evidence to the tribunal.

His name is Armando Lucini. His evidence is cold, flat, factual, to the point. There's a certain exasperation in his tone. Yes, he put thirty people into a lorry that night. Yes, they were the same thirty people later found dead. Yes, at the time he did consider it a "notable coincidence". He believed they were drugged before they were put into the lorry. He seems about to finish and step down when he is asked if he can remember the names of any of the people. No, he replies, thousands of people went through where he worked. Some were moved elsewhere, some were murdered. He can't remember names.

The judge asks if torture was practised in his detention centre. The answer comes calmly, deliberately. "What happened was a total aberration, it makes me sick just to think of the tortures I saw. Everyone who came in was tortured, not just for days but for months, every form of torture, they hit them, they burnt them, they raped them, especially the women, but also the men, they beat them with chains." Lucini's job was to take them back to the cells.

He mentions helicopters and, puzzled, the judge asks him to clarify what he means. Lucini tells the court that they put RAF after the names of the prisoners who were to be sent up on helicopters and thrown out into the Rio de la Plata.

The other policeman had told the court that it was common to wear swastikas in the detention centres. Lucini is asked about this. He confirms that there were many among the security forces with "nazi tendencies" and nazi literature overflowed in Coordination Federal, where he worked, as did anti-semitism, he claimed.

The military leaders who come to give evidence, unlike Lucini, give nothing away. They knew nothing, heard nothing, saw nothing. Only one thing becomes clear: no one in the army made any effort to find out what was going on. One general, asked by a neighbour to help find his daughter, told the court that he could do nothing: "I did not investigate because at that time military people were prohibited from making enquiries to find out the whereabouts of people who had been captured by the security forces".

His evidence was confirmed by, among others, a woman whose husband had been kidnapped in a swoop on a large number of directors of a bank which certain military gents wanted to take over. She went to see a general who told her he could do nothing. The general must have been watching too many movies: as soon as the woman entered he looked up from his desk and said: "Okay, so they've got your fat little husband. Don't worry, they won't do him any harm, just when you get him back he'll be a little bit thinner".

The most publicised disappearance during this period was that of Edgardo Sajon who had been the government press secretary up to

1972. He disappeared in September 1977. They phoned his wife to say he hadn't come in to work and she frantically went around police stations in the city trying to find him. She went to see one of the generals, now on trial, and he told her that the security forces had many sides and they all worked independently and he couldn't help her. She saw Videla who assured her that her husband had nothing to do with subversion. By the end of the year there was still no news; again she went to see Videla with her four children. His answers were vague. He told her there was a "pact of silence" in the army over disappearances. She decided not to pursue the case any further, realising, as she told the court, that those who talk too much about the disappeared tend to disappear themselves and she had her children to think about.

The search for Sajon was taken over by the former President of Argentina General Lanusse. Lanusse, in his own words, made a "vehement and long-lasting attempt to find out what happened to Edgardo Sajon". He had meetings with four senior members of the government, all of whom are now on trial. He was told that there was a small group which acted independently of the government in security matters. Lanusse sent the government a public telegram asking them for information about Sajon. They told him nothing. He had better luck when he searched for his cousin Elena Holmberg who was murdered while in detention. Lanusse was allowed identify the body. While he was waiting in the detention centre he heard a senior officer complain to a junior officer about the delay in finding Holmberg's body. He heard the junior officer reply: "How can you worry about one body when you have thrown eight thousand into the Rio de la Plata?"

They did not throw Edgardo Sajon's body into the Rio de la Plata. They took him into a room some months after his arrest and told him that they had orders to execute him. Former policeman Carlos Alberto Hours was in the room. He told the court that Sajon continued to abuse his captors as they took off his shoes and wet his clothes and wet the surface of a billiard table which was in the room. They tied him to the billiard table. They put electric wires around his little toe and into his mouth and they plugged in the electricity and that is how they killed him.

Three months before the generals took over power Carlos Alberto Hours had joined a special police squad to detain trade unionists. After the coup, he testified, things became looser and more brutal. Most of the policemen changed their names. Once, he told the court, they surrounded a house and told the occupant to come out; when he did they were ordered to shoot him. "Did you shoot too?" the judge asked Hours. "Of course I did", he replied.

The security forces stole from every house they visited. Every single witness has testified that this is so. Sometimes they took electrical goods, clothes, cameras. In the case of Selma Ocampo, taken away in August 1976, her entire flat was stripped of every single item of furniture down to the light bulbs. They stole cheque books and for months afterwards they wrote cheques in her name. "These are the spoils of war", one man was told when he complained. The wife of the torturer Colores could not use the sewing-machine which had been stolen from the house of Grasiella Trotte and Colores applied to her for instructions. Jorge Alberto Alega was an electrician and they brought him goods to repair which had been broken in transit. They also made him repair electric cattle prods which had broken. One man paid sixteen hundred dollars to a policeman to get his daughter out of the country. His daughter was never seen again.

They also stole cars. Edgardo Sajon was taken while driving to work and neither he nor the vehicle was ever seen again. Santiago Chiessa was held for almost four years. When he was arrested he was driving a car which was in such bad condition that it was, he told the court, "almost abandoned". Four years later when they gave him back his car it was almost new. They needed cars for other purposes; Marta Ocampo gave evidence that she lived opposite a centre of detention where stationary empty cars accelerated all night. They were using the power to drive the prods.

Sometimes it gets too much; sometimes you can't stay in there for more than an hour at a time listening to them tell what happened; sometimes you feel an urgent need to get the hell out of there. The court sits at three o'clock in the afternoon until late into the night; last Wednesday the court did not rise until four o'clock in the morning.

Outside is the city of Buenos Aires. Hints of summer still linger on the soft late autumn. Across the square from the court is the Teatro Colon, the city's luscious nineteenth century opera house, where the Argentine soprano Adelaida Negri is bringing down the house in a stunning production of *Norma*. Elsewhere Robert de Niro and Meryl Streep are having a love affair with a suburban train. Elsewhere are the tea rooms, the huge comfortable bars, the late night cinemas, the restaurants where the best steak in the world is served. The city is clean, rich, comfortable. The main streets are wide and crawling with taxis; the side streets on block after block are full of expensive shops where you don't get a shirt for less than thirty dollars. The city has turned its back on the huge harbour; the city has spread itself away from the Rio de la Plata; the city has modelled itself on Milan, on Madrid.

In one of the posh centre city hotels a team from the World Bank has installed itself. They are here to assist the Argentinian government to make serious cut-backs in public spending. Each one is an expert on such matters as the cost of public transport, health services and education. They spend the day in government buildings going through figures and plans for rationalisation.

The trains run all night out to the beautiful suburbs of Buenos Aires. I normally come home late and walk from the station through the opulent streets; the large detatched houses on either side are protected by high walls and gates, by armed security men, by guard dogs, who start to bark now at anyone passing in the night, alerting the security men who come to the gate and look out. It is hard to know how anyone living in these houses could get a good night's sleep.

At the weekend I go sailing on the Rio de la Plata in a boat owned by an executive of a multi-national company. He shows me the huge glass house down by the harbour where he used to live, but he had to move. The security firm commissioned by his employers did a trial run to see if it would be easy to kidnap him, and when they discovered that it would be dead simple, they forced him to move to an apartment block in the city centre with special security features.

It is a mild autumn Saturday; there is enough wind to take us over to Uruguay, but instead we set sail across the bay to the Yacht Club de Argentina. The swirling water is clear blue in the light of the South Atlantic. This is where the bodies were thrown, the wide water of the Rio de la Plata.

Our host at the Yacht Club is Argentinian, the economic and political adviser to one of the large multi-national companies with considerable investments in Argentina. When he hears I am reporting on the trial, he defends the generals, saying that they took over power in a difficult time, they did a difficult job. He has no time for the trial, and believes that most of the witnesses are unreliable.

His son was injured in the Falklands War. He is proud of his son, but ashamed of how badly the Argentinian military conducted the war. His grandfather was involved in one of the last campaigns against the Indians which finished them off, and he is glad to say that there are no Indians now in Argentina. They were not economically active, he says, they were like parasites.

Sometimes you wander around the city just to get away from what is happening in the court. Sometimes you don't want to hear any more about the time they took the students from the Arts Faculty in, selected one of them called Sergio and tortured him so badly that he lay there for days dying, and they brought the other students in to look at him and told them that if they didn't talk they would be tortured like Sergio was and left there on the metal grill to die.

Sometimes you don't want to hear any more. The man taken in with his wife and held together blindfolded for days and days, all they can hear is the sound of screaming from the torture rooms until one night they recognise the screams, their son is being tortured, the son who was dragged from the house three weeks earlier, until that moment they did not know he was in the prison with them, they never heard him scream again and they never saw him again and they can only guess what happened to him. Some time later their other son was taken in; they have never seen him since either.

After six or seven days their blindfolds were taken off and what they saw they could not believe: all of the torturers and the prison staff were less than twenty-five years old.

You walk through the city with the images of the day in your head: the Capuchin monk being tortured with the electric cattle prod and the torturers roaring "Where is God now? What can God do to help you?" The prisoners shot in reprisal for the terrorist bombing of a police station and their bodies left all over the city at random. The Obelisk is the main monument in the city; it was here right in the heart of the city at the height of the murdering that they took six prisoners in the middle of the night and shot them.

Each street name now has a certain resonance: the route the prisoners were taken on; the houses they were arrested in; where they were released, the lucky ones. Slowly you get to know the city through walking around and through the names mentioned in the court. Slowly the names of the tram stops into the city from San Isidro where you are staying take on a resonance too. *Olivos* is where the priest from Venezuela spent the day trying to get exit documents for the five Forti boys aged between seventeen and eight who, with their mother, were dragged from an airplane by the security forces. Their mother was never seen again. *Martinez* is where one of the worst detention centres was situated. *Belgrano* is where Edgardo Sajon's wife was told that she couldn't make a statement about her husband's disappearance, that he had probably left her, maybe they weren't getting on, they told her.

For many people now the city of Buenos Aires is a nightmare. Fernando Alvez still has marks on his left foot from June 1977 when they tied it to a cable and turned on the current. About a year ago he saw the man who tortured him from a bus. He got off and followed him. He walked along after him. He didn't know what to do and stopped when the man went into the house about a block away from where he stood. Jorge Alega, who was badly tortured by both Julian El Turco and Colores, met Colores in the street. Alega froze with fear but Colores seemed not to understand this and asked him how he was getting on, how his work was going and gave him a phone number (458836) in case he was ever in any trouble. Alega later phoned the number and asked for Colores; he was told he was busy but if he could ring back in about an hour.

For Alega the city didn't stop spewing up reminders of his year in detention. He met Julian El Turco on the street as well and was also greeted warmly. A guard from the detention centre moved into a flat in the same building. Julian El Turco began to telephone him first at his parents' house and later at his flat. He proposed that they might consider going into business together.

Some people broke under torture and told them what they wanted to know. Grasiella Trotte told them where they could find her husband and child and they took her with them when they went to get him; they left the child on the side of the road to be picked up by neighbours. One girl from the Arts faculty of the university gave them her boyfriend's address and they came back that night and told her that they had gone there and murdered him.

The third week of the trial was dominated by the following names. The names became like a chant in a Brian Friel play as each person listed them out; Liliana Garlaza, Pablo and Maria Magdelena Mainer, Domingo Moncalvillo, Martin Groeber, Susana de Salamone, Lilia Idiart, and Maria Moretini.

Last seen November 1977.

All of them arrested late in 1976. All of them held under extraordinary circumstances. They were all tortured in the early days of their captivity. They were all professional people, doctors, teachers, engineers, and if the hints of the court by parents and other witnesses can be treated seriously then they all either belonged to or supported the terrorist group the Monteneros. It looks as though they all broke under torture. Their parents were told that they could visit them any time, two of the women had babies during their time in prison and the babies were handed over to the grandparents.

They all had work to do every day: typing, writing, sewing, making clothes. The parents were told that they were being detained for their own protection.

Two men's names figure in everyone's evidence: Fredrico Assis and Christian Von Wernich. Assis ran the La Plata detention centre when these young people were held and Von Wernich was a police chaplain who saw a great deal of the young people and seemed to be deeply involved in their future. They use the word "assessor".

Several years ago evidence was given to the commission on the disappearances that Father Christain Von Wernich was in the room when these people were shot in late November 1977 but this evidence has not been given before this tribunal so it is not known if Father Christain Von Wernich was in the room when these young people were shot. It is not even known for certain how these young people died.

The following is clear. Towards the end of 1977 these eight young people believed that they were going to be allowed leave the country. They asked their parents for money, they would need dollars in Uruguay where they believed they were going first. They asked their parents for passports. They asked for their certificates, degrees, as they believed their exile was going to be long. The parents duly brought these. They gave them to the priest, who was going to look after them.

So that when the children disappeared, didn't write, when time went by, the parents appealed to Father Von Wernich and he told them not to give up hope, never to give up hope and that is eight years ago and they have nothing else to make them hope that they will ever see their children again.

The court awaited the entry of Father Christian Von Wernich with considerable interest.

He was tall, well-groomed, in his late forties. He explained how he was a police chaplain, how he came across a number of young people who were in detention and he offered them spiritual help and comfort. ("I offered them my spiritual services"). They had doubts, they had problems, they had fears, he said. He could not talk about what physical state they were in as he had only considered their spiritual state. He spoke with the utmost gravity. There was no torture, his voice became angry and he clenched his fists, in all those years when he worked for the police he never heard of a prisoner being tortured. It is something he would never have tolerated.

Did he know Federico Assis? There was silence for a moment. The angry voice denouncing torture had gone. Several witnesses had given evidence that they were tortured by Assis. Did he know Assis? He began to talk about the Catholic church and what an important and loving name Assisi is for members of the church. The judge looked puzzled. Did he know a man named Federico Assis?

29

No, said Von Wernich, who was a chaplain in the detention centre run by Assis as well as in others. He would always remember a name like Assis.

He found the young people were all going to leave the country and he counselled them on the perils of living abroad. He did not seem to understand the laughter in the court at this. He talked to them, he said, about the things they might miss if they went to Uruguay or Brazil. (The judge said he would clear the court if there was any further noise). He remembers it was November, because it was the month of the Virgin in Argentina, and he went on to tell of the importance of the Virgin and the month of the Virgin in his own life and the life of the church. Over and over he used the images and language of the Catholic church to sidestep questions about how these prisoners came to be murdered.

They all left the country, he swore, at the end of November, some by land, some by air. He saw them all off. He remembers the details. No, he cannot remember the name of a single person who came with them although he agrees there was a driver as well as several members of the security forces. No, he cannot even remember what any of these people looked like. Nor what sort of car.

There is no record of any of these people leaving the country on the date specified or on any other date. Father Von Wernich still thinks the parents shouldn't give up hope. Domingo Moncalvillo's parents are suing him for the disappearance of their son. The other parents also know they will never see their children again.

21 May 1985 Buenos Aires

There is big news today. All the newspapers have it as the lead story; radio and television are going to town on it. By the end of the week every single magazine in the country will have the story on the cover. Norma Aleandre has won the Best Actress Award at Cannes for her part in the all-Argentine film "La Historia Official". She plays the part of a woman who slowly begins to discover that her adopted daughter was stolen from a woman taken in by the security forces.

There are hundreds of missing children in Argentina, toddlers taken in with their parents and never seen again, babies born to mothers in prison and snatched away. Some of these were murdered, but others were taken home by childless policemen or prison officers, or handed over to right-wing groups. They are now being brought up by these people. There is a body now working solely to get these kids back.

"La Historia Official" was doing okay until Cannes and then all hell broke loose. All the seats in the cinema are numbered and you have to book days in advance. It is eleven o'clock now on Saturday night in Calle Lavelle, one of the two or three most fashionable streets in the centre of Buenos Aires. The foyer of the cinema is absolutely packed and resembles nothing as much as a fashion show. These are the Argentinian middle classes, famed in song and story, come to see their compatriot who made it in France.

They've all been to France. In the 1970s the entire population of Argentina, all twenty eight million of them, travelled all over the world. When an airplane came back from Europe to Argentina another one came behind with all the goods the people in the first plane had bought. This is called, with regret now and bitterness, *la epoca de la plata dulce*, the age of the sweet money, when the national debt rose to forty five billion dollars, almost two thousand dollars per man, woman and child in the country, when the peso, the national currency, was kept artificially high, so that if your money wouldn't buy much in Buenos Aires, it would be worth a fortune in New York, or Paris France.

The middle classes wish they could have the good times back again and they have little interest in the trial of the generals for grave breaches of human rights. It's the last thing Argentina needs, almost everyone I meet tells me this.

Eleven o'clock Saturday night. Silence. Lights down. "La Historia Official" is about to begin. Well-known scenes from the landscapes of Argentina appear on the screen and the audience stands up for the national anthem. They know every word, they sing it out loud and clear, dead serious, no slouchers. The movie opens with a small parody of this, but no one seems to notice.

The movie has a tug-of-war over a child, a beautiful woman, some nice houses and nice clothes. It can't go wrong, they love it. It would be easy to watch it without having to think about the murdered, the tortured, the maimed and the bereaved, the events in Argentina in the late 1970s.

No one wants to think about this. The trial will go on and convict some of the generals and lock them up. But many people seem set against knowing what happened, many don't even believe that anything occurred. And the longer the trial goes on the less interest there will be.

Anything could happen here again. And there is no evidence that people this time would do something to stop it. There is no evidence that what happened to the Forti boys, five of them aged between seventeen and eight when they were released from detention, would not happen again in Buenos Aires.

They were left blindfolded on the side of a main street in Buenos Aires with their hands tied. The police car sped away. Their mother had been murdered in the previous few days; their father had gone to Venezuela, they had been arrested in the airplane. At first they were not aware that they were being watched by the entire clientele of a bar who all stood at the window gazing out. No one left the bar. The boys took time to untie each other and take off the blindfolds. They looked behind and saw the bar but still no one came out. A man was walking towards them but when he saw them he turned back. They had never been in Buenos Aires before, but they picked themselves up and tried to walk along even though they had no idea where they were going.

In Dublin/The New Statesman, June 1985

THE PROMISED LAND

The rain has stopped now. I can hear it soaking through the luscious growth in the garden of the priest's house here in Promissao in the Mato Grosso of Brazil, twelve hours by train from Sao Paulo. We have taken chairs out onto the verandah, myself and the young seminarian who will be ordained in two years' time. The newspapers devote page after page to the state of health of Tancredo Neves, the President elect of Brazil, who has taken power from the military. Neves is dying. It is Good Friday.

The fact that it is Good Friday means that the papers can refer to the "Calvary" of Tancredo Neves, to his "martyrdom". The main Sao Paulo newspaper has a huge, detailed drawing of Tancredo's naked body, genitals and all, with loads of tubes coming in and out of various parts of him.

When he dies, as he will in a few weeks, they will call him a saint, they will compare him to Moses who brought his people within sight of the Promised Land, in Tancredo's case the Promised Land of democracy in Brazil, and then fell down dead. They will call his wife Risoleta a "symbol for Brazil".

The sound of singing comes from the church. I turn to the seminarian and ask him why he isn't at the ceremony. Religious ceremonies really bore him, he says and goes back to reading about Tancredo Neves. When he is a priest will he not have to spend his time at religious ceremonies? He shrugs his shoulders; there are other things a priest can do, he says. Like what? I ask.

He puts the paper down. Like help the people, like work with the people. Like work with the poor. Would he ever minister to the rich? I ask. No, he has clearly thought about this, no, he wouldn't. Does he think that the poor should rise up against the rich? Yes he does, and he seems to have thought about this too. What about sin? Sin is exploiting other people. What about heaven and hell? Does he believe in heaven and hell? He looks at me sharply and shrugs his shoulders. No, he doesn't.

After tea we stand outside the church and wait for the people to carry out the life-size statue of the crucified Christ on a wooden bier decked with flowers and leaves. The church is full and many people are standing outside.

Christ's mouth is open in anguish and pain. There are gaping wounds on his body; hands, feet, side, head. Through the streets of Promissao we follow the procession. We pass through the nice area of the town; people come out to look, or watch from the windows, but the owners of these low, comfortable houses will not join in. They have nothing to do with the church and will enter its portals only for weddings.

The poor of the town and the surrounding area are walking through Promissao back to the church where the new parish priest stands at the door and tells them that for the poor of Brazil the image of the suffering Christ is very important.

Behind him in the doorway of the church is a poster of a hungry child with a slogan saying "Bread for Those who are Hungry". This is the church's official slogan for Lent. The 250 Brazilian bishops in a long pastoral letter have defended their support for liberation theology, have emphasised the need for huge social reform in Brazil, have emphasised the church's right to teach this doctrine, have issued this slogan as a subject for discussion this Lent. Last year it was "Health for Those who are Sick". The slogan will be discussed not just in sermons from the pulpit, but in the small communities which the church has set up all over Brazil, the communities where the residents of a street of an area will meet once or twice a week to talk and pray. The talk this Lent has been about feeding the hungry; the talk in general is about raising the political consciousness of the people.

The new priest whom my father taught in school in Enniscorthy has been in Brazil for fifteen years now. His new job is not just to run the parish, hear confessions and say Mass. He has been posted to Promissao by the bishop to organise the agricultural workers in the whole area, to raise their political consciousness, to improve their lot. There is little stability in the lives of the farm workers in Brazil; they are forced to move so often that many of them have no idea where they were born, or where they were before, have no roots anywhere in the country, except roots in the struggle for survival. Several years ago the government introduced a law which gave certain rights to farm workers who had been on an estate for more than five years. This has made things much worse for farm workers: the estate owners remove them long before their five years are up.

Why is the Catholic church in Brazil so interested in the plight of farm workers? Is it because they are so poor and harassed that they can't practice their religion? Does the church want to improve their

34

lot to bring them back to the fold?

The priest looks puzzled at the question. No, no, that's not what he's trying to do. God made the world, let's just start with that. God made the world, and the church in Brazil is concerned with that world, how the men and women in it should be brothers and sisters and not exploit each other, how the resources in it should be used for the common good and not as a facility for exploitation. That is why a Brazilian bishop would send a priest to work with the farm labourers. Let's just stick to the world for the moment.

The church in Brazil, he says, wants to lend its power to the people.

What about heaven and hell? Does he believe in heaven and hell? His eyes light up with irony and amusement. Here is a journalist wanting a crude answer to a crude question. Here is the makings of a great headline: "Irish Priest Denies Existence Of Hell Shock". He tells me I am asking the wrong questions.

There will, he believes, have to be a revolution in Brazil in the end to get things right. And in the meantime things get worse; people pack up and move into the cities; inflation is raging; the debt to American banks is huge; there are no social services. Voodoo, black magic is increasing. At a crossroads now in the countryside you will see a tumbler of the local fire water, a candle and a black hen left there so the sick might be healed, so some evil might be warded off.

There are three priests from the diocese of Ferns now ministering in the diocese of Sao Paulo. One was the curate in Enniscorthy when I was a lad and later parish priest of Oylgate. Over a twenty year period he set up a superb service for the mentally and physically handicapped in Enniscorthy. He was known by everyone to be energetic, hardworking and concerned. In his mid-fifties, parish priest of a sleepy little village in Wexford, he decided to remove himself to Brazil, where he has been for four years.

Things are difficult, he says. In Ireland you had back-up from the state and from voluntary services; in Brazil you have no back-up. You are visiting people and trying to help them and suddenly a whole family will disappear, move elsewhere, no one knows where. There is no stability. The situation of any deprived group is truly appaling and hopeless. There is no possibility of starting a twenty year campaign to alleviate a problem; the state will give you nothing.

His own views have changed. In Ireland he would have viewed the dole with suspicion, as something of a handout to people for doing nothing. Now he sees it as something Brazil needs badly. He would see the word "love" now as including things he hadn't thought of before, like the rights of people and the dignity of man. He would see these now as very important.

They work hard. Another, in his mid-thirties, formerly curate in Gorey, is the parish priest. I go with him to two meetings of what they called "the basic communities", the meetings of a street or community to pray and discuss their problems. The church has to prepare all the children for communion and confirmation, as the state takes no part in the teaching of religion, there are masses, weddings, deaths, baptisms, all in a strange country, with strange people, in a foreign language.

I go to Rio where most of the sin in Brazil is committed. I stay around the corner from a long string of brothels and two-hour hotels. Every night I pass the couples sneaking into the hotels, the prostitutes standing in rows. One night just at the turn up to the hotel, at the crossroads, a woman is kneeling with her eyes shut, a candle lighting beside her, with a bunch of red roses, a little tumbler of pisco, the local fire water. This is the voodoo the priest has said is increasing, but here it is right in the heart of Rio de Janeiro, the woman is oblivious to everything, to the sexual tensions that fill the air in Rio, to all except what is on her mind.

Almost every day now I see such a scene, incongruous, powerful, heart-breaking.

Tomorrow I will be flying out to Buenos Aires. I wander out to Copacabana beach for a last swim. The sky is overcast and grey; there are at least fifty football matches going on along the beach; supporters send up fireworks when a goal is scored, blacks and whites are playing together and opposite each other without any problem. I go down to the shore.

There it is again. I see it everywhere. I can't take my eyes off it.

The woman is in her forties; the girl must be her daughter. They have left red roses on the sand and lit several candles around the roses. They have left a glass of alcohol on the sand. The fireworks and shouting from the football matches can be heard echoing back from the fancy hotels on the Copacabana. The two women are facing out to sea, watching the grey waves come in, wringing their hands in the hope that whatever awful thing is looming in their lives will not come to pass.

In Dublin, July 1985

THE TRAIN OF DEATH

"Put your trousers on!" He shone his torch into my eyes again and then back down to my bare legs. "Put your trousers on!" he said again. It was the fifth time he had disturbed me during the night; previously he had just wanted to see my passport, now he wanted me to take my shorts off and put my trousers on. I began to fumble in my bag. "Put your trousers on!" he said to a man who was picking his way among the sleeping bodies down the aisle. "Why?" the man said. "Why? For the reputation of our country," came the reply.

The first class carriage of El Tren de la Muerte. The Train of Death. Between the Brazilian border and Santa Cruz, the second city of Bolivia. The journey could take twenty hours; or it could take twenty-four hours depending on how fast the train would go.

The train went slow.

I had woken that morning still in Brazil, in the beautiful town of Corumba. I had walked down the hill from the hotel; I had caught glimpses of the floating islands of the river Paraguay way out towards the horizon. The air was serene, the sky perfectly blue, the day was like wide water without sound. Up there was the Pantanal: floating islands, wildlife, birdlife. Over there was Bolivia: floating pesos, wildlife, cocaine. Dream of days in a hammock on a boat up the Pantanal versus the corruption, evil and stench of Bolivia. I had to decide. I decided to go to Bolivia. There were no planes, the express train had been suspended, there were no roads, or maybe there were roads, but the roads were not passable.

El Tren de la Muerte. The Train of Death. The only means of transport to Santa Cruz.

The nasty little woman at the border told me that she would stamp my passport if I changed money with her. I gave her Brazilian currency, protesting that I had no dollars, and she gave me a fistful of Bolivian pesos. El Tren de la Muerte, first class to Santa Cruz, cost 800,000 pesos, which at first glance seemed a lot, and that was just one way.

800,000 pesos equalled less than five pounds, but it seemed like an awful lot more. As I handed it to the ticket man it felt like a million dollars. Just a few years ago fifty dollars was forty pesos; now fifty dollars is eight million pesos.

The windows on the train didn't open. There was hardly any room for your knees. There were mosquitos everywhere. The train left an hour late. At every village the locals ascended with all their wares: oranges, coffee, cakes, stew. All through the grim night the locals ascended, at one in the morning, at two in the morning, the locals ascended and wanted to know if you wanted coffee, oranges, stew, cakes, at three in the morning, locals. You began to wonder if you were dreaming the locals.

They turned the lights off at nine to try and keep the mosquitos away. The mosquitos crept up and bit you in the dark. They made me move to my properly numbered seat which was being occupied by a Brazilian basketball player as well as his own. The Brazilian basketball player resented my intrusion and diplomatic relations took hours to establish.

Hours! The very word is like a bell. For hours the train stopped at nowhere for no reason. For hours the dawn looked set to break and then didn't. For hours the man who had seen a woman who had very small breasts kept roaring down at her that his breasts were bigger than hers. For hours he wanted to know everyone's view on this, and was she a man? Did anyone think she was a man? For twenty-four hours El Tren de la Muerte tortured its passengers in every possible way.

Even the traffic police are corrupt. Say for example you're double parked because your father's gone into the bank. The cop comes up and you tell the cop your daddy'll be out in a minute, and if he wants you'll move around the corner. The cop sits into the car and says this is serious, double parking is serious, you'll have to come down to the station and so will your daddy. Busy today, the station, a few guys are off missing, there's a queue in the station, it's gonna take most of the afternoon. The cop is waiting for one word: Cuanto, how much? He gives a figure, you bargain for a while, and then the cop names the bottom line and goes off satisfied.

This is not just a story of something that happened once; it is how business is done in Santa Cruz.

There are only two ways of making money: currency speculation and cocaine. Along Calle Libertad dozens of men stand about with buckets of pesos wanting to exchange them for dollars. As we drive along Calle Libertad my friend in Santa Cruz pulls down the window and talks to one of the dealers.

"Fuck!" he says and bangs the steering wheel.

"What's wrong?" I want to know.

"The dollar's gone up again and I changed money this morning."

As we move around Santa Cruz everyone has heard. In the travel agent's everyone is talking about it. The dollar. How did you hear the news? A friend telephoned. Will it move again tomorrow? Or maybe in the afternoon? Or maybe it'll go the other way.

The rich are speeding around Santa Cruz in their huge cars. People point them out to you: look at him, he's one of the biggest dealers, his giant finned car, smuggled in from Brazil, slides by on cocaine. The talk moves from cocaine to dollars, from dollars to cocaine. The best place to change dollars, several people tell me, is at the back of the occulist's shop on the right hand side before you come to a post office in Calle Libertad. Do you want cocaine? someone asks me. No, I don't. I want to get out of here and this time I want to fly.

The airport is huge, bright, well-designed, full of snack bars, lounge bars, dining rooms, special rooms to view the tarmac. The money to build it was raised from international banks. The only problem is that there is no business; there are no international flights today. The elaborate arrivals and departures board is empty. There is only this domestic flight to La Paz, the capital, and even this is going to be four hours late.

So it is nearly ten o'clock at night when the plane lands in La Paz. Arriving like this fresh from the airport after a stop in Santa Cruz is profoundly unsettling. To have gone by road or rail would have been easier on the soul, but there are no roads and no railways between La Paz and Santa Cruz. La Paz is one of the most frightening places the Lord God ever waved his magic wand over. Firstly, there is the altitude - La Paz is the highest city in the world - which means that if you take one step you're out of breath. Then there is the cold which gets into your bones; Santa Cruz was in the eighties.

Street lights are sparse; there are large Indian families sitting on the side of the pavement eating their dinner. Indian women wear bowler hats and seem to giggle all the time. The altitude seems to make everyone giddy. Rubbish is thrown straight out onto the street and packs of huge dogs descend upon it and eat it. The only bar that I can find has run out of beer and wants to give me fire water with Canada Dry. Small boys tour the bar trying to rob the denizens. All streets are hills and the hills are murderous. I go back to the hotel and ask how quickly can I get out of here and where can I go. The man tells me I can book a seat on a bus to Peru for seven thirty the very next morning. I give the man the money.

Two days moving slowly across South America, on dirt tracks along the shores of Lake Titicaca with white clouds gathering on the horizon. And then on a train over the Andes, going higher and higher on a clear day until we reach the city of Cuzco, former capital of the Incas.

Tomorrow is election day in Peru and if all goes according to plan it will be the first time in over fifty years that one democratic government has handed over to another. Everyone says that Alan Garcia is going to win; his name has been etched into the mountain over the town. Posters everywhere call him Alan Peru. A man in a bar tells me that his campaign is being paid for by the CIA. A man in a bar tells me that his campaign is being paid for by the cocaine dealers. A man in a bar tells me that his campaign is being paid for by the Koreans. Either way, someone is paying for his campaign. Full colour posters everywhere, elaborate ads on television. I ask in the bars what he stands for, what his politics are. Nobody knows, he's young, in his thirties, he's nice, he didn't issue any policy statement, he's not left wing, no, he's not right wing, he's a family man.

On Sunday everyone goes to vote; the turnout all over the country is over ninety percent. Those who vote have to stick their finger in indelible ink. Alan Garcia, who also calls himself Alan Peru, will fail to get fifty percent of the vote, and will have to wait for a second round to win. Meanwhile, our friends the Sendero Luminoso, the shining path, the Peruvian terrorist organisation, have a night of fear in store for us all in Cuzco.

I am just leaving the main square when the bomb goes off; the lights go out all over the city. The streets have been full of people and now there is dead silence. Everyone is waiting for another bomb, watching, wondering is it close, wondering will it be better to run.

I run towards the church but a priest stands at the door and bars my way. Some of the vendors have left small kerosene lamps on and by this light I can see the square where everyone has voted, I can still see the stones of Cuzco, solid, grey, majestic. "Put out the lights". The soldier has a machine gun. "Put out the lights", he roars at the vendors and makes to smash the lamps with the butt of his machine gun. He has come into the street on a lorry, the headlamps turned down, the engine turned off, some of his colleagues are in camouflage.

"Put out the lights", they keep shouting. Another bomb goes off in the distance. Suddenly, a police jeep comes roaring down the street at maybe eighty miles an hour. The police have handguns.

Several of them approach us at the walls of the church.

"Go home, everybody, go home", they say, and point the guns at us.

I walked up through Cuzco in darkness. I can vaguely make out the mountains in the background. Just a few hours away now on a small train along a river is Machu Picchu, the last stronghold of the Incas and a city not discovered until 1911. You can spend all day there just wandering around. Near there is a little village called Aguas Calientes where there is a hot spring swimming pool and a decent place to stay. Tomorrow I am going to go there.

In Dublin, July 1985.

III.
WAITING FOR
THE 'REAGAN'

In 1985 a number of television programmes alerted the world to the plight of the people suffering from famine in Ethiopia and the Sudan. International concern culminated in "Live Aid", a concert organised by Bob Geldof. This article was written early the following year.

The landscape here seems like some outrageous parody of the plight of the refugees. The two northern provinces of Ethiopia, Tigre and Eritrea, which some of the refugees left over a year ago, are full of valleys and mountains. When they talk of home, they talk of a green landscape.

Here there is nothing except a long expanse of brown earth. There is not a single other feature in the landscape, except the mirages which appear on the horizon on all sides, the blue dream water, throbbing and shimmering in the distance.

The earth is burnt brown. In the rainy season the dry earth turns to mud, but now the clay is dry and brittle. Most of the small bushes which grow here have been removed for firewood. So the landscape is bare, made up of one colour, absolutely flat, featureless, dead, lifeless.

Every move you make, every move the refugees make, every move the aid workers make is watched closely, monitored and examined by COR, the Sudanese Committee for Refugees. All those coming into the camp and going out must seek permission; rules are made and re-made by the Sudanese. But the overall policy is clear: nobody must be encouraged to stay, this is a camp, not an embryo village.

The camp is called Shagarab East. It is near Girba, seven hours by road north of Khartoum, close to the Ethiopian border. It is divided into three parts. CONCERN is involved with the largest of these in which twenty thousand people live.

No structure is permanent. The refugees live in tents; the hospital and feeding centres are temporary structures, they could be moved in the morning and no one might know that they had been assembled.

One evening at about six thirty when the sun has gone down and we are crossing from the camp back to the CONCERN compound Miranna Quinlivan of CONCERN turns off the engine of the jeep and we get out and wander about as twenty thousand people cook their rations for the day on charcoal fires lit outside each tent. There is an extraordinary babble: babies whimpering against ordinary adult conversation, children still playing and the sound of the wind against the small fires. In a way, it is this everyone has been working for, that the day would end like this for the refugees from Tigre and Eritrea rather than in desperation and hunger.

Rumours are constant: that thousands of refugees are about to depart, that loads more are going to come. One thing is sure, however. The political refugees, unlike the farmers, will not return to Ethiopia in the near future. Most of them have been in prison in Addis Abbaba. Those interviewed claim to have witnessed random murders in the prison and regular torture.

One of the most serious problems facing the doctors is TB which requires treatment over a lengthy period. What do you do with refugees in a camp who might depart with their families without a moment's notice? Treating them for a brief period may only serve to make them immune from the drugs, may relieve them for a brief period, but will not prevent them from dying of the disease eventually. In Shagareb the doctors have now begun to treat TB sufferers, having made them promise to stay for at least a year.

Work starts early here. On certain days the whole camp has to be covered in anti-fly spray and this must begin at three-thirty in the morning. The sun comes up about two hours later and between five-thirty and six the whole sky is line with flocks of geese. All around is a sort of Platonic Africa: an absolutely cloudless sky, caravans of camels, lizards, snakes, thatched huts in compounds, heat and dust.

A group of nomads have made themselves at home between the CONCERN compound and the lake. They have built temporary dwellings of stalks and reeds, the lake is used by the hundreds of camels which they own. These days they have a huge party every second night. The darkness falls at six, it falls quickly with a twilight of only a few minutes. Some time later the party starts, twice this week it has gone on until near dawn. It is unclear if there is alcohol involved, or dope, or if the states of mind of the nomads on these nights are self-induced. Either way, they shriek, shout, dance up and down, roaring and create an enormous hullabaloo.

Oxfam and Save the Children issue a joint statement saying that four million Sudanese are at risk in the centre and west of the country unless urgent action is taken. The statement is widely reported. Peter Walker of OXFAM elaborates. Yes, there has been a bumper harvest in the Sudan, but only in certain areas. Getting food to the areas where there has been no harvest involves buying the food and transporting it. For this money is needed, hard cash. The country doesn't need grain flown in from Canada, the United States or the EEC. Requests for hard cash are being met with silence: "I would dearly like to know why it is people don't want to respond this year. All the money ploughed in last year will be wasted. Why not do something now since you know what's coming?"

USAID, the United States Government aid agency, have 100,000 tons of grain at Port Sudan which they are only now agreeing to release if someone else will put up half the cost of transporting it. The overall need is estimated to be 400,000 tons which will have to be in place by the end of April. No one is clear about who will come up with the money needed to buy the grain from the local farmers who have a surplus and then pay to transport it across the country.

Chris Aldridge of Save The Children remembers that just six months ago people were leaving the Sudan saying that the crisis was over, that the rains were good and the harvest was excellent. This was wrong, he says. The rains stopped one month early and the crop failed for the fourth year running in the north eastern part of the country. "Journalists and visiting UN people,"he says, "went back and made premature statements giving rise to the idea that things would not be bad here in 1986. There is still a need for a large scale relief operation."

Donor countries, he adds, want to give things, not money. They particularly want to give grain as it keeps the price of grain high in their own countries. "Sudan has a surplus," he says, "and we say buy it."

Samir Basta of UNICEF believes that the statement made by OXFAM and Save the Children about four million being at risk to be "slightly exaggerated". He shares the view taken by other agencies who have been in the Sudan for several years that the situation in 1986 is "very bad but normal for the Sudan. We don't think food aid is going to do anything to solve the problems, other than distort the basic economic system, you just create dependency." He points out that you cannot find labour this year in the rich cotton-picking areas of the country which used to bring in workers for the harvest.

Basta agrees, however, that there is a serious problem again this year. UNICEF, however, would put the figure of those who are at risk from undernourishment in the Sudan at one million in the north and one million in the south.

Everyone is depending on USAID. "In 1984", one senior aid official says, "they telexed to Washington in October and the reply came back very quickly. Between then and January 1985 USAID moved food very quickly." In late October 1985 they telexed again from Khartoum to Washington, saying that this time they didn't need grain, this time they needed money. By the end of January, three months later, they have not received a reply.

American officials here are now admitting privately that the reasons for the silence from Washington are not related to bureaucracy, or domestic budgetary problems or logistics of any sort. Officials here are now admitting privately that the reasons why the United States has not pledged aid to the Sudan in 1986 are political.

The Transitional Military Government, which took over from Nimeiri in a coup last April, has made radical changes in the Sudan's foreign policy. They have improved relations with Libya and have opened an embassy in Iran. The security situation, from the US point of view, has deteriorated and USAID has now handed much of its food distribution over to other non-government agencies and has moved many of its workers out of the country on advice from the American Embassy in Khartoum which believed, in the words of one official, that there were "terrorists in town", notably representatives of Libya and the PLO. There is tight security around American buildings here.

The Americans were also rather surprised, to say the least, when the Charge d'Affaires of the Embassy was invited to dinner by a senior official in the government of the Sudan in a Khartoum hotel to find sitting opposite him a Libyan who, according to American intelligence, was responsible for the assassination of an American diplomat in the late 1970's.

The US attitude to aid is understood to be shared somewhat by Britain. There is now enough food in the Sudan to feed the population; there is enough transport available as well to move what needs to be moved. What, then, is the problem? The government wants the United States, Britain and the EEC to buy grain in the country at market prices, exchanging dollars for Sudanese pounds at a punitively low rate, roughly half the street rate, then use more dollars to purchase transport and move the grain. The people will be fed, but perhaps more importantly, the country will have earned vast amounts in foreign currency. The government will have cashed in on the famine, so to speak.

45

The same government which is dealing openly with the "outlaws, looney-tunes and squalid criminals", in Ronald Reagan's phrase, such as Libya and Iran, which have caused American such grief.

"This is a kind of game," one senior figure involved in supplying aid to the Sudan says. "Time is now the crucial component. The Americans don't want to be seen as suckers. But they should not drag this out otherwise we'll be in the mud.

"These are all little pressures and little persuasions on the Sudanese," he goes on. "This country is in a transitional stage. We don't know how it will develop. The whole place isn't exactly up for grabs, it's what we call 'a major intangible'. Strategically, this is a key area. If someone started to control these two waterways [the Blue and White Nile] with evil intent ... There will be an excessive delay in releasing the money and it will put us back into the danger zone and we are fighting to avoid that."

Over the past few months there has been intense diplomatic pressure from the United Nations on donor countries. Several public statements from the United Nations and from OXFAM and Save The Children have been part of a concerted campaign of pressure on all donor countries but, most particularly, on the United States.

The food should be going out west at the rate of 1,000 tons a day. At the end of January nothing is going out. 400,000 tons have got to be out by the end of April, Winston Prattley, Assistant Secretary General of the United Nations Emergency Operation in the Sudan explains that the railways still can't be relied on. "We have to overcome tending procedures," he says, as the grain suppliers here refuse to stick to agreements made, thus making the local purchase of grain by tender burdensome and time-consuming. "We have to learn to do business the Sudanese way," he says. "This is a country in which everything tends to go wrong."

To the west of Khartoum the desert starts as soon as you leave the city. This is the way the trucks come with food. The journey is incredibly difficult. All along the route lie the half-rotted carcasses of animals dead from the drought, unable to make the rest of the journey to the market in Khartoum, half covered in sand, bits of them eaten by vultures.

The most important instrument in the jeep is a shovel for when the wheels get stuck in the sand. There is no level track to move along, no clear way through the sand.

CONCERN have come to work out here in the village of Umm Inderaba. When they moved in last September they found the people in an appalling state with over fifty severely malnourished children and all the children under the age of thirteen

46

undernourished.The landscape belongs to a dream world, a diagram by Jung. On the map used by CONCERN there is still an area marked "forest". There is no forest now; there is simply a collection of dead trees and tree stumps about the sand. It is like a world after a nuclear attack. Everyone can remember that it used to be green and fertile. They used to grow their own crops and keep their own animals. Now there is nothing, except money from seasonal labour in other parts of the Sudan. Now they live off the supplies of grain from America which they have been told are coming to an end. They call the grain "reagan", the word has become part of everyday Arabic as spoken in the Sudan.

The local chief goes into Omdurman, the city across the Nile from Khartoum, to get the grain. But the food he distributes isn't enough. CONCERN is involved with supplementary feeding and intensive feeding. Without the "reagan", the American grain, and CONCERN, there would be nothing to live on in Umm Inderaba, just two and a half hours by jeep from Khartoum.

We go one day to a nearby village where some of the Sudanese workers with CONCERN are from. They come every day to Umm Inderaba to work in the clinic and feeding centres. They are paid by CONCERN. Several of them speak English. They have made the decision to stay here in their villages rather than go to university in Khartoum, despite repeated warnings from CONCERN that their jobs will not always be there. There seems to be nothing for them to stay for. The villages will eventually have to be abandoned.

The wind is up tonight. The wind is blowing the loose sand about the desert which used to be arable land. There is no hope here. Just people being kept alive. The earth yields up nothing more than water which must be taken from wells cut deep down. Most people don't even have a bucket. You can travel west for days and it is like this. The desert is moving inexorably, covering the arable land.

In Khartoum the whites have formed a ghetto known as The New Extention which is a languid suburb to the south of the city. (Languid is a relative term; the streets remain unpaved.) This is where most of the aid agencies are sited, the embassies, the foreign companies. Here you can get a Chinese meal in a place where the only blacks are the waiters and the dominating voice is the voice of America. Here you can get a good party on certain feast days if you're lucky, know someone, and are white.

Here you can mix Ethiopian gin with real tonic water, drink American whiskey on the rocks. Here you can dance to the latest music and when you're tired dancing you can call the black waiter over for another drink. Here, at the American Marines' celebration of 210 years in existence, you could even drink cans of Carlsberg. Here, the walls are high enough so no one can look over them and there's a guard at the gate, a black guard, and if it's a good party in a posh place there may be a few black Sudanese guards. Here, if you're lucky you will also find pork on the food table. At one such function there was even a pig's head just to prove that in a Muslim country where pork is even more proscribed than alcohol you can eat and drink to your heart's content. If you're white.

Friday mornings are special in the Hilton Hotel. Here you can eat as much as you like for thirty-three Sudanese pounds - six dollars on the black market. Beef sausages, meatballs, scrambled eggs, fried eggs, omelettes of your choice, potato cakes, cold meats, salads. Almost every table is taken up by white people.

This is a world where you can ascertain someone's status by asking them how they came here: KLM, Swissair, Lufthansa, means you have a certain position; it also means you can probably get out in a hurry if you need to. Balkan Airlines or Sudanair means you are doing this on the cheap. You mustn't be very important. Long anecdotes are told of how so and so always travels Swissair, she won't touch another airline, and how right she was the time there was a coup in such and such a country.

Out at the swimming pool at the Hilton the Germans, Dutch and Scandinavians are displaying their blondness to the hot African sun. At intervals the sound of a splash interrupts the quietness of the afternoon as one of them dives into the pool.

Although the white population has increased enormously over the past year, aid agencies increasing their expatriate number from one to one hundred, from two to seventy, to give just two examples, you hardly ever see a white person in Khartoum or in the neighbouring city of Omdurman.

Khartoum: the name conjures up a huge colonial past, a legacy of fading old administrative buildings, palm trees, the white man's grave. In fact, Khartoum was, up to one hundred years ago, a centre of the slave trade. No one ever wanted the Sudan badly enough to make Khartoum into a colonial city.

Khartoum: the aura around the name comes not from years of governor generals and vice-regal parties but from a few days in January 1885 when Charles Gordon stood on the roof of his palace down by the river knowing that he was done for, knowing that he was surrounded by the forces of the Mahdi, knowing that help would not come in time. He is there as an exquisite symbol, where the Romantic ego meets the Imperial desire, just as a hundred yards away from his palace the White Nile and the Blue Nile mingle, "the longest kiss in history", as the Sudanese poet put it.

Gordon was dressed impeccably to meet his death. He had made sure that his diaries, full of recriminations and contradictions, had got out and the story of the brave, hopeless fight he put up. After they murdered him they put his severed head on show.

There is little of his spirit in Khartoum now (except the two guards at the door of the re-built palace, who are dressed in an extraordinary florid costume and stand to attention in the heat all day); the city is otherwise falling to pieces. Transport, run mainly by the private sector, is cheap and efficient. There are no muggings. The army is everywhere.

Anyone who wishes to travel outside the city must apply for a permit, sometimes also being required to alert the security police and fill in a separate form. Moving people is difficult here, but moving goods and money is fraught with danger as the aid agencies are finding out. Buying grain is not a simple operation. The money must be changed at a special low rate in a special bank, forms must be filled in and signed by the right people. Then you must wait. You must wait too for spare parts and other essential items to come from Port Sudan. CONCERN is still waiting for stuff which arrived last May at Port Sudan to be released by the authorities.

In this environment of bureaucracy, rules, hindrances, regulations, it is impossible to do much business and hardly any business exists in Khartoum beyond the artisan level. It is much easier and more productive to speculate in dollars than to invest money in an enterprise. In the city there is an extremely limited supply of commodities.

Petrol is rationed which means nothing, except that petrol is bought on the black market. These days the city closes down at ten o'clock in the evening although the official curfew was lifted in November. Alcohol is still banned which means nothing, except that alcohol is available and those caught drinking it, making it, or selling it, are liable to be flogged but more likely to spend a week in prison and even more likely to get off by bribing the police.

When the Truckers Association of the Sudan has its annual get-togethers in the future the members will raise their glasses to the year 1985, the year they cleaned up, the year when transporting grain a certain distance went up from eighty Sudanese pounds per ton to two hundred and fifty pounds per ton. (It is now one hundred and twenty pounds per ton).

The truckers will surely meet in the town of Wad Medani, where most of them are based. Wad Medani is three hours by road south of Khartoum. It is the capital of the area known as the Gezira, where prosperity reigns, rents are high and irrigation schemes operate. Most of the Transitional Military Council were born in the Gezira region, much to the disgust of Southerners.

The Gezira is the largest farm unit in the world. It is owned by the Sudanese government. It produces mainly cotton, which the country exports raw at very low prices.

Prosperity, however, is relative. One afternoon we drive across a barren landscape off the main road at Wad Medani. The village we are going to is an hour away. The land here again is difficult to drive on, the surface is full of bumps and dips.

Don McPhee of Foster Plan Care, a Canadian agency, is taking us to the official opening of a development project in the village. There is a reception committee to meet us and a tent has been specially put up.

There are three tables in the tent. One for the workers who built the new centre; one for the women and one for the khawajas, the foreigners, the whites, who have come from Wad Medani for the celebrations. At each place a bottle of Pepsi-Cola has been left, as well as an orange. There are sweets and biscuits on the table.

But first the khawajas must all meet the elders of the village who are seated on two lines of chairs at right angles to the tent. Behind them stand the male youth of the village who also greet the white visitors.

Speeches must be made. First, one of the elders makes a speech, and then two of the welcoming committee. Everyone listens attentively. Small groups of children who come to stare at the white people are sent on their way. The two longest speeches are made by two of the local women, one of whom has huge, deep tribal scars on her face.

It is getting dark. While Don conduct some business in the village we go for a walk. As the light fades completely, we become aware that we are being followed by as many as hundred people who are moving stealthily behind us, most of them children, the rest women. As soon as we turn around to go back most of them scatter in fright, racing back to the village.

As we get back into the jeep to go back to Wad Medani they crowd around us. As the jeep starts up they begin to applaud.

In March, 1985 Samir Basta, Head of UNICEF in the Sudan, travelled by helicopter up the Nile with the Sudanese Minister for Health. The Minister was shocked by what he saw in the villages.

He had not known the situation was so bad. Despite the Minister's shock, Samir Basta believes that a concerted effort was made by Nimeiri's government to keep the famine a secret. The government fell in April 1985.

Nimeiri is now the villain. They want him back from Egypt to put him on trial. Last September thousands marched on the Egyptian Embassy calling for his extradition. His cynical use of Islamic law seemed even worse when it was discovered that he had negotiated with Israel over the air-lifting of the falashas.

He introduced Islamic law in September, 1983, yet it took almost a year for the changes to affect ordinary life in the country. At first the Americans were alarmed by what they saw as the growth of Islam in the Sudan, but others who knew the country better, believed that Nimeiri had introduced sharia lawn as a last-ditch form of repression. People here were appalled when amputation of limbs, floggings and public executions became normal.

Since the fall of Nimeiri, the Transitional Military Government under Dr. Jazouli Dafalla has exercised great discretion in the use of sharia lawn, and there have been no amputations or public executions. They have also abandoned Islamic forms of taxation and the Islamic calendar, in which the year has 354 days.

The war in the south continues, costing the state an estimated million dollars a day, and presumably costs Ethiopia, who are financing the rebels, an equivalent sum. The south is Christian and animist, they do things differently there. The people's appearances are different, their skin is blacker, their clothes are different, they speak different languages. They have, since independence in 1956, believed themselves to be discriminated against by the north. They believe, with some justification, that important natural resources are being diverted away from them for the north's benefit. They greatly resent the imposition of Islamic law in the south which does not have a native Muslim population.

Everyone here wants to talk about the future. The aid people say that when the drought is over, and even now when there is still a danger of famine, people should be talking about development, about building up the infrastructure of the country. Bob Geldof is all for development.

The future of the country is not in the hands of Bob Geldof, despite his goodwill, nor in the hands of the aid agencies, nor in the hands of the incoming government. The future of the country is in the hands of a small number of banks and the International Monetary Fund. The country owes nine thousand million dollars to foreign banks. The country's annual exports bring in five hundred million dollars. Last year Sudan's debt service payments were 157% of its export earnings. One of the reasons for the shortage of food in 1984 and 1985 in the Sudan was its need to grow cotton rather than cereals, to earn foreign currency and pay back its debt. This is not to underestimate the importance of the drought.

"Nimeiri for his last ten years had been dealing with the IMF,"Prime Minister Dr. Jazouli Dafalla says in a recent issue of New Africa magazine. "They gave him a recipe. What had gone wrong? Either the recipe was good and the implementation was bad, because it led to one devaluation after the other and brought the Sudanese economy into a mess: the Sudanese pound is now nineteen per cent of what it used to be in 1970. Or the recipe is not correct. If the recipe was correct and the implementation was wrong, why was Nimeiri given money again and again? These questions have not been answered to our satisfaction.

"In many respects," he goes on, "IMF conditions are not suitable for a developing country. The IMF demands are too stringent, particularly when you inherit a collapsed economy. We told the IMF: Have the eggs but do not kill the goose!"

The arrears to the IMF now run at one hundred and sixty-seven million dollars, twice what Live Aid raised. The government is involved in negotiations with the US and Saudi Arabia over clearing this further addition to the debt, but there has been no conclusion, and there is unlikely to be any as long as the government continues to invite Libyan terrorists to dinner.

Magill, February 1986

HEART OF DARKNESS

Sometimes you feel you are not in the Sudan at all: that what you are looking at is an image from television, from a news report, a documentary, or from a book of photographs, or from a novel by Somerset Maugham, Graham Greene, V.S. Naipaul. Sometimes you feel that what you are dealing with is not here and now, not in the present, not actually happening: that it belongs to the well-worn, the cliche.

Take this one. Khartoum airport in the small hours. The soft heat of the night. A one-storey airport building, floodlit, soldiers in green uniforms with battered-looking machine guns. The flight comes from London, has stopped at Cairo and will stop again at Harare. There are just a few of us getting off. The sense of resentment against us in the arrivals room throbs like a headache.

They let me through as soon as my bags come in. I am thus in time to see the official, or the minister, or the VIP, drive by in his black mercedes. Young, suit and tie, short hair, glasses, sitting in the back of the brand new car, being driven back into the country which he helps to control.

All this could be imagined, conjured up by anyone who has read certain novels, watched certain television programmes. The African airport, the African dictator, the African heat. There is no need to go there to see this.

Nor is there any need to go there to see how battered the lone airport taxi looked, how five or six of them haggled with me and each other over the price; how it became clear that none of them actually owned the taxi; how they got the youngest and weakest-looking one to drive it.

The journey: that too, is easy. The road into the city, deserted now, but well-kept; the good buildings. And how the real city started when the roads became bumpier and the buildings seemed unfinished. The driver couldn't drive, he didn't know the way, he got lost down a dirt track, he got stopped by a soldier with a machine gun; how both of them, here now, in the dead of night began to question me in Arabic, how I didn't understand anything they said and keep repeating, like a prayer, the name of the hotel, the name of the hotel.

All sounds like part of someone else's dreams.

Maybe this will help. It was two, perhaps three in the morning, I made out the name of the hotel by the lights of the taxi as it approached. When it stopped the driver turned off the lights and there was darkness. No light from any of the surrounding buildings. No light from the moon. And no street lights. I knew we were in the centre of Khartoum. I could see nothing. I could hear nothing. I could hear the incessant barking of dogs; too close not to feel that they were coming closer.

I began to push doors to try and find some way of getting into the hotel. I had to feel along the wall. The taxi driver turned on the engine again; he was impatient for me to pay him and take my bag. I was afraid. Something moved behind me. I heard a sort of a groan. I could make out a pillar and below a figure lying stretched out. The figure groaned again. I could make a man out - skinny, old, dressed in night attire. He walked past me and pushed open a door, came back for my bag, which he took into the hall. He didn't speak. When he turned on a light I could look back and see that he had been lying on a spindly wooden bed out in the open. Upstairs another man was lying on a couch and had to be woken. The hostility from both of them was substantial, palpable.

The old man waited with my bag in his hand while the other entered the details of my passport on to a form. It was like the normal lobby of a small hotel, with notices up in English about tours on the Nile. I was not there to take tours on the Nile, but the fact that such things were available was reassuring, and helped to ease the silence from the two men.

"One night?" the guy at the counter said holding up his index finger.

"One night", I assented.

One night in a hotel room, the electric fan at full blast over the bed, only the sound of dogs outside, not a single car, or footfall, or sound of voices. The window looked onto the street, but there was not light enough to get any sense of the street.

The next morning, as I woke, confused by the unexpected heat, I contemplated the fact that every day from now to the time, two months hence, when I got back to Dublin, was going to involve hard work, constant meetings with strangers, difficulty, depression, exhaustion. Why was I doing it? What was it for?

In the early morning I stood in the centre of Khartoum. The streets were covered in sand. Even on the corners of the crossroads there were hardly any shops. Men in long white robes lounged about. No one got out of the way when cars approached. There was no sign of a cafe, or place where you could sit down and try to work out what in the name of God was going on.

I had read the novels and watched the television documentaries but I had no idea that a city could be like this. The more I got to know the place, the more disconcerting it became. Certain commodities were freely available: cotton, jewellery, fruit, vegetables. You could always get a taxi, at least in daylight. The buses worked.

But most of the buildings remained unfinished, the upper storeys were just shells, like hieroglyphics: messages of a future intention, or a past failure. Half the shops were shut up. There were blokes standing around wanting to change dollars. The official rate ranged from 2.2 Sudanese pounds per dollar to 3.3; the black market offered 4.7 to 4.8 for cash and four pounds flat for travellers' cheques.

The transactions were done openly. You would make your contact as you walked along and follow him into a shop or an empty space off the street. One of the spots I frequented was a sort of general meeting place for fellows who seemed like the princes of the Khartoum black market, with lackeys to run for them and questions to ask like: "Deutschmarks, you got any deutschmarks?"

Outside in the hot winter sun the desert sand seemed to be wreaking its revenge on the streets of the city. There were no colonial buildings, no sense of a whole legacy decaying slowly under the new regime. There was only the feeling that what had happened elsewhere in the cities of the world had not happened here. In Europe, North America, Canada, Australia, South America, everywhere, cities allowed access to greater ranges of commodities, social occasions, pleasures, outside influences. Here there was no such range, no such access, only the dead sand on the main streets, the run-down cars, the odd herd of goats or sheep coming through, the dullness.

Over the next four weeks I would tour this city in taxis talking to aid people about the drought, the famine, the relief work. Over the next four weeks I would deal regularly with CONCERN, the Irish relief agency, and I would find them efficient, hard-working, practical, tactful.

But the emergency aid business is essentially colonial. The natives are useful as drivers and cooks. They are good at making tea and running messages. But they are not to be trusted with serious tasks. Sudanese natives are not allowed to monitor food distribution for OXFAM. They are only allowed to drive the white man to monitor and interpret for him. "There are too many tribal loyalties", one British food monitor would explain.

The Sudanese learn nothing new while the aid workers gain skills and experience. ("You can't always be a volunteer", says one former aid worker, now earning a large salary here, living in a mansion with a private tutor for his children.)

But for those who, in a time of mass unemployment in Western Europe, want an outdoor life in a hot climate with servants, access to jeeps, a modicum of authority and no need to learn even the rudiments of the language, aid work offers an opportunity not available since the great days of the British Empire. In Khartoum you can see them, particularly in the New Extension, the white enclave, being driven about by natives in the only new cars and jeeps in the city.

The concept of superiority is deeply embedded in the white man's soul. At the office of the United Nations Emergency Operation in the Sudan in Khartoum there is a list of all employees, with names, addresses and other details. The seventeen Sudanese employees all come at the end of this list.

Yet when you see the aid workers in their offices, or go to meet the volunteers in desert outposts or refugee camps in the Sudan, people who have signed on for six months, a year, two years, when you watch their faces as letters from home arrive, you realise what an extraordinary sacrifice their coming here represents, working with strangers in a strange place. They too have their problems with journalists and visiting officials, people who are only too ready to make sweeping criticisms will also want to see starving people, and will even register disappointment when these are not available, who will be more interested in a weeping mother and her dead child than a new road built or a well dug.

On New Year's Day I stood in the bus station outside Khartoum like the boy on the burning deck. It was just before seven in the morning. I'd had less than two hours sleep. Between nine the previous evening and three in the morning I had drunk a large quantity of home-made beer, some whiskey and quite an amount of Ethiopian gin. I needed something cold and clear to drink. I would have given my return ticket for a Club Orange and a comfortable bed.

The journey north would take seven hours. I would be met by CONCERN volunteers who would take me to a refugee camp. All I needed was something to drink. I wandered about the market beside the station until I found a stall which sold drinks. I pointed at a covered bucket. The man took the lid off and displaced a swarm of flies. He poured the liquid into a tin mug and handed it to me. I paid him and started to drink. I had drunk half the mug before I realised it was thick, lukewarm mango juice, foul, evil-tasting.

On the bus I didn't know what was wrong. The seat was comfortable, I was sitting beside a window, the road was pretty good, I was feeling sleepy. But I kept feeling hot and then cold, particularly my head. I could feel my stomach contracting. But after a while I began to doze and it was only when I woke up that I realised I was going to be sick. I stood up and tried to stick my head out of the window but it wouldn't fit. I sat down again and thought I was going to be okay, no need to worry, the nausea had gone.

Suddenly it started again and this time it was serious. I got up as quickly as I could, just in time to emit a large stream of green puke, which completely covered my window and the window behind. I sat down, only to have to stand up again for more puking, retching, coughing and snivelling. My bag was in the back of the bus. I had no handkerchief, towel or tissue. Thick green puke covered my beard and my hands. I sat there. I didn't know what to do.

I tried to ascertain if there had been any reaction from my fellow passengers by turning my head slightly. Everyone looked straight ahead. No one, even the guy beside me, paid the slightest heed to me, the only white man on the bus. The puke had stuck to the window, had hardened on the glass, but it was still wet on my beard and there was no way I could think of getting it off short of stopping the bus. I hadn't the courage to stop the bus.

This was some sort of primary dread. To be covered in puke on a bus full of Sudanese with the hangover still gnawing away at one's insides, six hours still to go. To face arrival at a refugee camp and instead of being a business-like journalist with notebook in hand and all my wits about me, I was going to present myself to CONCERN as some sort of hobo, clearly alcoholic, lacking credibility of any sort or description.

Just three days previously I had been wandering about London without a care in the world. Just one week before I had been celebrating Christmas in the bosom of my family. Here I was amid the alien corn. When I looked out of the window through the chinks in the puke, I saw hundreds of camels stretching their long necks towards a shallow pool of water. I had forgotten where I was. Camels? There they were, just off the main road between Khartoum and Wad Medani. This came as an enormous shock. I hadn't thought of camels. They belonged to travel books of the coffee table variety, they belonged to zoos, documentaries and the eye of the needle. I had never expected to actually see a camel and here, now, were loads of them in front of me. It was deeply disconcerting.

When the bus stopped at a roadside eating place I edged around looking for a place to wash myself. There was a big queue at a water barrel, everyone taking a tin mug and drinking from it. I felt that if I put my grimy hands near the barrel or the mug there would be a riot, so I waited. I watched carefully as my fellow passengers formed another queue for food, this being the hour for fatur, the elaborate Sudanese breakfast.

When there was no one at the barrel I took the mug and filled it, making sure that no one was looking at me. I took the mug around the corner and used the water to rub the puke off my beard, but instead of removing the puke, the water only served to dilute it, soften it, spread it about a bit more. I went back several times and refilled the mug, trying desperately to restore the beard to its former pristine state. To no avail.

Someone had told me that the Sudanese were Muslims and I listened carefully and nodded. I had probably even written it down in my notebook. At the next stop, however, I was left in no doubt as to the religion of my fellow passengers. They all trooped out of the bus, queued once more at the water barrel - eyed by me - washed their hands, faces, feet and ears, rolled out their mats and faced Mecca, got down on their hunkers one and all and began to pray. They were all praying to Allah, letting their foreheads touch the ground, and then back up again. I stood there looking at them.

Kafka was a social realist. His world, an infinite complexity of offices, waiting rooms, a maze without cause and effect, was not a parable, it was real. Things are like that in certain places. I was living in Omburman, across the Nile from Khartoum. I was trying to find out how the famine was being dealt with, going into the desert where people live only on American grain, going to look at development work, lying in bed with dysentery, visiting aid officials.

Things were like Kafka in certain places. The Czech who wrote in German understood what it was like to try and travel from Khartoum to Port Sudan and from there to Egypt by boat.

First, the ticket and the ticket office. Yes, the large woman said, there was a boat from Port Sudan to Suez. No, they didn't know what day it went. Yes, this was the right office and, yes, indeed it was the only place where you could buy a ticket. Come back in a week.

A week later she was still sitting there: yes, she said the boat will leave on a certain Sunday, but it might leave on Monday, or

Tuesday, or any day, but you have to be there on Sunday. To buy a ticket, you have to take your dollars to a certain bank, no other bank will do, and change them at the lowest rate into Sudanese pounds. Then you take these pounds plus the certificate from the bank here and we will give you a ticket.

The following day I arrived with my dollars, showed them to her, was taken to the specified bank by the office boy, changed my money at half the street rate, was handed a certificate and marched back to get my ticket. She looked at the certificate then looked up at me in absolute contempt. I had been to the wrong bank. Yes she agreed that the boy from this very office had taken me, but he obviously had taken me to the wrong one, this certificate was wrong, it was no use, she handed it back to me, called the boy, had a brief conversation with him, then looked at me again, shrugged her shoulders pursed her lips and told me that I would have to go to the bank again, and no she didn't know if the first bank, the one I had been to, would change the money back for me into dollars. No new certificate, no ticket.

It was not clear, and it never became clear, if the man who was sitting behind me in the office worked in the place, owned it, or was just a man who happened to be sitting there. He began to take an interest in the row which had broken out. He spoke English too. He agreed to come with me to visit the right bank and the wrong bank, which were both beside each other.

First we went to the only bank which would be acceptable to the ticket agency and asked them if they would do a deal with the other bank about the certificate. We were interviewed by six different people. At one stage five of them stood together and discussed the matter while the sixth went into the bank. Various other bank officials were then consulted. The sixth bloke came back with the clerk who had dealt with me in bank number one. I didn't understand a word of the discussion, but I can testify that its tone was serious and its length was long.

At one stage an argument broke out and arms were raised to emphasise various points. I looked from one to the other, as they gestured fiercely, interrupted each other and discussed my case. Every time I asked the guy from the ticket office what was going on he told me to wait. I waited.

In the end it was agreed that I would take the Sudanese pounds and the certificate back to the first bank and they would return to me my travellers' cheques in dollars which I would take to the other bank. The other bank then would change money for me at an even lower rate, but a rate acceptable to the ticket office and give me a suitable certificate. But I couldn't do this today, as it was nearing one o'clock and both banks were closing for the day. I could come back tomorrow.

As I was walking out of the bank with the guy from the office, he asked me where I had been the previous Friday night. I told him I had been at a party to celebrate the 210th anniversary of the US Marines. He said he knew, he had given me a lift home from it. I remembered that there were four of us, we had been waiting for a taxi and we hitched a lift with this car which took us into town. I hadn't seen the guy's face as I had been in the back seat. This was him and what was he doing sitting in the office as I was trying to buy my ticket? Khartoum is a huge city; the chances of this were thin. He waved back to me as he walked off.

Now there was permission to be got from the Aliens Office and the Security Police to travel to Port Sudan, a bus ticket which would have to be purchased in advance, and a visa to go to Egypt. I would need five photos of myself. This would take days of visiting offices, finding them closed, being told to come back, wait, go somewhere else. Forms would be thrown at me by officials, I would have to tour Khartoum looking for a photo booth which also had an electricity generator - the supply of electricity came and went. There was a need, someone told me, to get used to it, this waiting, these days wasted in offices, this travelling from one official address to another, the long, hot, exasperating mornings.

In Port Sudan in the early afternoon on the road between the bus station and the town two Sudanese Arabs were beating up a black man. He seemed to have stolen a garment which he had over his shoulder, but this was not absolutely clear. The second of his assailants had a strong stick, but wasn't close enough to hit him with it.

The other caught up with the black guy, however, and tried to hold him while his companion hit him with a stick on the head and across the back. Our taxi driver stopped and started to laugh. By the time another car came behind the black guy was on the ground and was still being beaten. The driver and passenger ran across towards the scene. Instead of breaking it up, however, they began to kick the black guy. The kicks were vicious. We sat in the taxi, incredulous.

I caught a glimpse of his face. He was crying, his face in an agony of helplessness and desperation. Our taxi driver continued to point at the scene and laugh. More people arrived and joined in. We drove on. The taxi driver spoke no English so we couldn't ask him why he was laughing.

Later, on a ship on the Red Sea I would ask a young Sudanese bloke who spoke English whether such a scene was common. I did not mention that the victim was blacker than is normal in the north of the Sudan. "Was he black?" he asked me immediately. When I assented he told me that blacks come up from the south to rob. He was probably a thief. He shrugged. A few days later the BBC World Service would report a demonstration in Port Sudan by blacks from the south calling for civil rights.

One of our companions in Port Sudan was a member of the Sudan Club in Khartoum, a white man's stomping ground. This gave him the right to avail of the services of the Red Sea Club in Port Sudan, whither we repaired, having found our hotel, dropped our bags, performed our ablutions, and discussed the beating up of the black man, which, over a number of days we kept coming back to. It continued to hover. None of us had ever seen anything like it before.

The porter at the Port Sudan Club explained that today was Friday, the weekly day of rest, and members only were allowed, no guests. No matter what we did, no matter how much we explained that we were just here for a few days, et cetera, there was a rule, the committee had laid it down, he was only the man at the door. If we came back in an hour, however, he would let us in, he said. (Later, we would find out that Friday was the day when female aid workers like to come and sit around the salt water swimming-pool in their bikinis. The ban on guests lessened the chance of native boys coming to ogle them. The protection of the white woman's soft, delicate skin from the staring eyes of the black man has always been a primary ingredient of the colonial rhetoric).

An hour later, the man on the door had changed his mind. He said no guests at all. This was where he was interrupted by the representative of the British aid organisation, a member of the club, who roared at him to let us in. A photograph of the Queen of England on her wedding day hung inside the door.

Over the next few days we would be able to pick out the Red Sea Club a mile away because this was where all the jeeps were, the British aid workers' jeeps. Some of the guys were having a wonderful time: mountain-climbing, swimming, ordering natives about, driving jeeps, snorkling, as well as famine relief. Others were wilting: love sickness, sexual frustration, the runs, boredom, the sun, more runs.

One day, we borrowed all their snorkling gear and went down to Suakin, the old port, two hours south. Most of the other passengers on the mini-bus were nomads who had pitched their tents on the sandy terrain between Suakin and Port Sudan. When he wanted to get off the nomad would signal and the bus would stop. He would be wearing a long white jelabia, a turban and a sword, a real, heavy sword. He would stand and watch the bus move off before making for his tent, somewhere in the distance. If somebody moved into his territory, we were told, he would use his sword. This was a medieval world. Old costumes, old weapons, old wars.

The old port town of Suakin was joined to the land by a short causeway. When the harbour silted, the populace abandoned Suakin and moved to Port Sudan. They let Suakin fall. Stone by stone the place was crumbling, a whole densely built island. Some of the decorations and plasterwork could still be seen, some buildings were almost intact, the style of architecture was clearly more elaborate than in Khartoum, Port Sudan or points in between, but the place had been totally evacuated. There wasn't one person living on the island and the white stones fell one by one.

We spent the day wandering about this white shell. It looked as though it had been bombed, as though it had been through an air raid. Knowing that this was not so, knowing that the place had been left there, each and every house empty, gave the place a certain melancholy attraction: here was time at work, time that rots, crumbles and lays bare.

In many ways, this was a stranger world than Khartoum had been. The beating up of the black remained there, vicious, the work of a world we knew nothing about, a world led by some other spirit. The nomads with their swords and extraordinary good looks were living as though the Renaissance and the Reformation had occurred on some other continent (as indeed they had). And Suakin, old ghost of a place, beyond belief.

The offices of the good ship Syria were also beyond belief. On finally purchasing the ticket in Khartoum, I had been told that the boat might go on Sunday, or it might not, but it was necessary to be at Port Sudan on Saturday morning to alert the office there to one's possession of a first class ticket, or any other sort of ticket.

The office was dark, with three desks and one man sitting at each desk. It was just after nine in the morning and, immediately on my arrival, they announced they were closing for breakfast, I could come back in an hour.

An hour later the office was still closed up and a small crowd had gathered outside. When they eventually opened, we had to move from table to table, pay money at one table, show passports at a second table and show tickets at a third. At the third table we were told to come back at the same time tomorrow and no, they didn't know when the boat was going to leave.

Outside stood two people of the English-speaking, white-skinned persuasion. They had tickets for the good ship Syria as well, but I saw, to my relief, second class tickets. We will call the woman Lucy and the bloke Fred.

I had seen Lucy several days before in the town of Kassala as she pushed everyone out of the way to get her copious luggage on the bus. She kept roaring "Excuse me" at everyone in a loud, American accent. It was like the opening scene of a bad movie. I had kept out of her way. Here she was now.

Fred was Dutch. He wore an earring in his right ear. He was delighted that I was paying twenty-nine Sudanese pounds a night for my hotel; he was paying three in the student hostel. He was delighted that I had a first class ticket and kept going on about how much cheaper his own was. I didn't like Fred.

The following morning I arrived at the office. The same three men sat at the same three desks. There was silence. No one looked up. I asked about the boat. The first one shrugged. I asked the second one, who told me to come back at the same time, tomorrow, Monday. Would it leave tomorrow then? I asked. He didn't know. If I came back tomorrow, he would know. The next attempt at a question was greeted with "Tomorrow" and the man pointed at the door, and his face suggested that he thought it was time I left them alone.

Tomorrow, they were all slightly more chirpy. Yes, one of them said, the boat would leave today. Be there, at the port, at the good ship Syria at twelve, he said.

Down at the port all passengers were told to wait in a warehouse, unless they wanted to sit in the hot sun. Twelve became one, one half one. When I complained to the Dutch guy, Fred, he said if I was in a hurry why didn't I fly. I told Fred that people with second class tickets would be made stay in the hold. Lucy had not turned up. Please note two further things about Fred: he was still wearing his earring in his right ear; he had befriended a Sudanese boy, twenty years old, who was travelling to Europe for the first time.

Two o'clock became half two and everyone still sat in the warehouse waiting. Half the passengers were going to Jeddah, twelve hours across the Red Sea. The other half were going to Egypt. For some time now, for a number of reasons, flights from Port Sudan had been more or less closed. This was the only way of getting out of the country. At three o'clock they started to hand out our passports, which they had previously taken from us, and we stood in a long queue to go through customs, currency control, police and passport control, one as slow and deeply vigilant as the other.

By four o'clock we were all on the boat and were shown to our quarters. I was given the upper bunk in Room 31; a Sudanese doctor who worked in Cairo had the lower one. I spoke no Arabic; he spoke no English. The boat was old, worn and wonderful. I couldn't wait for it to start.

Lucy turned up. Through sheer determination to get out of the Sudan, she had seen the Syria coming in that morning, had battled her way down, past all concerned and sat in front of the ship with all her baggage. As I explored the three decks, I met her. "Do you know where the captain is?" she said.

"No", I replied.

"I'm in a room with three fat Egyptian women, I wanna move", she said. She walked on, an intent look in her watery eyes.

Next I met Fred.

"There are only three in our cabin", he said.

"There are only two in our cabin and we have our own bathroom", I replied.

"But think of what you paid", said Fred as he wandered past.

By six o'clock we were moving. We moved out of Port Sudan, past the small fishing boats and the big anchored Jugoslav ship, past the pier and the pilot boat, out to sea. By the time the light started to give, Port Sudan was back there in the distance. This was the magic time, when the dying light cast its spell over the world, when the air hovered with the coming darkness. I had seen it in Khartoum, the air changing colour almost every second. I had seen it close to the refugee camp - the sun's disc falling slowly over a lake, and the darkness coming in, just like that.

Graham Greene writes about it in 'The Heart of the Matter': 'In the evening the port became beautiful for perhaps five minutes ... It was the hour of content. Men who had left the port forever would sometimes remember on a grey wet London evening the bloom and glow that faded as soon as it was seen: they would wonder why they had hated the coast and for a space of a drink they would long to return.'

Every day I waited for it, took a shower beforehand to make sure I was fully alert, and sat on the lower deck, which was usually quiet, to watch the light as the sun went down. I saw it four times on the Red Sea, I witnessed that fifteen minutes of intensity, as day changed to night. I almost understood once or twice as the darkening air whispered all around, I almost understood what a different world this was.

When we arrived at Jeddah, the Sudanese immigrant workers got off and were replaced by Egyptian pilgrims coming from Mecca. This made little change to the routine already established. Breakfast at six thirty, lunch at twelve, dinner at six thirty pm. There was very little difference between two of these meals: they basically consisted of beans, those sort of hard beans that you have to soak, big plates of them, bread and chillis, real chillis which my table mates would take in their mouths and eat whole, and water. At dinner there would be two hard boiled eggs, cold, and a triangle of processed cheese plus rice and a stew followed by oranges, followed by tea.

Fred sneaked in from his second class one evening for a snoop and saw this. He was forced to confess that down in the hold they got beans and beans only for all their meals.

Lucy told me that she thought the captain wanted to sleep with her. I asked her for hard evidence. I had to repeat this several times. She told me that she had moved into his sitting-room and was sleeping on the couch, having complained bitterly about the three fat Egyptian women to the captain. He had not made any approaches yet, but she felt he was going to. "I'm not going to get laid on this ship", she said. "Even if I met Omar Sharif, I wouldn't get laid".

The muslims prayed five times a day in the bar, being called to do so by the extraordinary voice of an older man. (There was, of course no alcohol served in the bar).

Games of dominoes and backgammon were played in the downstairs and upstairs bars all day and much of the night. Luckily, neither Lucy nor Fred could play, which meant they stayed away. Playing for money was forbidden. One little Somalian began to have the most extraordinary luck in both games which he combined with skill to win over and over.

Each time I threw to decide who started the play in backgammon, I threw the same as my opponent, or he threw the same as me. This happened in almost every game I played. People began to notice it. Sometimes it was repeated. On a few occasions it happened three times. Once it happened four times. If I thought about it, or referred to it, or if people came to watch, it wouldn't happen.

For most of the day, however, I lay stretched out in the sun. I read for a while and then I stopped reading. I just lay there leaving my mind as empty as I could.

One Egyptian made various efforts to prevent me doing this. He had shaved his head in Mecca and was wearing an embroidered cap. He would come up to me and say: "Who was Jesus Christ?"

"He was the Son of God", I would reply.

"Not Son of God", he would say.

"Yes, he was the Son of God", I would say.

"Not Son of God", he would repeat. "'Prophet, like Mahommed".

"No, Son of God who saved the world", I would say, and would follow by explaining the mystery of the Holy Trinity to the poor Arab who would keep repeating "Not Son of God". This would go on until I got fed up. He would never get fed up.

One day he came to me and said he wanted to talk. I had been recalling all the theology I ever knew, so I was ready for him. The Assumption. The Ascension. The Infallibility of the Pope. The Resurrection. The Immaculate Conception. Confession. Extreme Unction. The Virgin Birth. The Annunciation. The Real Presence. The Christian Brothers. Good Friday. Knock Airport. I was ready for him. Don't think I wasn't well prepared.

No, this time he didn't want to discuss the evils of the infidel religion. He wanted to talk about Fred. I listened carefully.

Was I a friend of Fred's? he wanted to know. No, I told him. His bigot's eyes narrowed as he asked me: what was the meaning of the earring in Fred's right ear? I said it didn't have any meaning in particular, as far as I understood, except that Fred was young and foolish. He told me he knew what it meant.

"He do bad things with other men", he said. I told him I didn't think so. A few other Egyptians had gathered around us. Had I noticed, the bloke with the shaved head asked me, who Fred was sharing a cabin with? I said he was with the young Sudanese boy and the Somalian. Had I noticed that the Somalian was up and about the deck all day while Fred and the Sudanese boy were seldom to be seen? Did I know what they were doing down there?

Suddenly I realised that I had Fred's fate in my hands, not that they would throw him overboard, or anything, but they seemed to feel that he should be quarantined, or put into solitary confinement. But they needed confimation about the earring. What did an earring in the left ear mean? I said that it meant nothing much, except that the wearer was generally a bit of a fool. What did the right ear mean? I said that it meant more or less the same. They shook their heads in dissatisfaction. They wanted me to tell them that the earring meant what they thought it meant. They moved away.

That evening Fred and the Sudanese boy appeared in the bar after dinner, completely oblivious to the storm brewing all around the. It struck me, looking at them, that they probably were up to something down in the hold alright. The Arabs continued to conspire against them, but nothing came of it. Fred and the boy were left to their own devices.

Rumours began to fly around. The boat was going to arrive in Suez on Thursday afternoon, according to some. The doctor who shared my cabin, a most polite and sensible fellow, said it wouldn't arrive until Saturday. I met Lucy and she swore that the captain had told her that it would arrive on Thursday. This was very unsettling, and it was hard to decide whether one wanted the boat to sail up the Red Sea for ever or whether one wanted to arrive in Egypt this minute. We arrived in Port Suez at eight o'clock in the evening but the port had closed and it was announced that we would have to anchor in the harbour overnight. All foreigners were ordered back to their cabins to be interviewed by the police. I was in the middle of a game of backgammon when some fellow came and shouted at me to get down to my cabin.

Morning came and still no police. Neither was there any breakfast. By ten o'clock we were all starving. By eleven the crew were calming us down. It was Friday and the staff of the port were praying more than usual, we could hear the prayers bellowing out from loudspeakers. Eventually we started to move and we were all told to go down to the hold.

Down in the hold were a huge number of women gathered together, who had not appeared on the boat during the voyage. Most of them had their faces covered. They had not appeared for meals, nor had they taken a stroll around any of the decks. They had obviously stayed in their cabins for the whole journey, through all the long, hot days. It was an odd feeling looking at them now, finding out that they had been down here all this time.

We stood like cattle in the hold of the boat, waiting for someone to come and authorise our arrival on dry land. This authorisation had to be delivered from the port in writing. Through a small window I could see a platoon, or contingent of the Egyptian army trying to stand to attention on the dock. They looked scrawny, underfed and nasty.

Mini-buses and taxis waited to convey us to the customs office. The taxi driver kept roaring at me. "You change money, you change money". I looked out of the window and ignored him. The Egyptians were let go but us, the whites, the one Somalian and the Sudanese were told to wait in front of the fire brigade on a piece of waste ground. I was fed up waiting. It was now nearly two o'clock and prayers were still being shouted over the loudspeaker.

This was very like the day of the Blessed Sacrement procession in Enniscorthy. It would always be a hot Sunday and your feet would stick to the tar on the road, and there would always be delays. Your instinct always was to duck down a side street and go home.

The taxi driver suddenly came back and ordered the three whites, me, Lucy and Fred into his car to go and change money. All attempts to discover his motivation failed. I asked him if he was a policeman or a customs man. He said he wasn't. I asked him if he was a taxi driver. He assented. "Then don't be annoying me", I said.

A man came who said he was an official and he told the taxi driver to go away. Over the next hour this man was joined by eight other officials, all well-dressed, all looking as though they had serious business in hand. There were only about twenty-five of us and all we wanted them to do was let us go. Instead, they made an effort first of all to move us out of the shade and into the sun. The Sudanese refused to budge.

When this failed they called a young soldier who was guarding the fire brigade and told him to bring them chairs. The soldier carried out chairs for them. So here we were somewhere in the port area of Port Suez at three o'clock in the afternoon, it was hot, nine officials had got their chairs and were now being served tea. We had not eaten yet, most of us were sitting on the ground. No one had any idea when they would let us go.

Lucy became Biblical. She likened our plight to that of the Israelis, whom the Pharoah wouldn't release, and we tried to remember what the nine plagues were, so we could visit them on the nine officials.

Time went by. These guys still sat there on their chairs. We sat on the ground in front of them. Then a taxi came and they conferred with the driver and then ordered me, Lucy, Fred and the little Somalian who was lucky at backgammon to go and change money at the official rate. The official rate, we discovered was 1.3 Egyptian pounds per dollar; the rate on the street was 1.8 pounds. American Express would cash travellers' cheques into dollars in order to facilitate their customers who could then change the cash on the street, but before the Egyptians would stamp our passports we would have to change one hundred and fifty dollars in the bank. We would need this certificate before we paid a hotel bill, anyway.

We took our bags and moved towards the taxi. Release at last! We passed the nine officials. I had counted them carefully. They told us to leave our bags behind, that we were to go and change money, have our passports stamped and then come back here and wait for customs.

I walked up to the guy in charge. I was shaking with a mixture of temper, impatience and hunger. I came up very close to him. Why did we have to come back I wanted to know? To go through customs, he said. Why couldn't we go through customs now I asked? Because the customs men hadn't come yet, he replied. He had nine people here, I said, I counted them out for him - one, two, three, four, five, six, seven, eight, nine, ending with him, what were they doing, why were they just sitting around?

His face exploded. He went ape. Veins stood out where there had been no veins. Arteries throbbed. He went red and bits of him went blue. He screamed: "Don't speak to me like that!"

One of the nine came and held me. "He is a general", he said.

The general roared at him to let me go and told me to get into the taxi.

Fred was the first to speak as the taxi moved away. 'I told you if you are in a hurry you should fly', he said. I told Fred to shut up, just shut up.

Lucy was howling with laughter. Seemingly, as I spoke to the general, or whoever he was, she had said to Fred: "Oh look, he's shouting at the fat cat", and the taxi driver had interjected: "Yes, he fat cat, he very fat cat", in thick Egyptian tones, straight out of a movie.

It was generally agreed that the fat cat would be waiting for me when I got back.

"Shut your mouth", the Egyptian taxi driver said to the little Somalian. The taxi driver's English was confined to colloquialisms and odd phrases. As he started up the taxi the little Somalian looked as if he was going to cry. He hadn't even addressed the taxi driver. He had merely used some pleasantry to try and break the silence.

Changing one hundred and fifty dollars at an official rate, compulsory on entering Egypt, had taken an hour. First we were marched to an office somewhere in the port and told to wait outside; then, having waited while the officials inside did absolutely nothing, we were brought in one by one.

I was like a little lamb. All my arrogance and temper had been used up on shouting at the general. Now I was meek and humble, fawning and smiling at the officials and making myself agreeable to them. Had they said stand up, I would have stood up; had they said sit down I would have sat down. Instead they ignored me while they looked at every page of my passport, most of which were blank. Then a man escorted me down to the bank, where Lucy already was. Lucy and Fred, when he arrived, put up a big fight about changing their dollars at an official rate, saying they were just passing through Egypt. They lost their battle, as they knew they would, and we all changed our one hundred and fifty dollars and were led out to the taxi and told to wait there and our passports would be stamped and brought out to us.

The receipt from the bank was of major importance: to settle a hotel bill you could use Egyptian currency only if you could prove it had been changed at the official rate.

It was now getting towards half past three. We had now been in Suez since eight o'clock the previous evening and had still to go through customs. I still had to deal with the general. No one had eaten. Everyone we met so far had been deeply unpleasant.

During the next half hour as we waited in the taxi, which was being paid for by the port authorities, we learnt what the delay was about. The little Somalian hadn't got a hundred and fifty dollars and was being interrogated inside. The taxi driver said that they were going to send him back on the boat.

When he came out he seemed uneasy about facing us. The last half hour had been pretty rough, but he seemed to have won, and he had a stamp on his passport to prove it. No one spoke in the taxi at first and when he spoke it was as though nothing had happened.

"Shut your mouth", said the Egyptian taxi driver.

As we drove back through the port I had the general on my mind. I had seen 'Midnight Express' and my thoughts were full of damp cells and nasty jailers. I told Lucy to find out if there was an Irish consul and tell him to do something if I were taken in. Fred snorted.

Our bags lay there, like left-overs at a party, in front of the fire brigade building. The general and his friends had gone, as had the Sudanese. We were told to collect our bags and were driven to another customs shed. The taxi driver's main interest now was to drive us to Cairo for some exorbitant sum of money. Cairo was two hours away. He wanted fifty pounds.

We told him we would pay him half that, to the delight of the blokes at the customs office, who encouraged us no end and told us to pay him even less. We could get a bus for two pounds each, they said.In the end, we found a taxi to take us to the bus station. On the way, the taxi driver told us that he had a friend who would take us to Cairo for twenty pounds. After much discussion, and attempts to reduce the price, Fred, Lucy and the Somalian agreed. The taxi-man drove us into the centre of Suez and went to search for his friend.

The new taxi driver drove like an expert, fast, sure of himself, knowing when to slow down. The road between Suez and Cairo goes through what is a cross between a desert and a no man's land; there are no villages, or side roads, or turns off, or crossroads. This is not to say that no one lives between these two points.

Half way there we passed by a mini-bus which blew the horn at us frantically. When we looked behind, we saw that the bus was full of various Egyptians and Sudanese who had been on the boat with us. They were all waving and yelling. Our taxi slowed down and their vehicle passed us out only to be passed out again by us to the sound of more hooting and yelling. This was repeated several times until we all got bored with it and returned to the serious business of getting to Cairo.

No one had ever told me about Cairo. As we nudged our way through the traffic into the city, I caught myself looking out of the window in sheer amazement and wonder at some spectacular scene of urban blight. We told the taxi driver to drop us at Ramses Square in the city centre. It was getting dark and the thickening air served to add to the confusion.

Ramses Square was a disaster area. Every driver of every car honked the horn on a permanent basis. Lanes of traffic went in every direction. Although each lane was thick with cars the traffic never came to a standstill, never stopped moving. The people moved as well, on an elaborate set of footbridges which spanned the length and breadth of the square; the people moved into the train station, huge huddles of people; the people forced themselves into mini-buses on the waste ground in front of the station.

The relief of parting from Fred and Lucy was undermined somewhat by the surrounding confusion, by the sense of Cairo as one huge, unholy mess of a place. I waved farewell to them all and removed myself to the Fontana Hotel.

Having established myself and dropped my bags, I began to wander about the city. It was dark now. I turned off into a side street as soon as I could, feeling every so often the ground sway under me as though I were on a ship.

Cairo was still open for business. Everything under the sun was for sale. Most of the shops were tiny, most of the shops sold only one commodity. There was a wonderful sense of life here. Cars raced down the unpaved streets, scattering men, women and children. Motorbikes, vans, bicycles.

Every so often there was a bar, but there was no drink for sale, only Turkish coffee, tea and an elaborate glass contraption for smoking from, full of pipes, and water. Dominoes and backgammon, as well as card games, were being played with an exquisite seriousness by men, the domino slabs being slapped down on the table with great force and suddenness to maximum dramatic effect.

I never learned to play dominoes with so violent a sense of

challenge as these guys played and I decided I'd better not try. I played quietly, just timidly placing the slab down but usually I had two or three helpers behind me, who had worked out the percentages and the chances, and they made a great deal of noise.

I toured the halls, I listened for the sound of the throwing of dice. If you walked in and ordered a coffee, someone would come and ask you if you wanted a game and that was you set up. In Cairo, even more than in Khartoum, people stared at you because you were white, but in the rooms devoted to the sacred art of backgammon and dominoes the game was all important, not just winning it, but playing it faster and with greater passion than your opponent. There was no money involved. In those moments when luck came hovering over the board, as it can in backgammon, particularly towards the end of the game, when luck matters, the company would grow tense, there would be silence, all the European slowness, hesitancy and lack of passion would be made up for by double sixes and if you could get another double on the next throw and on the next they would watch you, keep their eyes on you, momentarily offer you honorary citizenship of the Middle East.

I wanted to get a boat from Alexandria to somewhere in Italy. I wasn't fussy about what part of Italy. I wandered up one day into the posh shopping quarters of Cairo to buy my ticket. I told the woman I wanted to get a boat to Italy. She told me I was in the right place. When? she asked. Next week, I told her. Sorry, she said. There are no boats from Alexandria for six weeks to Italy, Greece or anywhere else. From 1 February to 13 March there are no boats.

Imparting this information did not take much out of her. She was pretty smug about it, as though it was a speciality of the place. And to add insult, she took out a ticket and asked me when I wanted it for. I said I wanted to go next week. She said I couldn't, I couldn't go until 13 March. Did I want to go then? No, I said. I did not. Then she made it clear that there was nothing she could do for me.

All the agencies had the same news: no boats from Alexandria to Italy between 1 February and 13 March.

All the travel agencies and airline offices were in the same street. I wandered from one to the other in search of a cheap flight. Where did I want to go? they wanted to know. Anywhere; as long as the plane flew north and landed in Europe. Anywhere: but it had to be cheap.

No one had anything cheap. Everyone pointed out that a foreigner was required to have a certificate to prove that the money used to buy the air ticket was changed in a bank (at 1.3 per dollar) rather than on the black market (at 1.8 per dollar). .

I moved about Cairo trying to find something in the off-beat agencies, the run-down shops. Everyone had the same story.

The first chink in the great armour of the Egyptian travel trade came when the women in the airline office of one of the Soviet block countries said all she needed was the certificate with a sum of money written on it, she didn't require the same amount in cash. She whispered this to me.

"Where you want to go?" the little old man, pushing ninety, interrupted as I told my story to the woman behind the counter. "Anywhere", I said. His little bullet head looked at me "Where you want to go?" he said. "Europe, anywhere in Europe", I said. "Where?" he said. "Rome," I said. "Okay," he said. He sat there at the next counter nodding. "No certificate," I repeated. "No certificate," he said. Three hundred pounds was a hundred and eighty dollars on the black market. "I'll take that," I said. "Come back tomorrow with the money," he said.

At the top of the street stood the Egyptian Museum and the Hilton Hotel. Outside the museum stood large numbers of men, who wanted to be your guide in the museum. Having paid your money and avoided these fellows you could wander about this huge shambles of a place, room after room of mummies, tombs, ornaments, thrones, statues, jewellery, amazing stuff.

The staff had a special way of getting money out of you. One of them would call you over, with a conspiratorial look on his face, put his finger to his lips to call for silence and bring you down a corridor and would show something and lead you to believe it was very special, then he would put out his hand and demand money, baksheesh, a tip. What he was showing you would either be worthless or open to the public anyway. The security staff seemed to spend most of their time playing this game.

The treasures were just piled into rooms, there was no information on where they came from or what they meant, the museum's catalogue was out of print. Anything which could fit into a glass case was put into a glass case.

I went back three days in a row. There were two coffins in a room upstairs, each in a glass case on either side of a door. They were painted bright yellow, and different objects had been painted over the yellow: birds, men, women, hieroglyphics. But on both of them on a bottom corner were painted a pair of eyes, jet black, Egyptian, with eyebrows. Eyes staring out at you from the dead.

73

I met a German who told me that a few of those objects had been exhibited in Germany; a throne, a mummy, a coffin, one example of each thing. And each one had a room of its own, with special lighting and detailed explanations of its provenance and meaning. Here they were all jumbled together.

Yet the museum was a great labyrinthine haven, a shelter from the city outside. If you could get the staff to leave you alone, you could wander about these bits and pieces collected from the ruins, going back again and again to stare at the eyes in the coffin, a sign of death as something frightful - a sign, however dim, that the occasion of burial involved emotion, not apparent in any other of the monuments of death in these huge rooms, cold, ornate, placid, elaborate, stunningly beautiful.

The luxury train left Cairo for Luxor on the Nile, just across the river from the Valley of the Kings, at seven o'clock in the evening and arrived at seven in the morning. The ticket included dinner, bed and breakfast. There was a bar on the train.

The train looked like nothing on earth, or at least nothing on earth in Egypt. It was low and silver, like a Talgo. It looked weird in the railway station in Cairo, which was as ramshackle and overcrowded as the rest of the city. Everything was impeccably clean, everything was in order, there was a boy in uniform to show you to your compartment.

This train was nothing ordinary. You had to be there half an hour before the time, as though it was an aeroplane. The driver made an announcement over the loudspeakers, introducing himself and welcoming us aboard, as though we were about to take off at any moment. Before we took off, indeed, a youth in uniform appeared at the door and demanded baksheesh, a tip, from me and the French bloke who was sharing the compartment. I told him we would give him a tip at the end of the journey. He skulked off and we never saw him again.

Dinner came on a tray with tin foil over it an hour after the train started. The dinner was really good. Drinks came. The captain, or the driver of the train, informed us that the bar was open so we went down. The Egyptian waiter was doing a belly-dance, or some sort of snake dance, for the pleasure of the Germans and the Americans, who were egging him on and applauding him. This was deeply embarrassing.

In the morning the train arrived on time, like a little silver bullet, at Luxor. The French guy in the compartment had a guide to Egypt which announced that the best hotel in Luxor was called The Winter Palace, which was full of old charm, had excellent gardens, a

74

swimming pool, and a general air of opulence about it. I decided this was where I was going to stay, feck the expense.

We walked through Luxor in the early morning, the French guy went to a cheap hotel (two dollars a night) and I marched bravely down to the Winter Palace and presented myself at the reception desk of the old hotel - a new addition, called The New Winter Palace, I ignored. A room, the man said, would cost me twenty-nine pounds a night and I would have to show him a certificate to prove that I had changed my money at the official rate. This would work out at less than twenty-five dollars a night. I told him it was fine and immediately I was lit upon by a number of men in turbans and long white robes, one to carry my bag, one to carry the key, one to know if I wanted room service.

The hotel was splendid, incredibly posh, full of ante-rooms, wide, sweeping corridors, vestibules, carvings, statues, stained glass. Men in turbans sat all day along the corridors in case you wanted anything. Several of them ran towards me now, the new guest, being led along by the man with the key and the man with the bag. Five of them swarmed round me and would not go away until I had given each of them money. The window looked on to the Nile. The room had two large beds, armchairs, an escritoire and air-conditioning. Everything in the bathroom worked.

Downstairs, long gardens led to a swimming pool, supervised by several men in turbans who handed out towels and made sure that you were comfortable in your deck chair, or if you wanted a drink, they were in charge of it. The day was warm and the sun was getting hotter.

A whole new set of names and places had to be learned: Seti I; Thutmose III; Amenhotep II; Ramses III; Tutankhamon. It was all very complicated. Every time I walked out of the hotel I was surrounded by fellows who wanted to change money for me, take me to see these tombs and temples, bring me somewhere or other in a horse and carriage, sell me goods, souvenirs, rugs, jewellery. The main streets of Luxor were full of tourists being pursued by locals who wanted, in one way or another, to get their hands on some of the tourists' money.

Sometimes the civilities broke down and abuse broke out. The locals would block the way, follow you, harass you. Walking along the street became an ordeal; moving outside the hotel involved courage and bravery; the locals, of course, were brave too, and persistent, and exuded a genuine contempt for the tourists.

I had been reading Graham Greene's 'The Heart of the Matter' in which the phrase 'jig-jig' is used when sex is offered to foreigners in Africa. One day I was wandering back to the hotel along the bank of the river when a man came alongside. Did I want to change money? No. Did I want to go out on a boat on the river? No. Did I want to go to Karnak in a carriage? No. Did I want hashish? No. Did I want a guide? No. Did I want to see the tombs? No. He had exhausted every possibility, or almost, when he said: 'Do you want jig-jig?'

Along with two companions from the hotel, I rented a bicycle, and we crossed with the ferry, got our tickets for the tombs, which had to be bought here, and made our way uphill to the Valley of the Kings. The road made its way through hills of dry dust.

The tombs were wonderful. Each one was totally distinct, both in colours used and the images painted on the walls. Each tomb, too, had a different shape and size, some cut deep into the ground, others, such as Tutankhamon's, close to the surface.

The hieroglyphics, squiggles, odd shapes and designs stood confidently beside drawings made in the same colours, using the same materials, of dogs, beetles, snakes, human figures, plants. There was no sense of a tomb being a formula, decided beforehand and executed by an artisan. There was, instead, a sense of the mind at work: of a dog here, and let's put a little squiggle here, and a face below it, and what'll we put here, I know, a woman, or an eye.

One tomb was done to resemble a scroll. Another was painted an extraordinary seething blue. Some of the work was clever, even funny, as the human neck would be elongated along a ceiling to meet a head on the other side. The tomb artists had a great time with snakes coiling around each other. Most of the stuff was in an amazingly good state of preservation; the dry, dusty, dead air outside offered no threat.

We freewheeled all the way back down to the Nile and crossed on the rusty old ferry.

One day on our way back from looking at temples we wanted to go out on a boat, a felucca, and watch the light fading and the sun going down. The boatmen were having a bad time because there was no wind, and one of them came running after us, wanting us to come out with him. The price was agreed and this guy started talking to us. He brought the boat out a bit but he couldn't use the sails because there was no wind, so we were stuck there in the middle of the river with this fellow who began to quote Shakespeare at us: "Time and tide can wait for no man", "To be or not to be", "Tomorrow and tomorrow and tomorrow"

There seemed no way to stop him. He seemed to know every passage of any note by heart. More than that, he was delighted with himself, despite the fact that there was no wind. He had a captive audience in the middle of the Nile.

My companions were going to Aswan the following morning, but I was going nowhere. I was afraid that if I left the hotel for too long it would melt, or be taken away by Americans. The boatman asked me what I was going to do in Luxor on my own. Nothing, I said. He told me I should hire a donkey and a guide and trot about the mountains. He then went back to his Shakespeare. After a long passage, which we dutifully applauded, he said he would arrange the whole thing for me.

I felt ridiculous enough as it was, staying in this posh hotel, being pursued hotly by the locals every time I left its sanctuary, in receipt of constant abuse for not wanting a trip in a carriage, or change money or any other of the services and delicacies on offer. Sitting on a donkey would be the last straw. But I told the Shakespearean boatman that I would see him at nine thirty the following morning. Bring the donkey.

He was there at the appointed hour with another fellow whom he called Gemal. Gemal was going to look after me for the day for the price agreed. We went down to the ferry and at the other side were several boys who had two donkeys waiting for us. I felt like an awful eejit sitting up on this poor animal, and I told Gemal that if anyone laughed I was going home. Gemal said no one would laugh. The boy who was holding the reins let go; now I was on my own, sink or swim with this animal.

Every time a car approached, or a bus, or a motorbike, the donkey went faster. The faster the donkey went the more unsettled I became. Falling off a donkey would be no joke - it would have to remain a dark secret all your life. You could never tell anybody about it. ("What happened your head?" they would ask. "Oh just a small accident with a horse," I would say.)

We were going back to the Valley of the Kings. This time, however, we were not using the road, but going straight over the mountain. Donkeys look slow and stupid, which is why they have a bad name, but they know how to move. There were times, as we moved up the mountain, when one wrong step would have seen me and donkey in kingdom come. I kept asking Gemal if this was okay, and he kept saying that it was, not to worry, the donkey does this every day. I couldn't stop thinking that some day he was going to get fed up doing it. ("What happened to your leg?" they would ask. "Oh, I had a small accident when I was horse-riding in Egypt.")

I asked Gemal if there was one tomb or temple which was off the beaten track and better than the others. He said there was and, on our first day out, we went there. It was the tomb of Sennudjem, a room maybe ten feet by six, coloured in bright orange, depicting the most extraordinary scenes: the mummy being leaned over in a delicate gesture, almost of affection, by a god with an animal's head. The bed he is lying on is in the shape of a lion. Other scenes showed a feast, the underworld, fields of wheat and hashish. The low ceiling was also decorated. Nothing had faded or was incomplete. The place was perfect, a little gem stuck into the ground.

In the tombs and temples, the guards for the most part would let you do anything if you paid them particularly in the tombs of the nobles in the hills. One bloke really wanted me to use a flash in a tomb which would actually damage the walls. It occurred to me that if you wanted to make it with Cairo Jenny on the floor of one of these tombs with strobe lighting and Diana Ross and the Supremes singing 'Baby Love' in Dolby stereo with a Today Tonight team, reporter Pat Cox, there to record it all, you would just have to pay a guard some money.

We stopped for lunch at the same place each day. The second day everybody looked very busy. Those who had stood around were now running up and down the restaurant laying the top table, frantically cleaning everything, loud noises came from the kitchen. Gemal discovered that a millionaire from Cairo was being shown around the tombs and was stopping here to have lunch.

When the millionaire and his party trooped in, we saw that he had two fat sons, who when they had finished their lunch, came down to Gemal, handed him five pounds and said they wanted to use the donkeys; Gemal gave them back the money, told him he didn't want the money, but they could use the donkeys. He didn't want the millionaire's money, he said. Anyway, it wasn't very much.

He told me that once, a few years before, he had got a message to meet a small party of Swiss people at the airport in Luxor and arrange transport for them to the river and then donkeys to the Valley of the Kings. He did this and he found them pleasant enough, as foreigners go. They insisted that he come back to the airport with them, they were using a private plane. They gave him a tip in Swiss francs which equalled about eight hundred dollars. He couldn't believe his eyes. Eight hundred dollars bought him two donkeys of his own and a large extension to the family house. It changed everything.

I went to visit the extension. Two bedrooms upstairs had been built, which gave the family privacy they'd never had before, and a big sitting-room downstairs for visitors and gossiping in.

It was late when I went to cross the Nile to go back to the hotel and the ferry was on the other side. Gemal began to call across the river 'Mahmud, Mahmud' to the ferryman. The night was dark and there was a mist wallowing along the water. We could just make out the lights of Luxor. Gemal kept shouting 'Mahmud' at the ferryman and there was a faint echo from the opposite bank. The night was warm. Slowly, we could make out the ferry, the flat old boat, as it came towards us.

In Dublin, March/April 1986

IV.
THE QUEST FOR CONDOMS

In 1979 Charles Haughey, then Minister for Health, introduced a bill, which he called "an Irish solution to an Irish problem", legalising the sale of condoms for the first time in the Republic but limiting availability to married couples, forcing them to get a prescription from a compliant doctor and then find a chemist who stocked the offending objects.

On Tuesday 11 November I took out the Golden Pages, looked under "D" for doctor, and selected six, three on the north side of Dublin and three on the south side. I decided to visit them and ask them to prescribe condoms for me. I arranged with myself to use the name Richard Flanagan and, if asked, to tell the first and last doctor that I was married, the second and fifth that I was unmarried but indulging in a steady relationship; the third and fourth would be told, I decided, that I simply want to get my rocks off.

Out of the six doctors, three refused to write me a prescription, two on vaguely moral grounds. Of the three who complied with my request, two charged a fee. Four grinned when I told them what I wanted. And I must admit that despite the fact that I was acting in the course of my professional duty, there was a considerable amount of sweat on the palms of my hands as I went into the surgeries of all six. Only one asked me if I was married or not. I phoned each one before I visited them to ensure that they were trading that day.

The first doctor conducted his practice in the area of Dorset Street. He was a jaunty-looking man in his fifties. "Now what's the trouble?" said he. "Well, I just wanted a prescription for condoms" said I. He pulled his spectacles even further down his nose and looked at me. A broad grin came over his face. "French letters" he intoned and grinned defiantly. "Never" he roared. I looked behind me to make sure that the door was shut. "Over my dead body!" I smiled weakly and understandingly at him. "It's not a doctor's business. You can do what you like as far as I am concerned. But between doctors and chemists it'll be an expensive business for ye lads." He removed his glasses altogether. "Next it'll be abortion on demand." He looked sad. "Doctors and nurses killing babies. In this

80

little Catholic country." I asked how much I owed him. "You don't owe me anything. I'm terribly sorry. I wouldn't prescribe a French letter for anyone, not even for one of my own patients."

The second doctor's surgery was located in the area between Terenure and Rathgar. Having elicited my date of birth and my profession, he too asked what the trouble was and I told him. "Are you sure this is not a dare?" he asked and I assured him that it was not. "Can you not get them in the clinics?" he then asked. I told him that I thought it would be just as easy to go to a doctor. "It's a farce" he said "it's your T.D. you should be lobbying, not your doctor. It's just a way of blackmailing doctors, this law. Doctors are going to refuse to do it, you know." I nodded sympathetically. He was young and interested in his first patient to seek condoms. I felt it was a great pity that there wasn't something wrong with me. He smiled in a resigned sort of way. "How many do you want?" he enquired. "I don't know" I replied. I hadn't thought of that one. "They come in dozens, don't they?" I agreed. "Do you want a dozen or a gross?" I made motions to suggest that I would prefer the latter number. He wrote the prescription. "How much do I owe you?" I finally asked. "I'm not going to charge you for this. I'm a doctor" he told me.

In the region of Camden Street I sat for twenty minutes in the doctor's waiting room. He got himself into a state of great confusion when I told him what I wanted. He didn't know that the new law was in operation. He picked up the phone and dialled the number of another doctor, peering at me every so often in a state of disbelief. They talked for a while. Did I know that there was a family planning clinic quite close by? Could I not get them from there? The other doctor had told him that the chemist shops had not got the objects I was looking for in stock anyway. Was I resolute in not going to the clinic? I would certainly be able to obtain as many as I wanted there. The new law, he felt, had pros and cons; he wouldn't like his children to be able to get condoms from slot machines. But, of course, he would write me a prescription if I really wanted one. Was my general health all right? He took out his pad and wrote the prescription, telling me that he would have to charge a consultancy fee. I gave him a tenner, he took a wodge of notes from his back pocket and handed me a fiver as change. I put the prescription in my pocket and departed.

In a quiet, sedate, secluded area of Ballsbridge my fourth doctor held her surgery. I had the feeling as soon as I rang the bell that I was onto a wrong one. There was a piano in the waiting room and a fire was lighting. The receptionist sat with me in the room. Nobody else was waiting. Finally, the doctor herself appeared. She was in her late fifties. Her first reaction was firm. "No, I won't do it" she said. "Can you not go to the Universities? You can get them there in slot machines" she told me. "Are you married?" she then asked. Since she was the fourth, I replied in the negative. It didn't seem to matter. She sighed. "It does seem ridiculous to come to a doctor for that" she said with an air of finality and stood up. I didn't mention money. It would, somehow, have been even more offensive to the poor doctor's ears than my original request.

Fairview. A five minute wait. The doctor motioned me to sit down. I told him what I was looking for. His response was so business-like that I felt he was defying me to note that he looked surprised. But he didn't look even slightly surprised. He simply took his pad and wrote the prescription, asking, for the sake of conversation, if there was any problem with the clinics. He didn't pay any attention to whatever I mumbled. He handed me the prescription and told me that I could pay the receptionist and that the prescription was renewable six times over. The receptionist charged me four pounds.

My sixth and last doctor ran his surgery in the area of Amiens Street. He was youngish and his office was untidy. "What sort of condoms do you want?" he asked. "Ordinary ones" I told him. He grinned. "What's your own doctor's name?" "I haven't got a doctor in Dublin" He looked highly dubious. "There's nothing I can do for you. You can go to your own doctor. I'll have nothing to do with Mr Haughey's Bill but I'll look after my own patients. Go to your own doctor." I pointed out that it was a simple matter of a prescription. This didn't help. "You're the fifth person." he counted them on his fingers, "that I have never seen before who has come in here looking for condoms. And you all said that you hadn't a doctor in Dublin. Well you can go and find one." I didn't mention money and as I was going out the door, he repeated in tones both advisory and contrary "Go to your own doctor."

In Dublin, November 1980.

82

HAVE SPUC,
WILL TRAVEL

In the early 1980s a campaign began to insert an anti-abortion clause into the Irish Constitution, which resulted in a referendum won by the anti-abortion lobby.

The local curate was saying ten o'clock Mass on Christmas morning in Enniscorthy Cathedral. He had an announcement to make. He told his congregation that a bus would be leaving from the Abbey Square at a quarter past twelve on Monday morning. Its destination was Dublin and a march for the rights of the unborn child. The interest in the bus was disappointing so far, he said. He would like parents to consider it as a day out for themselves. He would like parents to consider bringing their children on the march.

It was Monday December 27 and there was no way of getting out of Enniscorthy. The trains weren't running, nor were the buses. CIE was staying at home that day. Thus was the priest's bus a godsend. He was my shepherd. He was a true friend to those in need of getting back to Dublin on December 27. But his bus, hereafter called the SPUC bus, had other distinct advantages. One, it wouldn't be stopping in every godforsaken village along the way. Two, it was cheap. The train cost £12. The bus £6.80. But the SPUC bus was just what this reporter needed. The SPUC bus cost £2. And that would take you all the way up and back. Travel SPUC. SPUC saves you time. SPUC saves you money. Every town should have one. See Ireland with SPUC. Three cheers for SPUC. There was a moral in this story.

The first thing I saw in the Abbey Square in Enniscorthy on Monday December 27 at a quarter past twelve was a Knight of Columbanus, a common enough breed about the town. The second thing I beheld was a Fianna Fail councillor, also common in their own way. There were two young blokes leaning against a monument to Thomas Rafter and there were about twenty women from the town. "We should have brought a pack of cards," said one. "I don't want to see another card until next Christmas," replied another. There was a priest, there were a few school girls. There were some little children. And a woman who as long as I remember has never been able to keep her nose out of the whole town's business. These were my fellow travellers. And then there were some late-comers. One of them was wondering how everyone got over the Christmas.

The bus arrived in the Square and we got on. There were still some empty seats. The Knight of Columbanus, apparently had merely come to offer the blessing of his august organisation to the bus and all its passengers. He did not get on the bus, and as it moved away he could be seen walking up Castle Hill.

The bloke who sat beside me looked about thirty. He was a farmer. He hadn't been in the movement long, just about six months and he hadn't had time to be very active in it. Why did he join? He thought for a moment and told me that his wife had had a miscarriage and he had realised that what she was carrying was a human being. He thought this amendment was going to work. It was a rough world, he said, and he was glad something good was going to happen. But the miscarriage wasn't the only reason he joined. There were other reasons. He supposed I had my reasons as well. He glanced at me. I could hardly tell him that I was only here for the bus. I looked out of the window.

We stopped in Ferns and more SPUC people got on. One woman sat in front of me beside the Fianna Fail councillor. They talked the rest of the way to Dublin. All their colleagues in SPUC also talked the rest of the way to Dublin. People like this reporter who had never been on a SPUC bus before may imagine that they say the Rosary, sing hymns or listen to sermons on SPUC buses. This is not the case. This SPUC bus was a day out, as the priest had promised, and the SPUC people blathered away to each other as though it was a day trip to Curracloe. The Fianna Fail councillor and the woman from Ferns, for example, got into a long discussion about women's lib and its ins and outs. "Women don't go for the sort of man who carries the shopping bag," said the councillor. The bloke beside me talked to another farmer about cows and fields and how to kill badgers. "Hit him on the nose with a bar,"was one suggestion.

"God, I didn't feel the journey," said the woman as the SPUC bus stopped in O'Connell Street. Everybody took out flasks of tea or coffee and everybody unwrapped sandwiches. There was going to be a sort of picnic on the SPUC bus. And then the passengers were going to join the march with other SPUC people. But there was no hurry. There was time enough.

The SPUC march was smaller than the anti-amendment march just one month before. There were no nuns on the anti-amendment march, but this march was creeping with nuns of every description.

There was one TD on the anti-amendment march. (The people of Limerick have since seen to that.) Jim Tunny, Sean Barrett and Alice Glenn were on this march.

There there was the woman the other marchers didn't want to go on the march. She was dressed all in black and had a big banner over her head. The banner proclaimed: ''Abortion is a Mortal Sin''. There was a photograph of Pope Paul VI on one side of the banner.

She had been asked by the organisers and a Capuchin priest not to go on the march. She might have put others off, and the movement was non-sectarian. She talked about the devil. "The devil is making hooks in the eyes of the world." She talked about the Pope. ""'Young people of Ireland, I love you," he said. Well, if he saw what I saw them doing last Saturday night he wouldn't say that." She went on more about the Pope. "I wouldn't thank him if he flew in this morning and out tonight. Where are the bishops? Why aren't they here? Abortion is the work of Satan."

She was following the march up Kildare Street where two children had left a wreath at the gates of Leinster House. She was following the nuns and the priests and fathers and mothers who had lit torches for SPUC and were going to carry them all the way down Grafton Street to the Central Bank. She was following the children who had been brought out for the day. One of the children, whose friends were probably at home watching Bosco, held a banner which declared "RTE: Regularly Touting Evil". The Enniscorthy branch of SPUC had the best banner. The woman in black, whom these people didn't want on the march, was born near there.

Then came the moment which Loretto Browne, the high priestess of SPUC, had been waiting for. A lorry was parked on Dame Street in front of the Central Bank and Loretto could address the crowd once Alice Glenn had finished. As the buses roared by Loretto told the SPUC people that politicians who said one thing in public and another in private should look out.

The march was over. SPUC moved away in peace. The Knight of Columbanus would be waiting in Enniscorthy for his family to come home. It had been a great day for SPUC. A Capuchin monk began to walk alongside. "Did you try and stop the woman dressed in black going on the march?" I asked him. He laughed. "I asked her not to march," he said. "If the media saw her, they'd make a haymes of it."

Magill, January 1983.

85

GAY BYRNE:
IRISH LIFE AS CABARET

For the past hour he will have held the nation in thrall: reading bits from the papers, playing the Mystery Sound, putting on records, talking to housewives on the telephone, using funny voices. Now he has moved across from the radio centre in RTE to the offices of the Late Late Show. For the rest of the morning he will function just as an editor in a newspaper office functions. He will talk to his staff, find out what they have been doing, how's that idea going, why doesn't someone go and see so-an-so. His team will have ideas, he will think about them, reject them, accept them, often he will change his mind.

He will be slightly on edge all the time about how things will go; he doesn't want to lose his audience or bore the people of Ireland. This part of him is different from what you see on the screen. He is like the priest who manages the affairs of the parish. Behind the mystery of the Mass lies cold hard work. He is generally quiet spoken, but he is also ruthless; he wants things done.

Beliefs? He is a practising Catholic, he thinks divorce should be allowed in certain circumstances, he believes in cleanliness, hard work. He writes a column for *The Sunday World*. He subscribes to a success ethic from which springs his complete and total lack of understanding of crime. He often patronises women. He has a thing about cranks and he has some difficulty distinguishing a crank from someone who merely harbours certain strong convictions. He has likes and dislikes rather than beliefs. But he has not established his influence because of his beliefs, or his caprices. He has never actually sought to influence anyone at all.

He doesn't have much patience. He dislikes people who have ideas fixed in their minds about things. The show in his view is not there to influence people or explain things to people, or select what is important and present it to the public. He would rather talk about showbusiness. He would rather talk about filling the hall. The show is there to entertain, to pack them in, to keep them watching.

It had worked in America; it had worked in England.

But something different could be done in Ireland. The place was changing fast. There was Vatican II, the Beatles' first LP, Edna

O'Brien, the Programme for Economic Expansion, RTE, John F. Kennedy, The Bungalow. There was also a large and established set of beliefs which belonged to a large and established set of people. For the next twenty years the Late Late Show would stage the drama of Irish life, the play between the established and the new whose intensity was only matched in the emerging countries of the Third World.

So you could have a woman on who had taken the pill and she could say she felt great after it and it had done her the world of good. A man in the audience would then attack her and then there would be a break for music and then there's someone you really must meet. After a while they found the formula: the row came at the end of the show after you'd met all the guests and listened to all the music. And the rows were often great and big. In Enniscorthy when I was a lad we all sat glued to it. We were often embarrassed that someone was talking about sex: there were older people in the room who didn't like sex being talked about. If the Late Late Show had not existed it is highly possible that many people would have lived their lives in Ireland in the twentieth century without ever having heard anyone talking about sex.

If any other programme had mentioned sex, it would have been turned off. Turn that rubbish off. But nobody ever turned the Late Late Show off. The show was too unpredictable: you just never knew what you might miss. The show was too central: topics too close to viewer's lives were being discussed or people were being introduced whom everyone had always wanted to have a good look at. And if you didn't want him to talk about sex, then your prayers might be answered and he might go on for three weeks without any mention of sex. One week he might have a few guests on and they'd be pretty dull, one week he might have a student on who thought priests should live among the people and another week he'd have the policeman from "The Fugitive', hated by man and beast, who spent his time on the popular TV series hunting an innocent man.

Then the show would be packed with women's libbers, roaring and screaming in this valley of tears. Fed up washing dishes, fed up having children. They talked about their bras. Life in Ireland had been very quiet since the Civil War.

People disliked him because he was lightweight. But he could never be accused of much more. He was a Catholic who had been known to defend the church on his show; he didn't seem to share any of the views being perpetrated by his more notorious guests. Maybe he was okay. The Show was the problem. The Show was immoral, not fit for children, a disgrace, a foreign influence. But somehow he himself managed to escape the worst of the attacks on the Late Late Show.

So the county council passed a motion condemning the show; Gay got away scot-free. He was a clean-looking fellow, married to nice respectable Kathleen Watkins who sang and played the harp. (Nice instrument, the harp).

Gay Byrne has talked since of how you can have an enormous impact if you get an issue on the crest of its wave. The show got contraception just when it was breaking and it got the North just at the right time.

Before the North happened we had the tension of life in the Republic between the reality and the perception of the reality, between those who wanted change and those who had never heard anything worse in their whole lives. It was a drama called the Republic of Ireland, in five parts, with ads in between, relayed to every household in the country. There were huge elements of O'Casey. Little songs, a few laughs here and there; but basically being played out before you were the life and death issues, being argued and presented by those protagonists who had been vetted the previous week by Gay Byrne's production team. It was Irish life as extravaganza.

The show played the North for all it was worth: special programmes on the North with Gay appealing at the end for more time. Two people were fanatically at odds and it was the sort of thing the Late Late Show lapped up. The horror, the horror.

The North upped the ante. You had fresh accents and a whole new set of people. There was real blood and there were real guts. And they sure knew how to fight up there. It was wonderful. Down here we got them on a Saturday night, they bickered viciously with each other. Ulick O'Connor and Denis Franks were tame compared to this shower of mad dogs. The fun we had.

One night the audience was full of life and had loads left to say. Gay offered them a choice. They could continue talking about the last issue or they could meet someone new. Which did they want, he said washing his hands, to talk more about the subject under discussion or meet...ladies and gentlemen...fresh from the barricades...can I present...Bernadette Devlin.

Did they want her? What are you talking about? Yes, they did.

In no other country in Western Europe were the arguments about national life so heated, were the contrasts so stark. In no other country was curiosity so great about which way things were going to swing. In no other country could so many be outraged by so few. Gay Byrne understood that. He put it in his show, mixed it with a bit of music, visiting movie stars from Hollywood, pop stars from England, people you have heard about and now you can see, odds and sods from around Dublin.

His influence arose not from any set of beliefs which he wished to present to the people of Ireland, but from the fact that the issues were presented in such a popular package. His belief in the end became simply that things should be discussed and brought out into the open. His talent was in knowing how fast the pulse of the country was beating and in knowing whose pulse he should be taking. In Ireland like nowhere else the airing of the problem was enough to cause a whole lot of trouble. Had he not come along with the instincts of a successful impresario and created a mass audience and then raised the issues he did, it is conceivable that dissent on the essential ingredients of Irish life would never have reached the ears of the majority of people in this country. No one else would have done it.

Over the past ten years, however, the show has had its problems. Not as many new things were coming to the surface. The show was often dull. A recent programme on marital breakdown was badly timed and had almost no impact at all. On the other hand the row over Reagan's visit was at its most vibrant on the Late Late Show. The only recent issue on which the Late Late Show will have a lasting impact is Gay Byrne's assault on the politicians who have been running the Republic. He raised the issue at the right time using the right people. He proved to his mass audience that the country was being run by a shower of incompetent and wilful politicians. Once again the gap has been narrowed between the reality and the public's perception of it.

The North is a turn-off. He won't do anything now on the North. The last time he did something on the North was when John Bowman's book on de Valera appeared and he was even unhappy about doing that. He really believes that no one wants to hear any more about the North. There's no sex in the North anymore; the North is an old bitch gone in the teeth. The Late Late Show begins and ends as showbusiness and the North just doesn't bring in the audiences it used to. Irish life, as presented on the Late Late Show, has always been half serious, half cabaret.

If the Late Late Show has waned in its power and impact over the last ten years then the radio show has come into its own over the same period. This is where you get Gay Byrne at his most intense. It is also where you get him at his worst: making sexist remarks, patronising women, making right-wing remarks about what should be done to young people who are involved in crime. He also spent a

89

period where he would berate women who phoned his show; this was at its worst, for some reason, in the spring of 1980. Since then he has calmed down somewhat.

Most of the time he is just superb. The radio programme is unique in that it doesn't treat a subject just because it has come into the producer's head. Gay reads a letter - it could be from a woman whose husband never talks to her, or a vicious attack on litter bugs, it could be about sex and teenagers. Sometimes he comments, sometimes he doesn't. Generally he invites listeners to comment. Sometimes there's no reaction; other times the reaction is incredible. (Recent reaction to an appeal from Gay Byrne on the Late Late Show brought in almost a million pounds for Colin MacStay who needed an expensive operation).

Then the discussion goes on for a week or so. Phone calls, letters, women giving their views, their experience. Middle Ireland rearing its complex head.

The team element in all Gay Byrne's work has always been important. June Levine, for example, was brought in to focus the attention of the show on the women's movement. Vincent Browne worked as a researcher at a time when the North was being covered. For a time Rocky de Valera brought in youth. ("Do you watch the show,' Gay asked Rocky. "No,' Rocky said. He got the job.) Tony Boland knows about music. Billy Wall, later head of Radio 2, was involved in setting up the whole consumer and light entertainment package that made the radio show so successful. This package has been hardened and politicised by John Caden who has produced the radio show over the past several years.

In the latter half of 1983 and the first half of 1984 three issues dominated the public imagination. There was the abortion amendment, the sacking of Eileen Flynn, a teacher in New Ross, and the death of Ann Lovett and her child in Granard. These are the stuff which Late Late Shows have been made of. It is useful to look at what Gay Byrne did on those three issues.

RTE is a difficult place to work. A producer of a programme is responsible to a sub-committee who is responsible to a controller of programmes who is responsible to the director general who is responsible to the RTE Authority who is responsible to the government who is responsible to the people. If one link in that chain dislikes an idea or an item, then memos and meetings are the order of the day. It is not that programme-makers are afraid to take risks or innovate or get really stuck into something, nor that they are too conservative to do so, it is simply that the repercussions take up too much time and are too much trouble. This is true in any large

90

organisation, but in RTE it is exacerbated by the fact that management can be influenced by political and, indeed, religious affiliations or influences.

Gay Byrne had been thinking of doing a programme on abortion for a long time. It was the sort of thing which could cause real trouble on the Late Late Show and give us all a night to remember. It is murder, you can hear a woman roar. You are a murderer. What the Holy Father said is good enough for me. And so on. Bridget Ruane, a researcher on the show, worked on the idea before the notion that we should have a referendum was ever mooted.

Then one night Gay Byrne announced that he was going to do a show on abortion. This was a mistake; he generally never let the public know in advance what he was going to do. The night of the announcement he had a woman on who'd had an abortion and she talked about the experience. He also had a wonderful woman from England called Madame Sin who used to run a brothel. It was all great stuff, the sort of thing which made the Late Late Show a part of what we are.

In his house in Howth sat Fred O'Donovan, the Chairman of the RTE Authority. O'Donovan was opposed to abortion and in favour of the referendum. ("We are talking about murder,' he said). O'Donovan decided that the Late Late Show should not discuss the referendum. If Gay hadn't mentioned it O'Donovan would not have known it was on the cards. O'Donovan announced, to the consternation of senior executives of RTE, that the show could not go ahead. Gay kept his head down. He was not going to resign, nor was he going to get into a row over whether his show could contain sensitive current affairs matters. During the EEC referendum he had introduced a courtroom scene to the Late Late Show with a real live judge, counsel for either side and no breaks for music. He was thinking of doing it again for the abortion referendum. Such a programme might have made a significant difference to the debate. It was not to be.

Eileen Flynn, a teacher in New Ross, was living in the town with a married man and had given birth to a child. When she was sacked by the local nuns she took the case to the Unfair Dismissals Trbunal. Gay Byrne ran two reports on the trial. Both were by Kevin O'Connor. Both were the best reports of their kind that this writer has ever heard on radio. O'Connor stood in the middle. Here, he told us, was a nun who had been in the convent all her life, responsible to the parents for the children's welfare, responsible to her order for the proper running of the school. What could she do? And here on the other side was a young woman who had fallen in love and become a surrogate mother to the man's children. What could she do?

It was as though a scene from a Thomas Hardy novel was being described: each character motivated towards doom by outside forces, by history itself, by happenstance. Kevin O'Connor is not a news journalist, and no news or current affairs programme would have carried the type of report he delivered. He simply managed to let the listener know of the utter complexity of the situation. It is the sort of currency Gay Byrne has been dealing in for a long time.

Then there was Ann Lovett. The day after the story broke Kevin O'Connor was despatched to Granard. His report was not as inspired as his report on the Eileen Flynn case had been. But it was factual and fair; he tried to give a sense of the town, of the context.

It was more than a week after the news broke that Gay Byrne did an hour-long programme on Ann Lovett, a programme which represents the apotheosis of his twenty years in Irish broadcasting. He used the old letters thing again. He did nothing, he just sat waiting for the letters. He sets great store by letters and he reads every single letter that comes into the radio show or the Late Late Show. At the same time as priests and people were complaining about the media coverage of the death of Ann Lovett, the letters poured in to Gay Byrne.

Just as the Eileen Flynn reports broke new ground in Irish journalism, so did the Ann Lovett coverage on the Gay Byrne Hour. The idea was thought out carefully. John Caden, the producer, gave it his full backing. Kevin O'Connor edited the letters. They found two actresses, one with a middle class Dublin accent and the other with a more country accent. What resulted was the most relentless assault which has ever been presented to a mass audience on the accepted version of reality in this country.

Gay read a letter. Then one of the actresses. Then the other actress. There were several breaks for commercials. Most of the letters were direct accounts of personal experiences. Most of the letters came from women who had given birth in rural Ireland outside marriage. Some of them were heart-breaking. One in particular, an account of how a servant in a house gave birth in a locked room and then murdered the child, was absolutely shocking.

Gay had a special tone that morning. He didn't comment on letters, but he spoke a few times to say here was another letter or we're stopping for a commercial break. There was an intense calm about the way he spoke, a controlled anger almost. Here it was in a nutshell in one hour what he had contributed to public life in Ireland. This is what we are: Ann Lovett's death came out of a context. I've been telling you about that context for twenty years. It has happened before and it will happen again. Don't blame me for not telling you.

There is a war in Ireland which Gay Byrne has been dramatising for the past twenty years. Between reality and the perception of reality, between de Valera's vision of Ireland and Patrick Kavanagh's "The Great Hunger', the world of people in power who believe that Ann Lovett will never happen again and the world where Ann Lovett happens all the time. In the middle of all the nonsense spoken about the media and Ann Lovett and should the story have been mentioned in the newspapers or should it not, Gay Byrne summed it up. He left us in no doubt. It has been his finest hour. Over the next twenty years he is likely to have plenty of opportunity to present more such hours.

The Crane Bag, 1984.

OUT OF THE DARK

A profile of John McGahern

The man who comes to the platform in the Arts Centre at Nun's Island in Galway is totally at ease. There is nothing of the shyness, slowness or hesitancy which seeps through his writing. The hall is full. His name means more than the writer of four novels and three books of stories. His name is still potent; its power is probably best described by himself in his new book *High Ground*. He is writing about a television producer who "made a series of documentary films about the darker aspects of Irish life".

He could equally be writing about his own novels. "As they were controversial, they won him a sort of fame: some thought they were serious, well made and compulsive viewing, bringing things to light that were in bad need of light; but others maintained that they were humourless, morbid, and restricted to a narrow view that was more revealing of private obsessions than any truth about Irish life in general".

Tonight he is funny. Tonight he does not select parts of his work which dwell on death, isolation, the loss of love. Tonight he is satirical, reading with enormous gusto, acting out the lines: the drunken teacher talking to the drunken locals in a pub; neighbours back-biting; the peculiarities of the gentry; a local politician. For over ten years he was, of course, a teacher. Standing there on the raised platform he has a teacher's command over his audience.

Eager questions come fast at the end of the reading. He mentions again that he was born into an Ireland which was going through the nineteenth century and that he now lives here in the late twentieth century - several decades are missing. The country has jumped ahead of itself.

His nineteenth century was set in Leitrim and Roscommon. Children still brought turf to the school where his mother taught. He went on a sidecar to make first communion. His mother and uncle had won scholarships but his uncle could not afford to leave the small farm in the mountains where he grew to know everything about the locality.

Both sides of the family had been involved in the War of Independence and there was always talk, hushed talk, of what had happened. If you asked a question you would be told nothing, but if you sat and waited and listened you would hear them talk of ambushes, of men followed to Australia and murdered there, of men dumped over the side of boats.

Religion offered solace, comfort. The candles and flowers on the altar, the luxury and ceremony of the Catholic church versus the brutality of the world outside, the brutish quality of things. His mother stayed on in Leitrim after she married. He was the oldest and then there were five girls and another boy. His father came over from Coothall, where he was stationed, whenever he could.

When his mother died his world fell apart. He felt a grief that maybe the younger children didn't feel; he was old enough to know what he had lost.

So she was gone, she would not move to any word or call; in her brown habit facing the plywood wardrobe she would lie quite horribly still; her raised feet would not sway or stir to any touch or fingers, her eyes would be closed, her white beads twined in her fingers, the wedding gold and the engagement ring with its one stone missing gone. O but if only I could have had back then that whole hour I had wasted down with the lorry on the cinders so that I could see her stir or smile. I would portion the hour out so that I would see her forever. "The Leavetaking"

They moved to Coothall and the barracks after her death. He didn't like the barracks. He had this feeling that the law was the enemy, this feeling of being tainted by being from the barracks. There was something against the law in the Irish character. Yet the crowds came when the Roscommon team was in its heyday in the early forties to listen to the barracks' radio; on a summer Sunday there would be as many as sixty or eighty of them glued to the set.

Early on he created his own world in Coothall. He could escape in a boat into the network of tributaries of the river Shannon. Sometimes he could take a book and read. There were no books in the house; reading was viewed with suspicion in that world. Had a family of gentleman Protestant farmers not lived nearby, he might not have been able to engross himself in the world of Scott and Dickens and Zane Grey. They gave him the run of the house. He could read what he liked; he still talks about the experience with wonder and the people with gratitude.

They played before the fire, twenty-one because it would take long to finish, and it was Elizabeth who kept the scores on the margins of the radio supplement. The night began to come as they played, the fire to flame brighter and to glitter on the glass of the pictures, on the shiny leaves of holly twisted with their scarlet berries into the cords. As always close to nightfall, the ghastly red glow from the Sacred Heart lamp grew stronger. Through the windows vague shapes of birds flew towards the wood. There was a pause in the game. the lamp was lit, the blinds drawn, the table laid for the tea, the kettle put to boil. None of them was hungry. They nervously searched each other's faces. The phone did not ring. The doors were open. no one would come. "The Barracks"

Every day he rode on his bicycle to secondary school in Carrick-on-Shannon. He knew he wanted to write, but he had no notion of getting published or becoming a writer. He had never seen a writer. He decided he wanted to become a national teacher because of the hours, because it would leave him free to write. He left Coothall, for St Patrick's Training College in Drumcondra.

It was the second shock. The first had been the move from Leitrim to the barracks; this move to Dublin was unbelievable; fiction, he says, has to be believable and he has never written about this. Anyone who missed daily mass at St Patrick's College in Drumcondra was expelled. Many of his fellow trainee teachers were half-savages who divided up on county and locality lines rather than on the basis of mutual interests and concerns. The crowd from the Gaeltacht were the worst.

They were being trained to become extensions of the police force. He watched a friend of his, nearly twenty years old, being beaten up by one of the staff. On Saturday nights they started putting on a show in the college. He wrote some of the scripts which had thinly veiled references to the staff, but the Dean was not amused and stopped the show. You needed ninety percent to get into the Training and thirty-five percent to get out. It was a relief to get out.

He didn't take a job immediately but went to England for six or eight months. It was the dawn of the 1950s in Ireland, nothing was about to happen, and it was marvellous to be out of the country.

Because of the rain we didn't go any farther than the few hundred yards down the Strand to Henekey's. Upstairs in the wine-room we found a table at the window, where we could watch the wet gleam of the Strand beneath its lamps, and the traffic come and go over Waterloo Bridge. "The Leavetaking"

He was writing then as well as doing labouring jobs, but it was more scribbling, more a reflection of what he was reading. He came back to Ireland and went to teach at the CBS in Drogheda. One day he asked the head brother why one of the brothers didn't contribute to *Our Boys*, the brothers' magazine. The answer was important: "Because we'd laugh him out of existence". He would soon understand even more fully that in a closed society writing is a dangerous activity.

He moved to Dublin. And just as it is possible to piece together his family, his childhood, his Coothall from "The Dark", "The Barracks", the first half of "The Leavetaking", certain short stories in "Nightlines" "Getting Through" and "High Ground", it is possible to chart his Dublin in "The Leavetaking", "The Pornographer" and other short stories from his three collections. Indeed, there is no evocation of Dublin in the 1950s and 1960s as powerful as his.

There is Fairview and Clontarf. *Spring was late, and when it came it was more like early summer. Fairview Park was full of flowers and young men, their trousers tucked into their socks, kicking football under the greening trees, using their cast-off clothes to mark the goal* "The Pornographer"

There are poets and pubs. *It was how we began, the wind blowing from the mouth of the river while the Blanchardstown Fife and Drum downed their first thirst-quencher in the Scotch House. They'd nothing but beef left in Mooney's after the weekend. We had stout with our beef sandwiches. Soon, in the drowsiness of the stout, we did little but watch the others drinking. I pointed out a poet to her. I recognised him from his pictures in the paper.* "My Love My Umbrella" - "Nightlines"

There are dancehalls. *I saw the boxer in evening dress leave the head of the stairs. The* House Full *notice must have gone up on the easel below. It was no longer possible to see onto the dance floor, the space at the head of the steps packed with men, and men on the steps below struggled to push through. Everywhere now there was the sense of the fair and the hunt and the racecourse, the heavy excitement of preying and vulnerable flesh.* "The Pornographer"

There are flats. *He showed her the rooms, the large living room with the oak table and worn red carpet, the brass fender, the white marble of the fireplace, the kitchen, the two bedrooms. He watched her go over the place, lift the sea shell off the mantlepiece, replace it differently.* "Bank Holiday" - "High Ground"

And there is sex. *"I won't hurt you", I said. "Be careful", she answered. "It only happened once before", and she guided me within, wincing whenever I touched the partly broken hymen. Within her there was this instant of rest, the glory and the awe, that one was as close as ever man could be to the presence of the mystery, and live, the caged bird in its moment of pure rest before it was about to be loosed into blinding light.* "The Pornographer"

He was living in Dublin. Over and over he went to the theatre, to the cheap seats in the Gate, where Lord Longford was putting on Shaw, Chekhov, Wilde, to the Gas Company where he saw Lorca's "The House of Bernarda Alba" maybe ten times. The library in Fairview was good, and beside Roche's Stores there was a man who sold books from a barrow at half-price. He sold no rubbish, but more importantly he sold banned books. On certain days people would congregate around the barrow and go on talking and discussing what they were reading.

He was still in his early twenties and he was writing. He finished a first novel, which he sent to Hutchinson. It was long - it might have been around nine hundred pages had it been published. He wrote in longhand. Hutchinson sent it back saying that maybe if he re-wrote it or wrote something else they would be interested. He published a section of it in the London magazine *X*. Faber saw it. He had written a second book "The Barracks" which Faber agreed to publish. Charles Monteith of Faber, to whom "Nightlines" is dedicated, encouraged him to enter the manuscript of "The Barracks" for a Macaulay Fellowship, which he won.

He travelled to Europe with the money from the award. Germany, Finland, Barcelona. *She walked the narrow streets, went to a few museums and churches, bought a newspaper on the Ramblas, vivid with the flower stalls under the leafless trees in the cold dry weather, and ate each evening at the Casa Agut, a Catalan restaurant a few minutes walk from the hotel.* "The Beginning of an Idea" - "Getting Through"

He survived the publication of "The Barracks". John D. Sheridan reviewed it in the *Irish Independent* and called it a classical tragedy. That was 1963. Two years later "The Dark" was published. He was in Barcelona when the book came out. He bought the *Sunday Times* on the Ramblas to find a glowing review by Julian Webb (to whose memory "High Ground" is dedicated). "The Dark" was banned in Ireland. There was no reason given; a member of the board would later state privately that people in Ireland couldn't be going about with their flies open, but that is all he knows about what went on behind closed doors.

He went to London where he found a telegram from the management of St John the Baptist School in Clontarf who tried to get him not to return for the new academic year; they offered to give him glowing references so he could find a school in England. He turned up on the first day of term and was suspended. At a meeting in the school at which everyone was even more embarrassed than he was, it was mentioned that he had been married in a registry office to a foreign woman. "What came over you," a school official said "to marry a foreigner when there are hundreds of thousands of women going around Ireland with their tongues hanging out for a husband." He was sacked; later, he found out he was sacked on the direct instructions of John Charles McQuaid, Archbishop of Dublin. *The Irish Times* ran the story for all it was worth. He became a *cause celebre*, the Eileen Flynn of his generation. People wanted to help him fight for his rights.

He didn't want any fight; he wanted to get the hell out. He expected nothing but abuse from his writing; he had been banned and fired. He's never had a job since. He went to London where he worked as a temporary teacher. Among his pupils in Clontarf were Declan Kiberd and Neil Jordan.

"You know that better than I do. If it got out that I let you go on teaching up there after what you've gone and done there'd be an uproar. The Archbishop wouldn't stand for it. The parents wouldn't stand for it. I couldn't stand for it." I notice there is a strong smell of whiskey in the room. *"Tell me this one fact. What entered your head to do such a thing? Didn't you know that it was flying in the face of God? You never caused me any trouble. I thought you'd see my days out at the school. Now you go and leave me no option but to get rid of you. Tell me this, what entered your head to do it?"* So this farce is another of the steps. *"I met someone I wanted to marry. There was no other way to do it." "God I always thought you were steady enough. Isn't there thousands of Irish Catholic girls crying out for a husband. Why couldn't you go and marry one of them?"* "The Leavetaking"

It was a while before he wrote again. "Nightlines", a collection of stories, appeared in 1970. "The Leavetaking" came out in 1974 and "The Pornographer" five years later. "The Pornographer" made the cover of the porn trade magazine *Fuckbooks*, much to his amusement and delight. *Fuckbooks* praised the book highly.

In the meantime he had married again, lived in Paris, London, Spain, the United States, Newcastle, Cleggan. In 1970 he bought a patch of land with a three-room cottage overlooking Laura Lake in Leitrim between Mohill and Ballinamore; four years later he and Madeline went to live there, and have been there most of the time ever since.

As you come out of Mohill you pass by the post office in Gorvagh and continue on until you come to a monument on the left at the top of a hill. The monument is to a number of locals who were ambushed by Black and Tans in the War of Independence. You turn left at the bottom of the hill towards the lake and follow a narrow path along the edge of the lake until you come to the house.

The house has been extended; three rooms have been added. The flat, grey light from the lake dominates everything: the front sitting room, the spare bedroom, his work room, their bedroom. Up beyond the house there is wood for the winter in a barn.

He now has fifty acres of bad land and says he is a rotten farmer: he gets attached to the animals, he finds he can't sell them when he's had them for a while. He is full of amusement and information about the area. He has a friend who lives across the lake and comes across once or twice a week. He hates meeting him by accident because then there's no more news, no reason for a visit until news becomes possible again.

His alertness, natural kindness, interest in everything that went on around him, made him instantly loved. What wasn't noticed at first was his insatiable thirst for news. "Oldfashioned" - "High Ground"

He himself is back in the news again for the first time in twenty years. Senator John Ellis of Fianna Fail wants to build a pet food factory beside his house; the fact that there are miles and miles of uninhabited ground all around makes no difference to Senator Ellis, who wants to build there and let the waste matter flow into the lake. The smell will be unbearable. He is opposing Ellis. His opposition has been reported in the papers.

His relationship with Fianna Fail politicians goes back a long way. Coothall is now famous not just for the barracks but for Sean Doherty's brand new bungalow with a state wall around it, and the pub which Sergeant Tully wanted to close on time.

The whole village seemed dead under a benign moon, but as I passed along the church wall I heard voices. They came from Ryan's bar. It was shut, the blinds down, but then I noticed cracks of yellow light along the edges of the big blue blind. They were drinking after hours. "High Ground"

His brother was in the same class as Doherty. He takes an interest in the doings of Doherty, as does the entire locality, ruled as it is by Ray McSharry in Sligo, Doherty in Roscommon and Albert Reynolds in Longford. He enjoyed "The Boss" immensely.

A politician lives outside the village, and the crowd that once flocked to the presbytery now go to him instead. Certain nights he holds "clinics". They are advertised. On "clinic" nights a line of cars can be seen standing for several hundred yards along the road past his house, the car radios playing. On cold nights the engines run. No one thinks it wasteful anymore. They come to look for grants, to try to get drunken driving convictions quashed, to get free medical cards, sickness benefit, to have planning application decisions that have gone against them reversed, to get children into jobs. "Oldfashioned"- "High Ground"

Two years ago he published a story in the *Irish Press*, which is also published in his new book as the title story. Anyone in the area would recognise the politician he was describing; it is as though he were writing about a national monument. The man, it should be added, is dead. His son, however, is alive. His son is a well-known politician.

He had come poor to the place, buying Lynch's small farm cheap, and soon afterwards the farmhouse burned down. At once, a bigger house was built with the insurance money, closer to the road, though that in its turn was due to burn down too, to be replaced by the present mansion, the avenue of Lawson cypresses now seven years old. "High Ground"

Life is quiet here. A prose writer, he muses, needs to live quietly. He doesn't enjoy functions, receptions, parties. Once a week they go to Enniskillen for an outing and shopping. They love Blake's pub in the town and have a small cache of Blake's twenty-five-year-old whiskey. They buy the week's supplies in Enniskillen.

The post comes, letters from all over the place, a present for Madeline of a book on Francis Bacon. He must catch the postman to hand him some letters to post. Outside the lake becomes somewhat choppy, slightly wild. He doesn't swim. There is no television in the house, no sign anywhere of newspapers or magazines.

He moves from the large issues of the locality to books. He, a most unliterary writer, talks incessantly about books.

He keeps going off to look for books in various parts of the house. He is delighted by books. Finishing a book leaves him vulnerable and open. The next time he wants to put the jumps up higher, to make it harder. Every five or six years, he says, a crisis comes, he has to sit there and fight for his right to speak. "Bank Holiday", recently published in the *Irish Times* he wrote over and over, as many as sixty or seventy times; he sees it as a watershed.

He agrees that there is no tradition of the novel in Ireland, and no fixed settled society from which the novelist can feed; no sharp world of manners and morals. He agrees that maybe this is where the peculiar desolation in his work comes from, that this is what saddens his work.

There is a new novel somewhere in his head. He needs to do one or two drafts to get where it hurts. He does the ending at an early stage. It is morning now, another grey flat day in Leitrim. He sits there, he won't go back to the novel until this new book is out. He is almost revelling in the dullness of the morning, smiling ironically while pointing out that maybe he won't do much today.

In Dublin, September 1985

THE GOLDEN VOICE OF TOMMY O'BRIEN

The two hands tense as he holds the script; when each piece of music is coming to an end he raises his left hand and quickly lowers it to his chest, with a look of professional pride and ease, as the red light comes on. The script is perfectly rehearsed. "Good evenin' listeners," he begins and even the g in "evening" is missing in the script. He has timed the introductions and the music so that his programme runs to just over 29 minutes. Every single pause, or inflection, or laugh has been prepared and rehearsed; the guy knows exactly what he is doing.

He is delighted to discover that his timing is right once more. He walks out into the control room. "If there's any problem, we can fade it," Johnny Devlin, the producer tells him and everybody looks up waiting for his reaction. Tommy O'Brien takes things seriously and fading a record is a matter of the utmost gravity. He rages against the fading of records. His speaking voice outside the studio is high-pitched; his speech comes fast and incessant, full of drama and conviction. "Fade it. I'll kill you."

Today is another milestone in Tommy O'Brien's great love affair with the microphone. Today he is going to record three programmes instead of the usual two. And in future he is going to record three. He has written Johnny Devlin a note to warn him of this; he has steeled his nerve that it is going to be done, even if it means getting a taxi to the station. There's no point in coming up every fortnight when you can come up every three weeks.

On the days he records his great programme "Your Choice and Mine" a car picks him up and takes him from his native Clonmel to Thurles; from there he gets the train - the dining car staff know when to expect him and have his breakfast ready for him. All the porters and most of the passengers know him and are aware of his sacred mission; his journey to Dublin with his box of records resembles nothing less than a royal progress. But this morning the roads have been icy and the car has had to go too slowly. He missed the train; he had to get a car in Thurles to take him the whole way to RTE. He can't remember this having happened before in his long career as a commuting broadcaster.

But his life has been a long struggle with the elements and the

103

great dramas: the death of Aida, the love between Romeo and Juliet, the wiles of Don Giovanni, the flashing eyes of Carmen. Even orchestral works have their own dramas to act out. All his life long he has been listening to these dramas. He recounts the missing of his train with an almost operatic verve and orchestral fluency.

He wants a dee-jay. Is there a dee-jay. Johnny Devlin thinks there is and wanders off to make sure. Is he, Tommy O'Brien not a dee-jay? The denial comes hot and heavy, followed by a degree of abuse. No, he isn't a dee-jay. He doesn't actually handle the records.

The dee-jay arrives in the person of Frank Corr. Tommy is pleased; now we can begin. He hands the script around to all concerned and opens up his box of records. "Be awful careful of this record, it's very rare," he admonishes Frank Corr. Suddenly, for the first time, he stops talking and stands to attention, his hands by his sides. Slowly he draws in his breath. Everybody waits for him to speak. Here we have the born performer and his captive audience. "Johnny," he says, "I'm going to play one I've never played before in my life." He looks around at everyone as though he has just delivered an important message from on high. There followed a conversation about music and who wrote what and when between Johnny Devlin and Tommy O'Brien, the elders in the temple.

Everything goes smoothly and according to the script. The battle to make three programmes instead of two seems to be well on the way to being won. But then the great Needle-Stuck-In-The-Record row begins. Tommy blames RTE. "It worked perfectly at home," he roars. But no matter what they do, the groove in the record resembles nothing as much as the Black Pig's Dyke. "I'll never finish three programmes with these whores," mumbles Tommy O'Brien.

Sometimes while the record is playing he sings along. Sometimes he talks: "Wait until you hear the second tune. It's got Verdi written all over it," or "If only Pavarotti could sing like this," or "There wasn't a tune in the whole opera." Then the singers, he knows everything about the singers. Ben Davis who made the recording when he was 76, Isobel Baillie who died last year.

It's time for the next number, the voice becomes disciplined, almost calm, controlled: he tells his listeners that the sound they are going to hear is the sound of pure enchantment. The dee-jay puts on the record. Tommy O'Brien grins in recognition when the music starts. He thinks for a moment. "Maybe it's a slight exaggeration to say it's 'pure enchantment'," he says and stops for a moment, "but it *is*."

Touring companies were common at the time. He remembers when he was twelve or thirteen and one came to Clonmel. They did concert scenes from operas. He remembers vividly that on the first night they did a scene from "Maritane" by William Vincent Wallace. It was the prison scene and there was a trio for tenor, contralto and baritone called "Turn On Old Time". Even now, and it must be sixty years later, he hums the tune and says that he was absolutely overcome. He keeps humming the tune to himself to help him recall what it was like to hear that sort of music for the first time.

Not long afterwards through an advertisement in a newspaper he paid fifty shillings for a hornless table grand, six records and a box of needles. It was Clonmel just after the war and when he left school he went to work for the *Clonmel Chronicle* as a junior reporter. One day when he had started making his own living he saw an advertisement in the *Daily Telegraph* for the International Opera Season at Covent Garden. He saw some of the names and they included a number of world famous figures whose records he had in his growing collection. Wouldn't it be great, he thought, to go and hear them in real life?

It was a long way from Tipperary. He was seventeen years old and five foot four. It was his first time in London. He arrived on a Monday morning and went straight to Covent Garden. A cross between Stephen Dedalus and Dick Whittington, he stood outside and stared at the Opera House. "Well there it is,' he thought. "Imagine I'll actually be in there tonight." Such is the stuff of almost half of the novels written in the nineteenth century.

Tommy O'Brien, our hero, went up to the tall attendant. "Excuse me," he said, "have you heard any of the singers tonight?" "Oh yes, sir," said the attendant, "I heard them all at rehearsal." The attendant continued, Tommy O'Brien remembers, and said: "There's one little fat Italian and she's great." "And that", says Tommy O'Brien, "of course, was Toti."

Toti was the coloratura soprano, Toti del Monte, "who could be said to be as broad as she was long; she was only five feet tall and she was very fat." On his first night in London he heard her sing in *Lucia*. The next night he saw *Tosca* and then *Butterfly* and then *Aida*. *Aida* is his favorite opera: he has seen it more often than any other. He witnessed the debut of many famous singers in that opera.

On that first visit he stayed for a fortnight and he was lucky because one of the touring opera companies had hired the Lyceum and Tommy O'Brien was able to go there as well as Covent Garden to see opera. But that wasn't all: on a Sunday afternoon, he won't say what year, he never gives dates, John McCormack gave a recital in the Albert Hall. There were seven thousand people there and loads of people turned away. McCormack sang 25 songs. For the first two songs the voice was dry and uninteresting, Tommy O'Brien felt. It was a phenomenon he was to notice with other singers. "But after the third song it was entirely different, it was glorious."

Back he went after his two weeks in London to his job as a junior reporter on the *Clonmel Chronicle*. When that newspaper folded he joined the *Clonmel Nationalist* and soon became a senior reporter. Every summer until the war he went back to London for two weeks. He saw all the great singers and musicians. Yet it seemed that those two weeks basking in the extraordinary pleasure he gets from music had to be paid for as though they were the golden fruits of some Faustian bargain. The rest of the year back in Clonmel was sheer slavery. He had taken on the job, in addition to that of reporter, as official court stenographer for County Tipperary Circuit Court. Sometimes he would start at 10.30 in the morning and work until 9.30 at night. He kept it up for ten years, taking down two hundred words a minute in impeccable shorthand, until he was ready to shout out loud in despair in the court. He gave it up.

He is still proud of his shorthand; he is still proud that he taught it to himself on his grandfather's farm in his beloved Comeraghs from a manual he bought for six old pence in Clonmel. He became editor of the *Clonmel Nationalist*. He enjoyed the job but hated when people asked, as they always did, to have their name kept out of the paper after court cases. He had to refuse and there are people in Clonmel who still don't speak to him because of it.

In those years between the two wars when he was going to London every summer there was an abiding passion in his life other than music. Billiards. He was crazy about billiards. He was three times Irish amateur champion, and four times runner-up. He was only in his twenties when he came up to Dublin and beat a man everybody thought was unbeatable. The man from the *Irish Independent* asked him if he had any hobbies besides billiards. Classical music, the reporter was told. The reporter from the *Indo* wouldn't believe this. "The last time I won," Tommy O'Brien remembers, "I played a great game. I was absolutely marvellous. I just knew that I'd win."

When he came to Dublin to play billiards he always stayed with a family called Kenny in Drumcondra. They were Northern Catholics and mad on opera. They had a gramophone and one day Tommy O'Brien told them: "The next time I'm coming up, when I'm playing in the second round, I'll bring up a lot of 78s and we'll play them."

He brought the records and the family would sit around as Tommy O'Brien, up in Dublin for the billiards, put on records and introduced each one with a short explanation. If it was an opera, he would tell the story, or maybe he had seen the singer in London, but for each piece of music he had an anecdote. Friends of the family began to drop in to hear him. Once Tommy O'Brien was about to play a piece without an explanation but a man stopped him. No, please talk about the record before you put it on.

So back home in Clonmel one day he had an idea. It worked up in Dublin in the Kenny's house - why the hell wouldn't it work on radio? He wrote to a man called Fachtna O hAnrachain in RTE and told him about his visits to Covent Garden and his record collection. "I think I could do some radio programmes," he said. He was engaged to do six quarter-hour programmes called "Covent Garden Memories". A star was born.

As the years went by the programmes he did increased and multiplied. A series of six, then a series of eight. Kevin Roche, the head of light entertainment, was a great believer in the snappy title. Tommy thought that if he could think up a snappy title he might be able to sell an idea to Kevin Roche. The title he had for years was "Tommy O'Brien and His Records" but he knew Kevin Roche would never buy that. He met him in the lavatory in Henry Street one day when Tommy was up in RTE to make a recording. "Kevin," he said, "I've thought of a great new title for a series which has never been used before, even by the BBC." The title was "Your Choice and Mine". Kevin Roche bought it.

He thought if he played ballads and well-known songs, that his audience would follow him wherever he went. He wanted to entice people who wouldn't normally listen to Mozart or Beethoven to listen to his programme so he could make them share his enthusiasm. Basically, he was a man with a mission.

There was no answer. Knock harder. Still no answer. It was difficult to just open the door, because there was no guarantee that this was the right house. There was a kitchen with an Aga cooker and there were two cats sitting on a chair. Hello. Anyone here? Still no answer.

Beyond the second door there was a hall and even in the hall the music could be heard. It was stunningly clear as though there were a huge orchestra planted in the living-room of this old house built high on a hill over Clonmel. The music was Beethoven's Pastoral Symphony and it was playing really loud. It took a long time to alert Tommy O'Brien to the fact that there were visitors.

Once aware of this, however, he was up on his feet, dancing around the room and talking. He never stopped talking except when music was playing. At one end of the room there were cabinets full of records and just in front of the cabinets there were two huge speakers which he recently acquired and he expressed his deep delight with these speakers. After he had put the meal on the table, he would demonstrate how the speakers work with 78s.

The two windows in the living-room look down on Clonmel; the view is spectacular and at night you can look out and see a mass of small lights. He moved here over ten years ago and he has been living here on his own since the death of his sister.

He has built up a huge collection of records over the years, although he has bought very few over the past decade. He still lives in some golden age of singers and records before the fall of man. He has not been back to Covent Garden since the war, for example, he doesn't like the singers. He hates the way they have perfected the system of recording; he likes recordings of live concerts. He has made great friends while buying records: one in particular was Rev David McCauseland, a Presbyterian minister, a kindred spirit in Clonmel who introduced him to Beethoven.

He has remembered the aria all evening since it was mentioned. Yes, he had three recordings of it. What's he saying, three, he has more than that, but three that he would like to choose between. He stops and thinks for a moment and then enumerates all the recordings of the aria and what he thinks of them, he names all the foreign singers in the rich tones of south Tipperary. He makes up his mind and sails down to a record cabinet. Within a few seconds he has the record in his hand. The duet from "The Pearl Fishers" sung by Jussi Bjoerling and Robert Merill. He walks up to the turntable and puts it on. The music starts. He knows all the French words and sings along for a while but he stops when one of the most magnificent arias of nineteenth century romantic opera bursts into full flower.

But soft, no, hold on, don't go yet, wait a minute. There is another matter. Sit down. The greatest Irish singer since McCormack and Burke-Sheridan. Who? Names are mentioned and dismissed by him. Suddenly he shouts out the name: Frank Ryan, the tenor from Tallow, Co Waterford. "Frank Ryan to my way of thinking had a world beating natural tenor voice. However he made very few recordings and he wasn't fully trained." Tommy O'Brien wants to play one last record by another man who stayed at home: he wants to play Frank Ryan singing "I'll Walk Beside You". He remarks on Ryan's ability to hit particular notes. The room fills with the voice of an old record, the room already full of a lifetime's obsession with the human voice. It is getting on towards midnight and he is old, but Tommy O'Brien is still listening with enormous intensity, waiting with bated breath, and a sense of wonder, for the singer to hit the top note.

Magill, May 1984

THE ISLAND THAT WOULDN'T GO TO SLEEP

It was Saturday night on Tory Island. Inside the shops in the West Town there were men sitting up at the counter looking out towards the street and making the odd remark to each other. The light was fading and the sky had clouded over. The shop was so near to the sea that you could hear the sound of the waves hitting the pier. The men were drinking cans of Tennents Lager; the cans had the brand name printed on one side and on the other side was depicted a woman who was scantily clad and in a seductive pose. Tennents, coupled with whiskey and poitín, is the staple diet of the drinkers on Tory Island.

In the tiny hall of the shop there was music playing out of a huge cassette player. Ballads, ceili music, but loud, really loud. Outside in the street loads of kids were having a great time throwing sticky burrs at each other and then running away.

Three girls came into the shop and sat down. This created a bit of a stir.

A bloke with an accordion appeared accompanied by another bloke with an accordion. Then a fellow with a guitar joined them. They were almost blocking the entrance to the shop as they began to play. A bodhrán player arrived shortly afterwards.

Then there was a huge commotion out in the street. Hens scattered squaking in all directions. Everybody who was standing outside in the street stood aside as a tractor and trailer bearing islanders from the East Town, which lacked a shop of its own, came down the hill from the church at breakneck speed and stopped, in true Hollywood fashion, with a sudden jerk.

It was clear that there was going to be a space problem in the shop, due to this and the fact that the night was fine benches were put on the street for the musicians to sit on and everybody stood around with cans of Tennents in their hands having the time of their lives. There was no thought of the winter in anyone's head. No thought that in early January not even helicopters would be able to brave the storm.

It was after eleven and the children were still up; a few older women from the island had joined the company. Every tune under

110

the sun was being played except "The Boys Of The Old Brigade" and it was this tune and no other which a fellow who had been staggering around the middle of the road for a while now wanted the band to play. He would do a bit of a dance about the road and then once more appeal to the musicians, nay demand, that they play "The Boys Of The Old Brigade".

There was a strange, almost Arctic edge to the darkness. A figure was moving slowly down the hill from the church. He seemed to have a limp. The musicians continued to play when they noticed him, but their playing was toned down somewhat. Several islanders averted their eyes when they saw him coming. He was not coming to join in the fun. He was a priest.

He made his way into the shop, muttering something to each individual as he passed. The music continued but nobody spoke or moved. Just as the priest came out of the shop the lights were turned off. He moved among the people and told them it was too late to be out on the street. Everyone was to go home.

"Why?" asked one of the musicians in English.

"You come and see me tomorrow," the priest told the only one who questioned his instruction. He turned and began to walk away.

The stunned silence was quickly broken.

"Go home," a man shouted after the priest. He said it quickly and l, as though it were one word.

'he priest turned around. "Who said that?" he asked. The man who had shouted looked ashamed. It was very like being in school. The priest made remarks about people not having the courage to own up to what they said. Still no one said anything.

The priest moved off on his own back to his house. The man who wanted the band to play "The Boys Of The Old Brigade" followed behind for a while doing a cruel imitation of the priest's walk.

This had never happened before; he had never gone this far. One of the accordion players started up again, but before more than a few shrill notes emerged from his box he was told to stop. Everyone would have to go home. The priest had gone too far but they would still have to do what he said. The doors of the shop closed up and everybody began to scatter.

Up a backstreet and in slightly to the left there was a door and more than half of those who had stood around the street went in this door after midnight. Inside was an ordinary living room with chairs around the wall. There was a counter in one corner and behind this counter stood our friend who had a burning desire to hear "The Boys Of The Old Brigade". He had sobered up no end and was now concentrating his mind on selling cans of Tennents at inflated prices. These were the same sort of cans as were for sale in the shop.

The party went on all night. All night people stood up and sang songs or the accordion player took over or a fellow with a guitar and a line in songs associated with Johnnie McEvoy.

All night boys and girls left for a while to caress each other up against the wall outside. All the night the fellow who wanted "The Boys Of The Old Brigade" sold Tennents Lager to the party. The party ended just before five.

The men sit on on one side and the women on the other. The mass is read in Irish and there is a choir at the back of the church. The priest must be in his late sixties or early seventies; a strong Dublin accent comes through in his Irish, but he does not seem to worry about this. There seems to be a rapport between him and the people he had ordered to bed the previous night. He gives them the news and mentions the names of various islanders. He tells them that Tony O'Reilly has given the island money to buy a bus. He appears very encouraged by this.

After mass the men stand around and debate the weather. Each day they have to watch the weather because their boats are tied up off the pier and if a storm blew up they would be broken to pieces. They agree that the weather looks dangerous and the six or seven boats must be hauled in one by one and pulled onto dry land by a tractor. It takes hours.

The priest can see this from his front window. If only there was a harbour on the island... The fishermen could use bigger boats and fish all the year round. A harbour would cost one and a half million pounds. The priest sees no reason why there shouldn't be a harbour.

He also wants a ferry. Cost: half a million pounds.

And an airstrip. Cost: half a million pounds.

And other services to bring the island in line with the mainland. Cost: £800,000.

Fr Diarmuid O Peicin is a Jesuit priest who had worked for a considerable number of years in Africa before he came back to Ireland and decided that he should spend a while learning Irish. Tory Island was an outpost, a place just like Purgatory, where curates were sent for a brief period before being allowed return to the mainland. Even Fr McDwyer of Glencolumbkille, who was posted there in 1947, wanted to get off the island. "I was young and energetic, and I fretted and felt frustrated that some of the best years of my life were being frittered away when there was so much work to be done elsewhere," he wrote in his autobiography.

Fr O Peicin came and wanted to stay. He saw that official policy seemed to be that the island should be cleared. He saw that the community, now down to 200, was nearly broken. He saw that in a few years, if nothing was done, this extraordinary place would be deserted.

"So rich is the island in lore and legend that hardly a rock or promontory does not bear a Gaelic name and in true Gaelic style each of these names is descriptive of some event, some personage or some geographical peculiarity," wrote Fr McDwyer in his autobiography.

In the late summer of 1980 Fr Diarmuid O Peicin S.J. came to stay. Soon afterwards he was presented with his first manna from heaven.

This was in the form of the first by-election which Charles Haughey fought as leader of Fianna Fail - the Donegal by-election. Fr O Peicin got a message one day that Mr Haughey would visit the island in a helicopter as part of his election tour. He would be accompanied by Maire Geoghegan-Quinn, then Minister for the Gaeltacht. "There were big things at stake" Fr O Peicin remembers. "We went to town."

Maire Geoghegan-Quinn was wearing a fur coat. Fr O Peicin had already had dealings with her and he didn't like her. A speech was made and Haughey stood still in that special way he has when Irish culture and heritage is being mentioned. A special song of welcome was sung. He was shown a picture of the island and the place where they wanted to build a harbour. "I see it faces south east," he said. Fr O Peicin was encouraged. The Taoiseach was listening to him. "If I've to go around the world with a begging bowl..." Fr O Peicin began. Haughey, he says, nearly collapsed laughing. Fr O Peicin wanted to get across to Haughey that the island was viable, that it could be saved. "Look Father, I won't forget you," Haughey said. He was presented with a lobster pot and a painting by one of the second generation of the famous primitive school of art on Tory Island.

Haughey kept his word. He had several further meetings with Fr O Peicin. The following year when he was leader of the opposition he tabled a question for Garret FitzGerald: "To ask the Taoiseach if it is Government policy that the island community on Tory Island off the coast of Donegal will be given every encouragement to continue to remain there as long as they wish to do so; and that the necessary level of services, facilities and amenities for this purpose should be provided for them; and if he will give direction to all Government departments, state agencies and semi-state bodies to have due regard to this policy in all aspects of their operations relevant to the situation."

Garret FitzGerald said he would give such direction. Haughey sent a load of photocopies of the question and answer to Fr O Peicin. "I would hope," he wrote, "that the question and answer given may be of some assistance to you from time to time in your dealings with the various Departments and Bodies concerned. If there is any other way in which I can be of assistance to you in your endeavours, please do not hesitate to let me know."

Yet there was no encouragement for the islanders to stay. Fr O Peicin got the distinct impression that the local authority and the Department of the Gaeltacht had already decided that the island would be cleared in the near future.

"Father, I've bad news for you," the caller was the late Clem Coughlan who had won the by-election in November 1980. It was December 1981. Fr O Peicin listened and slammed the phone down when he heard the news. Ten houses on the mainland had been allotted to families on Tory Island. It meant 80 people would go. Fr O Peicin didn't sleep for a week. There was no point in trying to convince the families not to go. If they didn't take the houses, some other Tory family would and the opportunity might never be presented again. It was a huge blow to morale on the island. Those who stayed felt it wouldn't be for long.

Just as Fr O Peicin was making some progress the horse had bolted and he would have to busy himself trying to entice it back as well as everything else. A knitting factory was set up with a grant from Udaras na Gaeltachta. Other grants came for other small schemes: from the Youth Employment Agency, from AnCo, from Roinn na Gaeltachta. Fr O Peicin was full of plans, both large and small, to keep the island going and to give the islanders something to do.

There isn't much to do and nobody does much. Everyone gets the dole; there is a bit of fishing, a small bit of farming, although the islanders are not keeping as many cows as they used to. Milk in a carton is much handier. They get all six channels on television and stay in bed a lot in the winter. Channel Four, one islander told me, is the best thing to come to the island for years. A man is reported to have come out from the mainland a few years ago looking for rates, he was told to go away and not be annoying everyone. He did just that.

They burnt the island, according to one verdict. And indeed if you go up to the top of the lighthouse on the western side of the island and look down at the island, you can see that the earth looks scorched. To walk on, it is soft; nothing grows on it.

The lighthouse is a monument to the great beauty of Victorian engineering. Stone walls six feet deep, stone stairs, cut stone floors, shining brass. It is a world apart from the rest of the island. The vegetable garden flourishes. There is even a patch of rich green grass. It is as though the very soil itself around the lighthouse were different. And the answer comes, yes, it is different. They burnt the island, so nothing grows on their soil. The islanders dug down deep for turf and they burnt the turf. They dug down too far and they are left with barren soil that looks like moonscape.

Fr O Peicin doesn't care whether this is true or not. He is full of hope. He lobbies every agency he can think of for money, for moral support. "We want to spiritualise the politicians," he says. the island has shown it is unique: its school of painters, its actors, its folklore, its use of the Irish language. Fr O Peicin has found his true vocation as he travels from Tory to Dublin to talk to civil servants and politicians or to Strasbourg to seek money from the EEC. He has the look of a man who will not rest.

There was a chair on the stage and on the chair sat an old half-broken-down radio. There was a microphone right up against the radio so that you could hear Radio Luxembourg loud and clear in every part of the hall. They were doing an hour of Golden Oldies; Dusty Springfield was singing her heart out.

It was to be the last ceili of the season. Soon it would be too wet and windy for all the islanders to come to the community hall. And even though it was after ten no one had turned up yet. There was just a bloke to take your money and sell you drink and two other fellows wandering about the hall. Radio Luxembourg played "In Them Old Cotton Fields Back Home". It was getting near eleven but still no one had turned up.

On the mainland now the pubs were well closed; and anyone who was going to a dance or disco was already dancing the night away. On Tory Island, however, they do things differently. It was after midnight befor the islanders and all their children arrived at the hall. By this time a man with an accordion had replaced Radio Luxembourg.

Fr O Peicin moved among the people keeping a distance that any outsider must maintain. However, there was a grin on his face which was caused by the presence of a family who had left for the mainland when they were offered a house. It was the first time they had been back. That was a sign of hope and Fr O Peicin is always looking out for a sign of hope.

There was to be ceili dancing. The Waves Of Tory; The Walls Of Limerick; The Siege Of Ennis. All of the islanders knew the steps, as did some of the visitors. Everybody watched the dancing and talked among themselves. Fr O Peicin knew everybody and what they had contributed to the island since he had arrived and what they might still contribute. He talked about how a BBC team had come and filmed the painter, Derek Hill, who has a small cabin up beside the lighthouse on the island. they had filmed him dancing with the islanders at the ceili. It was Derek Hill who had encouraged the school of primitive painting on the island.

At a certain point the dancing stopped and the music stopped. Patsy Dan Rogers, who had been playing, stood on the stage and welcomed everybody; he then called on someone to sing. For the next hour the islanders sang.

Among the dancers one man had been remarkable. He knew the steps inside out and he performed them with incredible skill and some small flourishes. He danced with an extraordinary seriousness and intensity.

When it came to his turn to sing he took the middle of the floor. The accordion began to play a fast tune and he did a dance on his own to this tune. He then stopped and the music stopped. He began to sing a version of a song about a fox. When he stopped the music started again and his dance was an acting out of the hunt for the fox and the fox in full flight. He had invented the dance himself.

A woman sang "An Irish Soldier Boy" and another woman followed with another song to the same air. A few children came and did Irish dancing on their own. A German tourist who was staying in the hostel sang a song.

It was way after two when the singing stopped and the dancing resumed. Fr O Peicin remarked that there was nothing he could do to make the islanders go to bed earlier. He had tried to get the ceili started earlier but no one paid any attention. Cans of Tennents Lager were still on offer and all the children sat around the hall. There were a group of lads sitting around the hall as well, and it was clear that at some stage they intended to start dancing.

But it was just after half past three in the morning, however, before they moved from the bench they had commandeered and asked a few girls to dance. Around four o'clock the ceili ended and everyone began to walk home.

One song sung that night by a woman who was sitting on the edge of the stage was a lament called "Sean Ban Mo Grath". It was taught to the woman by Jimmy Duggan, the man who had invented the hunting dance. It was to be sung by a woman who was pregnant and whose lover was marrying another woman. The tradition on the island was that the older women would all dress up and turn up at a party before the wedding ceremony with the bride and groom. They would each sing a song.

The pregnant woman determined to disguise herself, attend this party and sing her song. The song was the story of her plight, verse after verse of it. She knew that if she sang it well enough her lover might change his mind. Everything depended on how she sang the song. So the song "Sean Ban Mo Grath" contains both the song she sang and the story of how she sang it at the party and changed her lover's mind, how he threw over the other woman and married the singer.

They needed a play one winter, the actors on Tory. Jimmy Duggan remembered this song and got the verse he was missing from his mother-in-law. He doesn't know how many songs he knows, an infinite number maybe. Jimmy Duggan wrote the play around the song and all the drama in the song is acted out. They brought the play to the mainland and to Dublin. It was good for the island's morale. Jimmy Duggan explained that the first verse of the song was to be sung when the lights were down before the curtain came up, "like on television".

The song has been both an agent in keeping the island together and a metaphor for its survival. Because like the abandoned woman, if Tory Island can sing its song and make its case well enough, something will be done. a harbour, a ferry, an airstrip. Fr O Peicin will sing his song for anyone who will listen.

Magill, January 1984

FEAR IN THE VALLEY
John Hanrahan v. Merck Sharp & Dohme

All along the valley people have noticed rust. Ray Foley, who lives next door to the Merck Sharp & Dohme factory in Ballydine, has noticed recently that metals seem to rust very quickly in the area around his house. John Hanrahan, on whose farm 114 cattle have died mysteriously in the past two and a half years, has a metal lamp which hung outside for nine months: one side is completely corroded, the other is unaffected. He says that the rusted side was the side which faced the Merck Sharp & Dohme factory in Ballydine, which is about a mile down the hill from his farm.

The metal sheet which covered the rainwater barrel in Tommy Rockett's yard, opposite John Hanrahan's farm, was there for years with no rust on it. Over the past two years it has corroded. Even Tommy Walshe, who lives five miles away from the factory on the Clonmel side, says that he noticed rusting on an unusual scale.

The church in Ballyneale is less than a mile up the road from Hanrahan's farm. The church railings have corroded too, but only part of them. The other part, people have noticed, is given shelter by a house from the wind which blows from the factory; there is no rust on the sheltered railings.

People say the factory is blamed for everything that goes wrong. If there's a sick child, it's the factory or if a farmer has problems, the factory is blamed. Or the rust on the railings in the church in Ballyneale. Some people blame John Hanrahan for working up feeling against the factory.

In the church in Balllyneale they have been saying a novena for Bertie Kennedy, whose doctor has told him that Lourdes might offer him more than any medical attention could. He is a popular man in the area, and the church was full on the nine nights of the novena.

Bertie Kennedy has cancer. Last year his wife thought he wasn't well. She made an appointment with the doctor for him on the last day of August 1982. The doctor told him he had cancer of the lungs. He didn't smoke or didn't drink and he had never been sick before. He is 37.

His problems started in 1981, when his cattle began to behave strangely: "I heard them in the barn one night and I went out to see

118

what was happening. When I went in they were holding their heads up and sniffing the air. Then they all suddenly bolted down to the bottom of the shed and started to pile on top of each other. Three and four high they were. I've never seen anything like it before and I've been in Ballyneale for 27 years. One bullock got his back broken with all of them piling on top of one another. The shed was 135 feet long and they all piled themselves into the top 15 feet."

The problems recurred the following winter. "These were different cattle in different sheds. They started to tremble and then bolted into the corner. They could be standing there looking like they were dead to the world and then they'd go all of a sudden. One day they were standing in the field and they started shaking and one bullock ran and they all bolted out of the field. But then they came back into the yard and gathered around me like flies."

In August 1982 Bertie Kennedy began to get pains in his chest and suffered from breathlessness. He had been kicked by a bullock earlier in the month and he put his trouble down to that.

He went to a doctor in Carrick-on-Suir, and the following day he was sent to Galway for tests. In all he has been seen by six doctors. According to his wife, all the doctors have asked him where he came in contact with chemicals. One doctor in Galway said that he had never seen that type of cancer before in a farmer, according to Mrs Kennedy. "The doctor in Galway said that it had something to do with chemicals", Bertie Kennedy says. His wife says that one doctor asked where her husband had come in contact with asbestos. None of the doctors will make any comment.

"I'm not blaming Merck Sharp & Dohme for my illness", Bertie Kennedy says. "But I think it should definitely be monitored. I'd back any committee set up to investigate it."

At 1.45 on the morning of Sunday 10 April 1983 John Hanrahan made a telephone call to the home of the county engineer for South Tipperary. When his wife answered the phone she asked Hanrahan why he always phoned at night to complain about smells from the factory. He told her that emmissions from the Merck Sharp & Dohme plant at Ballydine - emissions which he believes have killed 114 of his cattle over the past two and a half years - only came at night. There would be no point in complaining at any other time.

The following Wednesday the county secretary for South Tipperary wrote to John Hanrahan. He reminded him of his phone call to the county engineer and claimed that there were no emissions from the factory on that night. And furthermore, he wrote, that Hanrahan couldn't have seen any because the factory wasn't in operation that night. And also the factory, on being notified by the county engineer, had inspected the area around Hanrahan's farm that night and had seen nothing. And anyway, wrote the county secretary, the wind was blowing in another direction.

John Hanrahan was not surprised that the council thought he was imagining things. Nor was he surprised that they based their opinion entirely on facts provided by Merck Sharp & Dohme. ("I didn't even bother replying to the letter it was so foolish.") He talked about it with bitter incredulity, which is how he talks all the time about what is happening on his farm.

From the council's point of view Hanrahan's phone call was just another example of the man's nuisance value.

John Hanrahan's mother inherited the farm in Ballydine, now 270 acres, from her uncles. Her mother's name was Mandeville and the Mandevilles have held land in the area for 700 years. The Hanrahans are, in the words of a neighbour, "real old gentry".

"Mrs Hanrahan was really the power behind the wheel", according to David Hurley, the former county agricultural officer, who first visited the farm in the early 1950s. "I would say that the mother was as good a farmer as there was in South Tipperary", he says. "Everything was done according to the best scientific advice. Mrs Hanrahan is a terrific manager."

John Hanrahan, his wife and their two children, have moved out of Ballycurkeen House, which is now inhabited only by Mrs Hanrahan and her sister. They have moved to Piltown, about ten miles away. "When I think of the nights I spent lying in bed in that house rolling around looking for a breath of air", comments John's wife Selina. "If I had my life again I would run as soon as I saw that factory coming", she adds. They have moved to Piltown because they believe that the Merck Sharp & Dohme factory has adversely affected their health. The children's ponies and rabbits have all died in the past two years. The Hanrahans' dog died of cancer in August 1982. (Bertie Kennedy's dog died in the same month. "He just wasted away.")

All the neighbours agree that the cattle deaths on the Hanrahan's farm could not be due to bad farming. There is general agreement that the Hanrahans are excellent farmers; everyone we spoke to shared this view. David Hurley says it is a model farm.

John Hanrahan's reputation changes slightly as you move from Ballydine to Clonmel. One trade union official in Clonmel laughs when he hears that John Hanrahan has health problems. He says that he might do better if he stopped drinking. Others, when asked, insist that John Hanrahan never takes more than one or two drinks. The personnel manager of Merck Sharp & Dohme doesn't want to comment on John Hanrahan's personality but he wonders why we should believe that all his cattle have died.

In Clonmel the view is that John Hanrahan is mad, that he's a lunatic. One official, who has visited the farm constantly over the past few years, says that "he wasn't a difficult man until he had a problem and found that no one was going to help him". His neighbours, even those who are friends of the family, say that he's hot tempered, highly strung. Scientists who have visited the farm over extended periods have found him to be perfectly normal.

His mother has a reputation for being lucid, tough, dependable, solid. She makes no excuse for the family's unpopularity in the area: she says they never courted popularity, and they made sure that they never needed help from other farmers. Many of their neighbours say that if the problem had occurred on the same scale on another farm, the neighbours would have rallied around and the problems would have been solved. But not the Hanrahans.

In the County Council offices in Clonmel and in Merck Sharp & Dohme in Ballydine they will tell you the same story. The same story contains two truths which have taken the shape of precepts in the minds of the officials as though they had been brought down on tablets from Slievenamon. The first truth is that there are no unusual health problems in the Ballydine area, the second truth is that the animal problems are confined to John Hanrahan's farm.

Paddy O'Meara has a farm on the opposite side of the river to the Merck Sharp & Dohme factory in Ballydine. In November 1981 he was visited by an official of the Department of the Environment and the county engineer. He says that he gave them the same evidence as he gave *Magill* and they noted it down. In October 1982 he told the deputy chief medical officer of the Department of Health, what happened to him. His neighbours have confirmed various parts of his story.

At five o'clock in the morning on the last Sunday of May 1981 O'Meara was in a field with his cattle and his sheep. The first thing he noticed was the cattle sniffing in the air. Then he noticed the sheep running up the field. The air was thick with a kind of fog, he says. He had noticed a touch of the same thing the previous year.

This time he felt it in his chest. He says he could feel it burning him. That afternoon when he went back to the cattle, he says he felt weak and sore. "I went to bed early and woke up at three or four in the morning. I thought I was done. I couldn't draw breath." Because Monday was a bank holiday he waited until Tuesday to go to a doctor.

"He examined me up and down first. 'God', he said, 'I don't

know what it is.' He said then:'Where did you come in contact with poison? Your system is poisoned. You're rotten with it', he said. I mentioned the factory in Ballydine. 'O bejaysus it is', he said. I mentioned the factory in Ballydine and how the smell had burned me. 'Oh that's it', he said."

When O'Meara returned to the doctor in Clonmel later that week he was told he was slightly better. He made several other visits to the doctor. "The flesh melted off me. I was sick for two months. That was May. All June and all July I couldn't catch a bale of hay or anything. I lost weight. I got out of it gradually. But I was never the same since, though."

His doctor in Clonmel refuses to comment on this case.

According to Paddy O'Meara the cows which were in the field that day faded away. At the end of the year he sold them to a dealer for half their value. Of the 24 sheep which were in the field that day, all but two of them were barren the following year. He sold off the barren sheep. The cows which he has at the moment are still not thriving, but he has no interest in them any more. "Trying to do anything about it is useless. I see Hanrahan across there trying to fight against them all and I say "What's the use?" We got no hearing at any of the meetings. We just want a bit of clean air, that's all we want."

At the end of last October Paddy O'Meara put seventeen bullocks in a field opposite the factory. After two days they broke out. He found that they would not stay in the field. He had similar problems in 1981. "What ever it was in the grass the cattle wouldn't stop in the field", he says. Last October he put barbed wire up to keep them in the field. One of the animals tore its chest open while trying to get out of the field. Paddy O'Meara claims that the smell still comes from the factory. He has asked for monitors to be put on his land. This has not been done.

The County Council received the first complaint from John Hanrahan on 14 September 1978. He said that he himself had difficulty breathing. He also said that his cows' eyes were streaming. Complaints from John Hanrahan have persisted from then until now.

In 1979 the Council received different complaints from various people in the Ballydine area about bad smells. "Towards the end of 1979", says a Council spokesman, "we could see that Hanrahan himself seemed to have a problem which seemed to persist". In February 1980 the county manager decided to undertake an independent investigation and contacted An Foras Forbartha.

He asked them to conduct an investigation into pollution in the area around the Merck Sharp & Dohme factory in Ballydine. The factory had opened in 1976 and had expanded in 1978. In 1978 Merck began producing a drug called "sulindec" prescribed for the treatment of arthritis. A substance called "thioanisole", the "odour of which can be detected from very small amounts", according to Merck, is emitted into the atmosphere during the manufacture of "sulindec". In order to modify the waste treatment area Merck had spent £200,000. In addition they also set up a monitoring system in 1979.

Dr Ian Jamieson began an investigation for An Foras Forbartha in May 1980. This investigation cost the County Council £2,000. The atmosphere in the vicinity of the factory was tested for various air pollutants.

The report, published in October 1980, found no evidence of serious air pollution and found that acid vapour emissions from the Merck Sharp & Dohme plant were within the proposed EC health protection standards.

Dr Ian Jamieson recommended that further monitoring be carried out and that complaints continue to be "regarded seriously and investigated". He also recommended that "selected persons" be given sample containers to obtain "grab" samples of the air. These containers operate in the same way as the normal aerosol spray but, on depression of the valve, air is drawn into the container.

The Ballydine farmers were never supplied with these.

The Council met local residents to discuss this report on 18 December 1980. They agreed that further monitoring was needed. In the spring of 1981 the Council decided to commission another report from Ian Jamieson. The monitoring began again in April 1981 and continued until May 1982. This report cost £13,000.

The Council had a second meeting with the residents on 20 February 1981. The IFA was represented, the county agricultural officer was present as were the county manager and other local officials.

It was suggested at this meeting that a special committee be set up of technical experts in the pollution, agricultural, medical, veterinary and other areas to sort out what the problem was. The county manager agreed to do this. Everybody left the meeting feeling that this would be done. It has never been done.

February 1981 was the month the problems started in earnest on John Hanrahan's farm. February was the month when he and his vet Tom de Lacy began to record the deaths of cattle. At first they thought it was just bad luck, but more and more they realised that there was something wrong. The cows had been stampeding and getting sick, their eyes were streaming.

They were going to send the records to Dublin but were advised to send them to the County Council. They sent them to the county manager. A few days later on 17 February, three days before the locals had their meeting with the County Council, an inspector from the Tipperary Veterinary Office called and said the cows had brucellosis. Neither Hanrahan nor de Lacy had given any evidence that this was the case. Both were sure that this was not the case.

An inspector came from Kilkenny to see the animals. There was a greater incidence of twins than is normal, and calves were being born dead and deformed. The Hanrahans were watching the destruction of their dairy herd.

John Hanrahan sent part or whole caracasses of 26 cattle to the veterinary laboratory in Kilkenny. He got back reports to say that they could find nothing. He asked if the lab had a list of chemicals to look for. The lab did not. Nor did the lab have facilities for testing cattle for toxic substances. These facilities are not available in this country. The Department of Agriculture usually sends such samples abroad for testing. But they did not send any samples abroad for testing from the Hanrahan farm in 1981. Nor in 1982.

In mid 1981 the Council asked one of its vets to visit the farm and look at affected animals. He did this and he wrote a report for the Council. This report remains on file in the Council's offices. It has never been released or commented on.

67 cattle died on the Hanrahan farm in 1981. Tom de Lacy has records of 300 visits to the farm that year. In November Ian Jamieson informed South Tipperary County Council that his findings seemed likely to confirm what he had found in his previous report. He suggested a further study to be done using other methods. The Council agreed, and in March 1981 another report was commissioned at a cost of £6,000.

In January 1982 Tom de Lacy became seriously worried about the implications of what was happening on Hanrahan's farm. He believed, as he still does, that the problems were being caused by Merck Sharp & Dohme. On 18 January he wrote three letters - to the county manager, to the factory and to the county medical officer - to ask if they could inform him what substances Merck used.

On 1 February he received a reply from the county manager telling him to contact Merck Sharp & Dohme for the information. ("The information requested in your letter can best be obtained from Merck Sharp &Dohme.")

On 24 February Tom de Lacy received two replies to his letters of 18 January. One was from Merck Sharp & Dohme, who said they could not make any information available.

The other letter was from the county medical officer, who wrote: "I confirm that the management of Merck Sharp & Dohme have informed me that I am not at liberty to disclose confidential information which they have supplied to me." Earlier in the month John Hanrahan had issued court proceedings against Merck Sharp & Dohme.

The following month was March and Fianna Fail were returned to power. John Hanrahan was in Dublin one day and happened to be in Buswells Hotel where he happened to see Brian Lenihan whom he approached and informed what was happening on his farm. Lenihan was at that time Minister for Agriculture. He urged Hanrahan to stay in Dublin overnight and come to his office in the morning. At the meeting the following morning there was a promise of a committee from the Departments of Health, Agriculture and Environment to be set up to investigate the problem.

This committee was never set up.

On 24 June 1982 Merck Sharp & Dohme invited some of the local residents into the plant and presented information on how the plant operated. Details were also furnished of donations which Merck Sharp & Dohme had given to various projects since 1976. These donations amounted to a quarter of a million pounds. The company estimated that it would give £70,000 in donations in 1982 alone. The following have been among the recipients of money: Irish Heart Foundation (£50,000); St Vincents Hospital (£5,000); UCD (£10,000); Presentation Convent, Clonmel (£20,000); St Mary's School, Clonmel (£20,000); Loreto Convent School, Clonmel (£20,000); Kilcash, Kilshelin and Ballyneale National Schools (£2,000); Carrick-on-Suir Development Association (£5,000).

On 6 July 1982 the County Council held another meeting with local residents. John Hanrahan and his mother were excluded from this meeting on the orders of the county manager. Apparently, the county manager felt that, since the Hanrahans were sueing Merck Sharp & Dohme, they could not form part of the deputation to meet the Council.

Tom de Lacy, the Hanrahan's vet, however, attended the meeting and informed the Council that he and John Hanrahan believed they had definite information which would prove that Merck Sharp & Dohme were causing the deaths of John Hanrahan's cattle.

De Lacy refused to disclose what this information was. The Council and the Department of Agriculture have sought this information since de Lacy's statement. The information in question is understood to have been commissioned by the Hanrahans from

Rory Finegan, a Cork scientist, formerly based in Canada, now based in Tripoli. Hanrahan says he will release it in the High Court.

The following month Dr Ian Jamieson published the results of a further study, carried out between April 1981 and April 1982, of the air in the vicinity of the Merck Sharp & Dohme plant in Ballydine. He found that the acid vapour concentrations were within health protection standards, although during the summer of 1981 (when Hanrahan's problems were at their most severe) they were considered high for a rural area. The report stated: "It is considered that the relatively high acid concentrations were possibly due to emissions from chemical processes or the handling, transporting etc of acid substances in the factory."

Jamieson himself mentioned in the report that on two of his visits to Hanrahan's farm he had suffered from minor skin irritations and odours, which he said were not severe, with the exception of odours from thioanisole, which were "prolonged and very unpleasant".

Jamieson's main recommendations were that as a matter of urgency the animal health problems on Hanrahan's farm be fully investigated by veterinary and other appropriate authorities, and that the monitoring of emissions from the factory continue. He also stated that complaints should be properly recorded and monitored by the County Council and subjected to serious investigation. "Until an explanation for the health problems is found the possibility that some serious toxic substance, from whatever source, is responsible should not be ignored."

The monitoring of emissions from the factory did not continue.

John Hanrahan did not receive a copy of Ian Jamieson's 1982 report. His vet, Tom de Lacy, however, managed to procure it through a contact. The same contact turned up trumps when the next report was presented to Tipperary County Council. Had his contact not given de Lacy the report it is unlikely that it would have seen the light of day.

The purpose of the next report, written by the members of the Trinity College Botany Department was to assess the impact of the factory's emissions on the surrounding countryside by examining leaf yeasts (which are particularly sensitive to air pollution), lichens, grass, soil, silage and samples of animal hair.

From the leaf yeast study, the report deduced that certain locations in the area "are exposed to high pollution levels". The examination of grass and soil on Hanrahan's farm indicated a higher level of bromine and chlorine than would be expected, and the silage study showed that higher levels of bromine had been present during the summer of 1981.

126

On the basis of the lichen study, the report stated that: "evidence that chronic levels of pollution are present was derived from (a) observations of discolourations and algal overgrowth on some specimens, (b) high levels of some elements, especially sulphur in the lichen thalli. It is therefore expected that over the next few years the more pollution sensitive lichens will be killed."

The report further stated: "There was clear evidence...that sulphur was being taken up by the lichens from the sulphur dioxide emissions of the Merck Sharp & Dohme factory."

The results of the animal hair studies showed a relatively high level of bromine and chlorine, particularly during the summer of 1981, and provided "circumstantial evidence implicating a pollutant emitted by the Merck Sharp & Dohme company during 1981."

The report stated that the area around Ballydine has suffered a decline in air quality as a result of the emissions from the Merck Sharp & Dohme factory, and recommended continuing study and more detailed analysis of the hair samples, lichens, grass and leaf yeasts.

It also recommended that as conifers are more sensitive to air pollution than broad-leafed trees, the conifers in nearby Kilcash wood be surveyed, and that the nature and quantity of the chlorinated and brominated compounds in the factory be investigated.

Rumours were flying around about the report and what it contained in the weeks before a meeting was held in John Hanrahan's house on 27 September 1982. The county medical officer told the meeting that he was unable to procure a copy. An official from the Department of Agriculture, who was present, said he had been unable to get a copy.

When nobody was looking Tom de Lacy put the report on the table. When it was noticed there was consternation.

The following day the county engineer, and the assistant county manager, travelled to Dublin where they had a meeting with the scientists who compiled the report and Dr Ian Jamieson. It had originally been intended not to release the report but to incorporate its findings with those of Ian Jamieson.

Now they realised, however, that the report would have to be released, particularly since a copy had been received anonymously by the *Irish Times*. The representatives of the County Council wanted changes made in the report. They said that if it were released in full it would allow Merck Sharp & Dohme to take an action. In particular they wanted Merck's name left out as much as possible.

At one stage local gardai mounted an investigation into who had leaked the report and who had put it on the table. Merck Sharp & Dohme still express great concern that the report was leaked.

One of the Trinity scientists comments: "A potentially serious air pollution problem exists in Ballydine because of the siting of the factory, because of the height of the stack and because of the nature of the process carried out on the factory." He continues: "If the effluent from the factory were nothing more than sulphur dioxide and carbon dioxide there would be no worry, but if they contained unspecified substances obtained from processes involving chlorinated and brominated organic compounds - as they do - the potential exists for the release of toxic substances into the air which, because of the siting of the factory, might not be effectively dispersed. The prevailing wind is south-westerly, and what comes from the stack ends up on Hanrahan's farm."

The scientists all talk about inversion. Inversion is a meteorlogical situation which occurs in a valley where the air near the ground is cooler than the air above it and therefore it will tend to be trapped; it won't rise. The scientists claim that inversion exists in this valley.

"This could ruin the country", comments one scientist. "It could ruin Ireland's beef and milk export trade. There has been enough about antibiotics in Irish products, let alone toxic chemicals. This could close down Irish agriculture overnight."

In the autumn of 1982 both the Department of Agriculture and Tipperary County Council produced their own separate interpretations of the various surveys and reports produced on pollution in the Ballydine area.

Some aspects of their interpretations were inaccurate. An official's report for the Department of Agriculture stated that the TCD study on lichens " does not indicate any pollution". The TCD study stated that the lichen study had indicated "chronic levels of pollution".

The Tipperary county engineer, in his report for the County Council stated that "...the lichen species in the Ballydine area are high pollution sensitive types which do not flourish in polluted areas". This is nowhere stated in the TCD report.

On the leaf yeast study undertaken by TCD, the Department of Agriculture official states the following: "The data can be interpreted as indicative of airborne pollutants occurring over a wide area around Ballydine. This interpretation is untenable in the context of meteorological conditions if the Merck Sharp & Dohme plant is the source." None of the studies undertaken have stated this, and he gives no reasons whatsoever for his conclusion.

The county engineer states that "the results of the Leaf Yeast counts...do not purport to be scientifically accurate". At no stage in their report did the TCD scientists give any indication that this was the case. Quite the opposite. The engineer gives no explanation for his assertion.

On the TCD animal hair studies, the official from the Department of Agriculture states that: "The methodology used was deficient. No conclusions can be drawn." The conclusions of the TCD scientists were that these studies showed a high level of bromine and chlorine which reached a peak during the summer of 1981. The official gives no reasons for his dismissal of the TCD animal hair studies.

The Department of Agriculture report suggested that no further money should be spent on monitoring the factory until further veterinary information could be obtained. Both the county engineer and the county manager agreed with this.

Tom de Lacy confirms that they have a private report which they will not give to the Council or the Department.

The Department of Agriculture has written to John Hanrahan promising absolute confidentiality if he will release information on the cause of his cattle's death. The Department says that it needs this information so that it knows what to look for in the cattle.

John Hanrahan refused to give this information to a number of vets who visited his farm on 25 January this year. Both the Council and Merck Sharp & Dohme are concerned that John Hanrahan will not hand over this information. However, a senior official in Clonmel wonders why the Department, the factory and the Council are now complaining about Hanrahan's lack of co-operation "since they had access to everything they wanted for two fucking years and they didn't use it".

In October last year the IFA drew the attention of Charles Haughey, who was then Taoiseach, to what was happening on Hanrahan's farm. Haughey wanted to know if Merck Sharp & Dohme had ever admitted causing a problem.

Later that month, during the general election campaign, John Hanrahan went to see Michael Woods, then Minister for Health. He told him that a man in his early forties had died of a sudden heart attack. There had been a remarkable number of sudden deaths due to heart attacks along the river Suir near the factory. The following day was a Sunday and Michael Woods contacted the deputy chief medical officer in the Department of Health, and asked him to investigate the case immediately. He drove down to Clonmel the following day and was in the office of the medical officer when John Hanrahan phoned to ask him why he hadn't turned up to the meeting in his house.

He had been told nothing about a meeting in Hanrahan's house. He found Hanrahan rude. However, he drove to Ballydine and found a roomful of local people at Hanrahan's house. He got the impression that they were frightened. They talked of sudden heart attacks, of cancer, of deafness among children. (*Magill* has investigated incidents of deafness among children and has found no evidence to connect this problem with the Merck factory.) He found the meeting very difficult.

"People were talking a lot of bloody-minded codology", he says. Paddy O'Meara mentioned that he had to sell his cattle and his sheep. The official asked him if he was now breeding racehorses. Another man said that his health had been ruined by one whiff of the emission from the factory which had knocked him over. "You don't look too bad to me", the official told him. The man's name was Gussie Lyons. He died suddenly in Clonmel on 21 March 1983. He died of a heart attack.

The Schering Plough controversy raged in the valley between Carrick-on-Suir and Clonmel from 1974 to 1976. Everybody remembers it and everybody still talks about it.

It was to be another chemical plant on the Clonmel side of Merck. "We had the experience of Merck (which was being built during this period) and we saw Merck was good and we thought Schering Plough would be another Merck", says a local trade union official. At first there were two hundred objectors to Schering Plough: bit by bit the number dwindled to eight.

One of the eight had his cows maliciously poisoned, others had their cows let out on the road. One found broken glass on his driveway, another's house was threatened by a mob. There was garda protection for some of them. Their children were threatened. At a meeting in Cahir with public representatives and local officials they were told that if they did not withdraw their protest they would be ostracised from the community.

They issued the following statement on 17 December 1975: "For the safety of our families and property we individually and collectively bow to the pressure of serious intimidation and threats of violence, which forces us to forego our constitutional rights as citizens of this country. In these circumstances we individually and collectively withdraw our objections to the proposed industry and will take no further action."

However, because of the delays and the protests, Schering Plough decided not to build the plant at Clonmel. They moved the plant to Puerto Rico. The IDA warned that Ireland could not afford to have a bad label in international industrial circles. The objectors were called "cranks and publicity-seekers" in the Senate by James Tully, the then Minister for Local Government. They were also castigated by Noel Davern, Brendan Griffin and Michael Ferris.

The experience has left its mark on both sides. Some are sensitive that complaints about the Merck factory will put the jobs of the 250 workers there in jeopardy. Others are aware that if they complain about the factory they will be open to the treatment which was given to the earlier objectors. Several farmers mentioned to *Magill* that they could not comment on the problems in the area as they had been involved with the Schering Plough protest and did not want to go through the same experiences again.

There are many farmers around the Merck Sharp & Dohme plant in Ballydine who do not have any problems. Ray Foley lives next door to the plant; his farm stretches up the hill and adjoins John Hanrahan's land. There is just a road between the two farms. Ray Foley, who has a suckling herd and is thus in a position to observe cows over a period of years, has had no problems with his animals. His son often gets a headache when he works in certain fields, but headaches can be caused by anything, he says. But there are two things which might be caused by the factory: the problem with Mrs Foley's eyes and the rust around the house. Mrs Foley's eyes stream sometimes, and she has been to see an eye specialist in Clonmel. There are often smells from the factory, but everyone in the area gets those; a spokesman for Merck Sharp & Dohme comments: "I don't think people expect us to be an odourless plant. We can't survive without making an odour."

Pat Walshe of Kilmurry owns the only other herd of cows in the area, aside from Foley and Hanrahan. His, like John Hanrahan's, is a dairy herd. His fields adjoin Hanrahan's land for a length of 600 yards. His land, however, is in a dip, while Hanrahan's is on a hill. His land is further away from the factory than Hanrahan's.

The Walshes have had problems with their animals but they consider these problems to be due to natural causes. Their children have had problems due to ill health, but they believe that none of these problems can be blamed on the factory. Siobhan Walshe, Pat Walshe's wife, comments: "We are watching the whole time. We are concerned both for our children's health and our own health. We get the smell, but we can't say that we have had any problems. We can't honestly see anything wrong. We are keeping our eyes open."

Tommy Rockett has a farm opposite Hanrahan's land. Last summer his cattle refused to eat the grass, but he says that the situation at the moment is not as bad as it was in 1981. In 1981 he says that the cattle had continuous coughing from April onwards. (This was also the time when Hanrahan experienced his most serious problems.) Rockett thinks that they were poisoned by the chemicals in the factory, but none died on his farm. "They died in the meat factory, chemicals and all", he says. He says that he would never leave a window open in his house.

John Callanan's farm is off the main road from Carrick and Clonmel. He talks about the emissions from the factory: "It's like fallout from an atom bomb." His cows had problems with internal bleeding and last spring they were fading away. His vet advised him to sell them to the meat factory, which he did. In 1980 his wife had a nose bleed which she couldn't stop. John Callanan says that other people in the area had nose bleeds at the same time. He refuses to name these people.

Another farmer who lives about five miles on the Clonmel side of the factory says: "We get an awful tiredness. If the east wind blows up we get this awful tiredness." For the past three or four years he has got spasms of deafness, of which John Hanrahan has also complained.

This farmer was a butcher before he married into the farm. In 1981 they killed a sick yearling. He says that he has "never seen anything like the state of it". "In the spring of 1981 we had dreadful calving problems. We don't know if it's the factory," he says. Out of 80 cows who calved that year they lost 20. The children had chest ailments. Last September the cattle had problems with their eyes running. He says that he suspects that one cow they have is fading away. "If I'd the money I'd look into it."

Up the river from Paddy O'Meara's are the Longs. Michael Long doesn't believe that they have any problems which could be connected with John Hanrahan's problems. In 1980, however, there was an unusually high incidence of death among lambing sheep, for which there was no explanation. In 1981, the same year as Bertie Kennedy, John Hanrahan and Paddy O'Meara had problems with cattle and sheep stampeding, the Longs also had problems with cattle and sheep stampeding. Otherwise, they say, they had no problems.

Tommy Walshe, who lives five miles away, has no problems from the factory, he says, except the smell that sometimes seeps down the river. Himself and his wife also have problems with tiredness and have noticed rusting, but he is not sure that these can be ascribed to the factory; Paddy Stokes who lives near him says he has problems only with the smell.

There is no unusual human health problem in the area around the

Merck Sharp & Dohme factory in Ballydine, according to the county medical officer. "There doesn't seem to be any greater instance of illness than in any other part of the country", he says. He asked anyone who thought they had health problems which might be related to the factory to come forward. He has had six complaints, five of which he considers to be "of nuisance value". These involve running noses and watering eyes. One family has come forward with respiratory problems, but the county medical officer has no evidence that these are caused by the Merck Sharp & Dohme factory.

He has asked all the doctors in the area if they have had any complaints which could be put down to Merck Sharp & Dohme. All of them have said no.

Dr Michael Carey is both the doctor for the factory and a local general practitioner. "There is no problem whatsoever. I have not seen anything that I could consider a health hazard. There's more pollution in Clonmel than in Ballydine. Nobody in Ballydine has anything to fear", he says.

Dr Carey states that there is no health problem within the factory, and this is confirmed by an official of the ITGWU: "The plant is probably one of the most sophisticated plants in this country as regards health matters. We have nothing but the highest praise for them." The same official is not aware of any problems outside Hanrahan's farm. "What Hanrahan seems to lack is solid evidence, and I think it behoves him to get proof", he says. A spokesman for Merck Sharp & Dohme comments: "There is no other farmer who has come into us and said they are having problems with their cattle."

Dr Oister is a homeopathic doctor who practises in Bolton Street in Clonmel. He comments: "In my 37 years of practice, I have never seen so many people coming to me with skin problems. Nearly one in every three patients that I see suffers from one sort of skin problem or other. I have practised in England and Scotland and I also have clinics in Roscommon and Kilkenny. On average, one in every forty patients would have skin problems, nothing like the numbers I have come across in the few weeks I have been in Clonmel."

Other doctors in the area, however, claim that there is no unusual health problem in the area. To conclude that there was a problem, one doctor pointed out, they would need to do a survey in the valley and a similar survey in another valley of the same size. Until they did that they were not in a position to say whether there was a human health problem in the area. According to the Department of Health this is being done at the moment. It will be some time before it is finished.

"They set out on the wrong basis. They wanted at all stages to insist that it was happening on one farm only. I think they set out with a fairly closed mind and they wanted to prove themselves right. It could have been handled better and it should have been handled better. I think they've put too much trust in Merck. I'm fairly certain that something is wrong," says a senior official in Clonmel who refused to be named.

He is talking about his colleagues. Like many other officials both in Dublin and Clonmel, this man has a file on the problems in Ballydine. He keeps the following quotation at the beginning of the file. It is from Joyce Eggington's book "Bitter Harvest": "It happened at the same time as Watergate and they called it Cattlegate. But there was no big cover-up. It was not what was done that was wrong, but what was not done by people in authority who did not realise the magnitude of the problem.

"All the relevant institutions of democracy failed to solve the problem. Rather than working together to solve the problem they operated individually and did not share their knowledge. This was not due to malice but simply because this was an event outside their experience and beyond their budgetary means to resolve.

"They under estimated the seriousness of the problem and its implications and when they finally acknowledged it they tried to pass it on as being someone else's responsibility to find the cause.

"A properly co-ordinated approach of all the relevant groups involved with authority to involve some others who may have specialised equipment or knowledge would have been a better approach."

(Bertie Kennedy died later that year. In 1988 John Hanrahan won his case against the factory in the Supreme Court.)

Magill, June 1983
Additional research on this article was done by Maggie O'Kane and Mary Raftery.

V.
TONY GREGORY:
THE MAKING OF AN
INDEPENDENT TD

In the February 1982 General Election Tony Gregory, a left-wing independent candidate, won a seat in Dublin Central and found himself holding the balance of power. This resulted in a deal with Fianna Fail, known as The Gregory Deal, which created employment and improved social services in Gregory's constituency.

It was the evening of Tuesday 23 February. Garret FitzGerald was in the National Gallery to open an exhibition of three hundred paintings from the cellar. He seemed at home: he was among friends; Gemma Hussey, Nuala Fennell and John Kelly were among the guests. He made a vague, meandering and unprepared speech. It was difficult as one watched him standing at the podium not to think of Charles Haughey. It was difficult not to imagine how Charles Haughey would have comported himself on such an occasion. How he would have spoken of art, of Ireland, of our great traditions. How he would have gazed implacably into the future as he spoke. How he would have enjoyed being shown around the exhibition. How Charles Haughey would have loved to have been in the National Gallery that evening.

Charles Haughey was elsewhere that evening. Charles Haughey was in an upstairs room in 20 Summerhill Parade. There was a red ladder leaning against the wall. The light-bulb was bare. There was only a wooden table and some chairs. He was alone with four people he had never met before. He was there because Tony Gregory had won a seat in Dublin Central. Tony Gregory was there, as was his brother Noel. The other two were Mick Rafferty, Project leader of the North City Centre Community Action Project and Fergus McCabe, a social worker with the Eastern Health Board. 20 Summerhill Parade is the headquarters of the North City Centre Community Action Project; it is also where Tony Gregory holds his advice clinics.

Tony Gregory spends his life at meetings. He had arranged to attend another when he was finished talking to the leader of the

Fianna Fail Party. So this meeting had to stop after an hour and three-quarters. At first Mr Haughey found himself sitting between Tony Gregory and Mick Rafferty, but he soon moved to the head of the table. "This is not a Cabinet meeting" joked one of his interlocutors. The letters C.J.H. were monogrammed on Charles J. Haughey's white shirt.

Gregory and his companions had prepared policy proposals under five headings, and they found Haughey to be well briefed on most of these. He came across as very shrewd, very cool. He gave them no sense that he needed an urgent commitment from Gregory because he was fighting for his political future. He told them that he believed it was important in a time of recession to invest in infrastructure. They felt they were meeting an official, a managing director of a large company rather than a leader or a statesman. He did not dismiss any of their proposals. He agreed to several of them immediately. When 20 million was mentioned as a sum needed to reduce unemployment in the inner city, he pointed out that, with inflation, the figure would be closer to 30 million. He didn't see any problem about this. He didn't see many problems about the proposals which were put forward. He seemed to have no theories. He seemed to dislike ideas.

He discussed derelict sites. He talked about putting a tax on derelict sites. The others said that this wouldn't solve anything, that property speculation itself was the problem. Haughey said he would look into that, and come back to it when they met again. He said this about anything on which he wasn't briefed. He exuded an easygoing charm. As he was leaving, it was mentioned to him that he seemed to be having problems with his party. He explained that during a time of uncertainty people have an opportunity to knock you, but he wasn't worried about it. He seemed to be confident.

"No one is to shout" said Mick Rafferty. The count in Dublin Central in the 1982 General Election was over: Gregory had taken the fourth seat and O'Leary the fifth. George Colley was making a speech about how other countries could be envious of our democracy. "El Salvador" roared Mick Rafferty. Mick Rafferty roared anything that came into his head. "No one is to shout." Tony Gregory had been elected, and Mick was going to celebrate, he was going to do what he wanted. He was going to walk straight over and tell a certain aide of George Colley's what he thought of him. He was going to tell a fat boy from Fianna Fail to go away and not be annoying him. He was going to put his hand on Tony Gregory's head and toss Tony Gregory's hair, despite Tony Gregory's protestations.

An hour earlier, Tony Gregory had watched the ninth count. He didn't look like someone who was winning. He looked exactly the same as on 12 June 1981 when he was losing. No, he told Forbes McFall of Today Tonight, he didn't want to be interviewed until all the counts were over. He was told he would definitely be elected. "I'll believe it when I see it up there" he replied. He looked almost bored. He leaned against the barriers and watched the tenth count. The Returning Officer told Kevin O'Kelly of RTE that Gregory was elected and so was O'Leary. This was conveyed to Gregory, but the expression on his face remained the same. He didn't show much emotion; it is possible that he didn't feel much emotion.

Mick Rafferty, on the other hand, was on top of the world. He followed Tony Gregory, who was to be interviewed on the radio. There was a tug-of-war going on. Television wanted Tony Gregory; radio wanted Tony Gregory. Tony Gregory was brought into a room to be interviewed for radio. After a few moments, Mick Rafferty came out and shouted "They're interviewing him in Irish." Mick had nothing against Irish, but he felt it was a bit of an anti-climax. The inner city elects its TD, and what do RTE do? They interview him in Irish. Mick thought it was a bit much. He wanted to have a party. Earlier, Gregory's women supporters had left the count; they gave their passes to the men so the men could get into Bolton Street. The women were now waiting in a nearby pub. Mick wanted to collect them, get into his van and go home and have a party. He didn't think Gregory would come to the party; it wasn't his style. He would probably just go home. "They're interviewing him in Irish."

The election of Tony Gregory was important for Mick Rafferty. By day, and often by night, he is Project Leader of the North City Centre Community Action Project. His brief is to revitalize the north inner city. He organizes full-time drama courses as part of Youth Training Schemes, photography courses, catering courses. He looks after specific problems that people have. He organizes festivals. He is a mine of ideas. He understands resources: where the money is and where the energy is. He has learnt how to tap both. The day before the election he got a letter from the Department of Health and Social Welfare to tell him that funds for the NCCCAP would stop at the end of March. Nine days after the election he got cheques to fund various specific projects. He is not sure if the election of Gregory was the cause, but he knows that the NCCCAP will not close down as long as Gregory is a TD. He also knows that the election of Gregory confirms everything that himself

137

and Fergus McCabe have done over the past ten years. Politics has not failed him.

"Just say Tony Gregory TD" advised Mick Rafferty, as an attempt was made to join the women for some after-hours drinking after the count. But the doors of the pub wouldn't open. No one was sure if the women were inside or not. Mick just wanted to get into his van and go home and have a party. Someone slipped across the road to his house and came back with a bottle of whiskey. Fergus McCabe had some drink at home as well, so the van moved in the direction of his house. "Where are the women?" wondered Mick Rafferty. The van pulled up outside Fergus McCabe's house. Mick and Fergus went in to get the drink. Suddenly, someone came to the door and shouted "He's on the telly." The van emptied only to find that Joe Sherlock was attacking Gregory on RTE. Everyone was stunned. First he's interviewed in Irish, then he's attacked. Back in the van, Mick Rafferty was only warming up. "If I ever meet that Joe Sherlock I'll give him a slap across the face" he exclaimed. He looked at a bollard in the middle of the road and laughed: "I don't like that bollard and I'm going to have it removed." The van cheered up. "Do you see that church?" someone said. "I'm going to have that knocked down and a community hall put in its place." "Let's go home and see what the national situation is" said Mick Rafferty. He thought this was hilarious. It was only later he realized that the national situation was going to mean something to both him and to Tony Gregory. The entire van sang a song about Alice Glenn.

Everyone was surprised when Tony Gregory turned up at Mick Rafferty's house. And Gregory was amazed when Albert Reynolds said on television that Fianna Fail would probably get his support. He couldn't believe his ears.

Without warning, the door opened. The women had come back from the pub and Mick Rafferty wanted the party to begin. More specifically, he wanted the television turned off. He wanted everyone to sing a song. He made up a song about Tony Gregory who is now a TD. Gregory wondered when the Dail met but no one knew. Gregory had hurt his wrist when he fell off a ladder while putting up posters, and it seemed to be paining him. He didn't sing and no one asked him to. But Mick Rafferty sang. He sang Roy Orbison's "It's Over"; he sang "Summertime"; he sang "Twenty-four Hours from Tulsa". Fergus McCabe played his guitar and sang "I'm a Union Man". Mick Rafferty wanted everyone to sing a song from the 1960s. By this time Tony Gregory had gone home. His phone would ring incessantly for two weeks. The first call came at four in the morning. A few hours later he would get a call from Michael Woods of Fianna Fail.

Tony Gregory was a student of Irish and History in UCD when the split occurred between Official and Provisional Sinn Fein. He had helped to set up the Republican Club in UCD, and, on leaving university, continued his involvement with Official Sinn Fein. He began to devote himself almost full-time to its activities: "pickets and protests and paper-sellings and any activity under the sun that you could think of." He felt that Seamus Costello was the only member of the leadership who was actively trying to implement and pursue the politics of the party. He admired him as someone who got things done, who did not deviate from the official line of the party. He felt Costello set an example and gave leadership. Costello became involved in local issues in Bray, he set up Housing Action Committees, he started Tenants' Associations, he stood for local elections. He became chairman of Bray Trades Council. He became popular in the party, so popular, Tony Gregory claims, that it was impossible for the leaders of the party to get rid of him at the 1972 Ard Fheis. Gregory was dissatisfied with Official Sinn Fein. He thought its policies were being diluted by the leadership. He saw another split coming in the party. He talks about "smear campaigns" and "purges". He left in 1973 before the split which gave rise to the IRSP. "Not too long after I left" he says "they began to shoot each other."

Gregory became a loner and remains one. He moved his base from a political party to a local movement. He made a decision that he would never again become actively involved with any other political organisation: his connections with the IRSP and the SLP were slight and short-lived. In 1974, a leaflet was dropped in his door to announce the setting up of a local Tenants' Association. He attended the first meeting. At about the same time, other such associations were being set up in the north inner city. This was how Gregory met his closest associates - Mick Rafferty and Fergus McCabe, who had both become involved in Tenants' Associations in the North Wall and Summerhill. They joined forces.

Tony Gregory worked as a teacher in Colaiste Eoin and had free time to devote to local politics. Fergus McCabe was a full-time social worker in the area. Mick Rafferty soon ceased to be involved in local activities on a regular basis due to personal commitments. All three felt a need for a full-time office and full-time staff to deal with the problems of the north inner city. According to Tony Gregory, they wasted a year trying to convince various agencies to provide funding. In the end, Combat Poverty, set up by the Coalition in 1974, agreed to give them money, despite violent protests from local TDs and councillors who said, according to

Gregory, that they were "communists, and bankrobbers and all sorts of things". The result was the North City Centre Community Action Project which was set up early in 1978; Mick Rafferty was employed on a full-time basis.

The usefulness of funds, a full-time officer and an office became clear when the Corporation, on 1 August 1978, announced its plans for the north inner city which would involve moving people out of the area. Gregory and his colleagues opposed the plans and organized an alternative plan. They cajoled the Corporation. They even sat on Gardiner Street during rush-hour to protest about the decay of the inner city. They were very nearly put in prison for this. Their campaign was extremely effective.

Gregory was determined to run in the local elections in the spring of 1979. He had become known in the area; there was a clear need for a non-party representative on the City Council; he also saw the issues in the area as a useful vehicle for a left-wing politician to get elected. Mick Rafferty, on the other hand, went about for an entire week trying to convince everyone that Kermit the Frog should be their candidate in the election and someone should change their name by deed poll. He lost the argument and put his considerable energy behind Gregory's campaign. Gregory took a seat on the City Council.

He chose to sit in the Council chamber between Labour and Fianna Fail, as far away from Tomas MacGiolla and the Community Councillors as possible. He looked cynical and bored at meetings. He did not seem to have much respect for his fellow councillors. He seldom spoke, but when he did he was brief and pointed. He saved his breath for meetings with Corporation officials. He knew how to get what he wanted. He put pressure on other councillors to support him. "I don't think my two-and-a-half years on the City Council so far have been wasted" he says. "We stopped the motorway, to start off with. We certainly highlighted the whole housing situation in the city. We made fairly significant changes in the Development Plan for Dublin. Eventually, we won out on changing the development of Gardiner Street and Sean McDermott Street from blanket commercial use to almost blanket residential use. When I say 'we' I mean myself as a representative of people."

When he says he is not interested in personalities, he means it. He does not inspire affection, and he is not interested in doing so. His admiration for Seamus Costello was based on Costello's policies and his activities, not on his personal qualities. His single-mindedness in pursuing his policies and not deviating from them is

140

supreme. He spends his life going to meetings. He would not see his election as a personal triumph, but as a victory for the policies he stands for.

On the evening of Thursday 25 February Tony Gregory received a telegram from Michael O'Leary, asking him for a meeting in the Dail the following day. The wording of the telegram suggested that Jim Kemmy and Sinn Fein The Workers' Party would also attend. Jim Kemmy, however, was in Limerick, and was unable to come to Dublin at such short notice; SFWP told O'Leary that they hadn't time to attend. When Gregory turned up at the Dail, he did not want to have a meeting alone with O'Leary so they arranged to meet the following morning in Wynn's Hotel. Kemmy would also be there, but not SFWP.

Gregory arrived with his brother Noel, Mick Rafferty and Fergus McCabe. O'Leary gave them the impression that they were a delegation from his constituency. He was not briefed in any way, and had nothing to say to Gregory's policies. Kemmy did not speak very much, and O'Leary's aide, ex-UCD revolutionary, ex-Dail librarian Dave Grafton, only uttered a brief justification for tax on short-term social welfare benefits.

O'Leary behaved not as the leader of the Labour Party in the company of fellow socialists, but as someone who would have to discuss matters with Garret FitzGerald. He remarked at one stage that Labour would be better in opposition; it would be able to become more radical. He thought it would be better if "the other crowd" took over power. When they came out of the hotel, they found that the Evening Herald had a headline about "The Gang of Five" Independents forming an alliance. They thought this was surprising, to put it mildly.

Gregory and his colleagues went to see Michael Mullen, General Secretary of the ITGWU, who offered to act as witness to any promises which might be made to Tony Gregory in exchange for his vote.

On the evening of Friday 26 February a letter from Garret FitzGerald was delivered to Tony Gregory. "Dear Deputy Gregory," it went "My party has authorised me to have discussions with you. I shall be happy to meet you at your convenience, and should be glad if you could ring my office next week to arrange a suitable time. Yours sincerely, Garret FitzGerald." The letter was hand written. Tony Gregory thought FitzGerald had left it rather late.

Dublin's Port and Docks Board are putting twenty-seven acres of land on the market. The site is beside the Custom House; the Port and Docks Board is insisting on its right as an autonomous body to sell the property on the open market for office development. They have been granted outline planning permission by the Corporation, and have appealed to An Bord Pleanala against the conditions which the Corporation has imposed upon any development. The twenty-seven acre site is the largest development ever planned in Dublin. It is, according to Fintan O'Toole, "Dublin's most important opportunity for redevelopment this century". This twenty-seven acre site is the kernel of Tony Gregory's bargaining position. He wants the state to take the twenty-seven acres over for a mixture of housing, light industries and amenities. He believes "it is the key to the whole future of the inner city." Michael O'Leary, TD for the area on which the land lies, has told Gregory that he "will look into it." On Tuesday 23 February Charles Haughey promised Tony Gregory that he would nationalize it.

Any industrial development on this site will involve the IDA. "Our dealings either on local level or on the City Council with the IDA have never been satisfactory" Gregory says. He believes that they expressed an interest in finding sites in the inner city in the belief that such sites were not available. "We feel that they have no commitment at all to inner city renewal" he says. When he met them to discuss the twenty-seven acre site, they did not seem interested. Gregory thinks his election to the Dail will change this.

Tony Gregory sees the development of the Port and Docks site as long-term. In the immediate future he wants to see the Corporation resume its Environmental Works scheme in the inner city. He see this as offering over two hundred people immediate employment. There is also maintenance work on Corporation flat schemes.

Reducing unemployment is Charles Haughey's first stated priority. It is also Tony Gregory's. Housing is Tony Gregory's second priority. He wants the Corporation to get more finance to continue its housing programme. He will be looking for changes in the way rents on Corporation flats are increased. He does not accept that there is no money available for these schemes, that the country is in a financial crisis. "How can they get £20 million for Knock? How can the banks make huge profits? How can the financial institutions make such huge profits? How can property speculators make such huge profits? There's no shortage of money in this country. It's just a matter of tapping it where it is and not where it's not."

Tony Gregory supports the general principle of armed struggle in the North against the British presence there. He believes that the

British presence is the root cause of the problems in the North. His closest advisers, however, do not support his views on the North. Mick Rafferty and Fergus McCabe would tend toward Jim Kemmy's anti-republican views on the North.

He believes in the restoration of the Irish language: "Every sacrifice should be made to try and save it. But I certainly wouldn't see myself carrying out a crusade to restore it."

Except for Articles Two and Three of the Consitiution, he supports the general principles of Dr FitzGerald's crusade for liberalization of the country's laws. He is also vehemently opposed to giving the police any further powers. One of those close to him is convinced that he would bring down a Government which tried to change the law governing the right to silence, or tried to increase the statutory powers of the police.

He says he would have voted against the Budget. He says he would have voted against the increase in the school-entry age. He will not abstain in the vote for Taoiseach. He has not yet met SFWP, although he remains willing to do so, despite his mistrust of the party. He doesn't know who he is going to vote for. Monday 8 March could be a long day in Irish politics. Gregory sees the negotiations becoming extremely intense, but at the moment he thinks the progress is slow, particularly with Labour and Fine Gael. He wonders if they haven't thrown in the towel.

"My policy would be to vote on issues as issues arise. I couldn't see myself voting for issues that I disagreed with. I'm not for sale. I would expect there to be a great deal of consultation. But at the moment there are people looking for my support for a vote on a Taoiseach, and I'm establishing what the policies of that Taoiseach would be. It's as simple as that and that's where it ends."

In Dublin, February 1982.

THE PRODIGAL SON

Early in 1983 the new Coalition government released details of the phone-tapping of journalists' telephones by Sean Doherty during his term as Minister for Justice.

There were old men wandering about the ballroom of the Forest Park Hotel in Boyle that Friday night with a pint of Smithwicks in one hand and a cup of tea in the other. Drink flowed from the huge tea-pots that were hauled from table to table. Drink flowed from the bar. There were queues four deep at the bar.

The tables were strewn with sandwiches and apple tarts. Women were wandering about with biscuit-tins full of more sandwiches and more apple tarts. This was the night they killed the fatted calf. This was the night the Prodigal Son came home.

Over a thousand of them had paid three pounds each. They were here to support Sean Doherty. Two of them had driven down from the next constituency, from Ray McSharry country, from Mattie Brennan country. Charlie Haughey was the only leader of Fianna Fail, they were sure about that. The others couldn't hold a candle to him. They pointed over at Ray Devine, Ray, they said, he's the man responsible for where Sean Doherty is today. Ray Devine came over. They shook his hand and said again that he was the one responsible for Sean Doherty and where he was today. Ray Devine smiled. Doherty would be along soon.

At five to eleven there was a cheer from near the door. The Prodigal Son was carried in shoulder-high. He was grinning and waving. Everybody wanted to see him and pat his back and shake his hand. Welcome home, Sean. Sean Doherty, all is forgiven.

He got down from the shoulders of his supporters and began to move among his people. Everywhere he went, he was followed by a group of people. He moved slowly towards where the band were getting ready to play. He was a likely lad out on the town on a Friday night. His face was scrubbed, his shoes were polished and his shirt was as white as the driven snow. His eyes played with the crowd, picking out a face and then he would move forward and shake a hand. This was a ceremony of touching. Of putting your arm around people's shoulders, of catching their hand. Doherty talked to his constituents. He got up close to them, put his arm around them and whispered in their ear. He would whisper a few sentences and then look at them straight in the eye. Every so often, himself and his constituent would burst out laughing. He did this maybe two hundred times that Friday night. The story he whispered into his constituents' ears was clearly very funny, although there is no evidence that he whispered the same story into each ear. The story was shocking in some way, alarming perhaps, and almost certainly it was a dirty story. The band started to play "Ramona" as Sean Doherty blessed and caressed the people of Roscommon.

This modern dancing hasn't caught on at all among the Fianna Fail supporters and cumann members in Boyle. If the song is slow ("Stranger on the Shore"), the Fianna Failers all waltz, as though the world had stood still since 1927, the year the party was founded. And if the song is fast ("My Bonnie Lies Over the Ocean"), they jive. The Fianna Failers jive as though the First Programme for Economic Expansion had never been published. And Sean Doherty, the former Minister for Justice and TD for Boyle, sure knew how to jive. The man moved as though it were some enchanted evening in the 1950s and his mother had let him go to his first dance. He loved it.

Then it was time for pictures to be taken to record this great event. Ray Devine kept close to Doherty. A man wanted his wife to pose for a photo with Doherty. But she wouldn't, she moved away. The man persisted. Doherty grinned. "What are they doing to my girl?" he said and lunged at her. He began to tickle her. She squealed with laughter. The band played "Spanish Eyes". At midnight Doherty shook hands with a constituent who had a problem. He stood in the middle of the ballroom as people danced and shouted and drank beer and ate sandwiches all around him and he noted down the details. Ray Devine was still following him closely. How did Ray Devine put Sean Doherty where he is today? Ray Devine explained that when Doherty's father died, there was a move to co-opt his mother to the county council, but Devine had the meeting postponed and he went to Dublin and persuaded Sean to leave the Guards and come home to Roscommon and Fianna Fail. A politician was born.

It was after one o'clock. There was still a queue at the bar. Sean Doherty had now been everywhere. He had done a full circle of the hall; he had shaken the men's hands and kissed the women. Now it was time for action; now it was time to give people their money's worth. The bands stopped playing and all the local Fianna Fail politicians, with the exception of Terry Leydon, made their way to the platform. Terry Leydon hadn't turned up.

"Every man, woman and child in the constituency can stand behind Sean now. He's on the way back. There's no doubt about that," said the first speaker. "Before this night 12 months we will have Sean back in the parliamentary party. I hope to God I live to see the day when Sean comes down the road in another Mercedes." There was a cheer. "Yahoo," roared one Doherty supporter.

Then it was Doherty's turn to speak. Doherty, the genial local TD who would pat you on the back, and whisper stories into your ear was a changed man. The hale fellow well met became a man at the microphone full of sound and fury. His eyes flashed with anger.

"I did not kidnap Shergar," he began. "I promise you." The voice rose. "I swear to you." The voice rose again. "Do you believe me?" he shouted. Yes, yes, yes, they replied. They believed him. "It's the only thing I haven't been accused of this year." He thanked them for all their support, for letters, messages, phone calls. He was grateful for these. But not for the other letters which didn't offer support. These he was going to dispose of when "the requirements of nature" came upon him.

"I hope that not ever again will I be pursued like a wounded animal. That's what they did to me and I know that," roared Sean Doherty. He went on to talk about law and order. To cheers and shouts he said: "Let it be two journalists or anyone else, if I think they're entitled to be tapped, I'll tap them. Because they associate with people who are a threat in one form or another to this state, I would do it again, if necessary."

He went on to denounce RTE who "attacked me as if I were the only evil-doer in the land." "I did not have the favour of the gossip columnists or the gossip journalists," he said. He talked about the need for a press council and the need to stop leaks to the press. "If a government attacks you, and the media and the people in your own party, where the hell can you go." He looked at the crowd. "You are the only people on my side at the moment," he said and the people on his side lifted him once more up on their shoulders, high into the air. One of his supporters stood back for a moment and watched him. "He's a great little trier," the man said. "You'd feel sorry for him. And you know, he'd help a tinker on the side of the road."

Magill, February 1983.

SO FAREWELL THEN, GARRET FITZGABBLE

The Coalition government fell in January 1987. Garret FitzGerald
was fighting his last campaign as leader of Fine Gael. Fianna Fail
won the election.

On a Sunday morning during the election campaign of November
1982, Fine Gael held a press conference in the penthouse suite of
one of the posh Dublin hotels, which was poorly attended. Jim
Dooge was in the chair. The main focus was Garret. Someone asked
him almost casually about the sinking of the Belgrano and he
roundly denounced Charlie Haughey and Fianna Fail for not
supporting Margaret Thatcher and her Falklands War. It was the
usual stuff.

A few journalists who had been slouching in their seats now sat
up, however. What would Dr FitzGerald have done had he been
Taoiseach during the sinking of the Belgrano, one of them asked.
Would he have blindly supported the British? Of course he would
he said, Britain was our ally. But would he have supported the
sinking of the Belgrano had he known it was an act of aggression,
that the ship was at the time sailing away from the British? Himself
and Jim Dooge smiled in wonder at our incomprehension. It wasn't
a question of right or wrong, they explained, it was a matter of
diplomacy. You supported your ally.

Just for a few minutes all the high-mindedness had gone, all
Garret's reasons for "coming into politics" had been left aside. A
wind of sheer pragmatism blew around the room. He seemed to be
saying that, under certain circumstances, the holding and wielding
of power did not have a moral constraint. It was a bit of a shock
coming from someone whose moral superiority, goodness and
truthfulness was a matter of personal pride and public record.

His aim from 1977 onwards was simple and direct, everything
was subservient. His aim was to make Fine Gael the largest political
party in the state. He was the right man to do it, with the right team
around him. People who knew about presentation and marketing,
who understood the importance of women and young people in any
campaign, who were seriously embarrassed by having the likes of
Gene Fitzgerald, Ray MacSharry, Gerry Collins and Sean Doherty

147

running the country, who detested the old, moribund Fine Gael, who delighted in marketing and manipulative techniques.

The fact that Garret FitzGerald has contributed nothing substantial to Irish society since he became leader of Fine Gael ten years ago arises from his subsuming all serious policy commitment into marketing and manipulation. Did he, or did he not want an abortion referendum for example? He promised SPUC that he would hold one. In power he said that the time wasn't ripe. In an election campaign he once more supported the referendum and the Fianna Fail wording. In power again, he no longer supported the Fianna Fail wording, and thereafter ceased to support a referendum.

Did he support the coming together of the Catholics and Protestants in the North for example? He always said he did, and, indeed, offered it as one of his reasons for coming into politics. His constitutional crusade would bring us all together. Yet his Anglo-Irish Agreement did exactly the opposite. It sought to isolate the Catholic community in the North as having a separate grievance which could only be solved by a separate form of representation. In doing so, it introduced an arbitrary authority in the North, which is the very antithesis of Protestant doctrine and the precise object of Protestant fear.

He "came into politics" to win power, like most politicians. But he was easier to sell because of his own view that he was somehow above politics, explaining over and over what he "came into politics" to do, as though he would of his own accord, vanish out of politics if these things no longer seemed capable of being achieved. He was full of a bloated rhetoric of goodwill. He would say anything. Even at the first press conference of this campaign he sounded like someone who was going to get things done. He sounded as though he had never been in power, as though he hadn't doubled the National Debt, as though all his life he was waiting for this great opportunity to solve the problems of the poor and the down-trodden. If only someone would give him the chance.

Then there was "Building On Reality", a long-term plan produced half-way through the government's term of office. We don't hear much about it anymore. The launching of the document was an event full of glitter and splendour. The marketing men must have been meeting way into the night. The venue was Iveagh House. The television lights gave a sense of urgency and importance. The heads of the semi-state bodies, by their very presence, underlined the sheer seriousness of the occasion. And just so nothing could go wrong, the questions from the press were to come in private sessions, where specialist journalists could be specially briefed by politicians. Specialist journalists are generally timid and conservative, thus keeping the people of Ireland safe for Fine Gael. In one of these private sessions Garret was asked to name one thing he had done in power which he had promised to do. The drowning man looking back on his whole life, all those promises, tax bands at twenty-five per cent, tax relief on rented accommodation, £9.60 for wives, the status of illegitimacy being abolished, the current budget deficit abolished in four years, all those things he had faithfully sworn to do, now nothing, little embarrassments, things no one had yet mentioned in this campaign, while he blathers on about how you can't trust Charlie Haughey. At that private session he had to admit that there was nothing. He had done nothing he had promised.

There was something very Garret about "Building on Reality", the long preparation of the document, the elaborate presentation of its content, the elongated tour of the country to explain it to the faithful, and then within six months the abandonment of its targets, the shifting to some new set of hopes and dreams. The ultimate Garret event, of course, was the New Ireland Forum, full of sound and fury, lengthy submissions, long talks, more meetings, historic proposals, a massive waste of time, producing a document which like "Building on Reality" should only be read for laughs.

I went to Cashel one night in November 1984 when Garret was explaining "Building on Reality" to the people of Tipperary. He began by having a press conference for the local and national press. He seemed content sitting back in his armchair in the warm room of the hotel, explaining things to us, fielding questions. Later, for more than three hours he sat at the top of the convent hall answering questions on career guidance, the Enterprise Allowance Scheme, the need for an open university, side roads, main roads, local government, disadvantaged areas, tourism, the public service, Bula, the pub opening hours, and many other matters.

He would have talked all night. He seemed immensely happy there at the top of the hall with an audience of about two hundred, explaining things to people. The fact that two years later he would still be in power and the pub opening hours would remain unchanged, despite his constant promises to do something about it, did not bother him much. He loves talking, like others love drinking. Plans and promises, explanations and long conversations. It seemed an odd thing for the head of the country to be doing, hanging around a hall in Cashel until after midnight, instead of drafting legislation, or shutting up for a while and just thinking. Yet he moved around the country night after night, like an alcoholic looking for a place to drink in.

During this period I often had occasion, in the course of my professional duty, to see a bit of one of Garret's special helpers, who used to feed me tea and little bits of information, most of them harmless. My main interest in these meetings was to observe the extent to which this fellow would use what our parents used to call "bad language". Every second word was "fuck", or "fucking", "shag" or "shagging", "whore" or "cunt". I enquired from others who also had meetings with the same man, but I discovered that he only spoke like that to me. Maybe he thought that because I had a beard I liked people talking like that.

They were smart people Garret had around him. They had long meetings to plan what was to be done. They knew their policies this time around were almost identical to the PDs', so they arranged to hold a press conference on the very first day of the campaign, thus stopping the PDs getting in before them. They thought all this out. Someone noticed that Garret's glasses were thick and looked particularly bad on television, so they got him a pair of light glasses which they kept in readiness for Garret's appearances on the box. The only problem was that they kept slipping off, so they had to warn Garret that he was wearing these light glasses and to try to keep them up on the bridge of his nose. They're a happy bunch of men and women, they feel they've worked hard for Garret, the country and Fine Gael. Every single thing in this campaign has gone according to plan. Even if they lost twenty seats, one of them says in a moment of candour, they wouldn't feel too bad, they'd know it wasn't their fault, all the work had been done, the meetings held, everything was in place, from the first helicopter ordered under a false name to the soccer match which they moved the election to avoid.

Garret went to Bray on the DART in the second week of the campaign. It was a photo opportunity. He was interviewed for the News at One-thirty at Sandymount Station. No, he wasn't worried about the polls, that was what he predicted. The DART came and he got on to a specially reserved compartment. He put his foot up on the seat (which he shouldn't have done) and if there had been any reporters there, this would have made the headlines. Instead, there was 'Today Tonight', the programme which makes public relations films about politicians, doing a bit of filming, and two RTE reporters. The place was coming down with photographers, *The Irish Times* printed a photograph of the photographers photographing Garret. *The Irish Independent*, however, had a photograph of Garret waving from the DART. The worst part was when Garret drove the DART. This should have caused great excitement, and indeed all the photographers ran into the driver's cabin to snap Garret with his hands on the wheel. The only serious event of the day was when a woman accosted Garret on a street in Bray while Cillian De Paor's tape recorder was on for 'Today At Five'. She explained that her daughter was ill and attended an outpatients department of a hospital several times a week. Garret, excited by the sheer joy of explaining, told her that she would only have to pay once a week. The woman knew this. It was ten pounds extra a week. Where was she going to get this? But Garret likes explanations only when they're technical, and he didn't know what to say, so he moved on.

In explaining the joys of Hillsborough, he was joined by Peter Barry and Alan Dukes and a whole bevy of lads from the Department of Foreign Affairs. Chief among them was a fellow whom Garret personally selected to be sent to London to butter up the Tories. So they rented him a house in Montpelier Square, where he wined and dined the Tory party. (Incidentally, this house in Montpelier Square is large and extremely comfortable. It would be a great place for anyone stuck in London with no place to go. The telephone number is: 584-2635.)

I was in Hillsborough on the day and can attest to the excellence of the stew provided to the press. Outside in the cold, Paisley and his mob protested. It wasn't just that his mob contained James Molyneaux which was disturbing. His mob contained Dowager Lady Brookeborough. There we all were inside: telephones everywhere, telex machines, sandwiches, the aforementioned stew, all sorts of drinks, RUC protection. Outside, in the cold, on the other hand, stood Dowager Lady Brookeborough. There was something funny going on. This was hardly an exercise in bringing the two communities in the north together.

All year we heard about the great successes of the Agreement. Not a week went by without Garret, or Peter Barry, or Alan Dukes telling us of the great breakthrough it represented, how the nationalist community was now supporting the RUC. It just happened that I was wandering around the North during four months of the summer while these gents were making pronouncements about what was and what was not happening there. I was talking to people all day about what was going on. Not one word which emanated from Dublin about the success, impact or beneficial effects of the Agreement was based on fact. It was an odd experience listening to all this disinformation; even odder for the people who lived in the North. The oddest thing of all was Garret's interview with the *Belfast Telegraph* where he said that the only reason for the Anglo-Irish Agreement was to defeat the IRA. Nothing else. This was so patently untrue that no one paid it the slightest attention.

This was followed by a speech where he said that one of the politicians he most admired was Kevin O'Higgins. His liberalism had gone, it meant nothing. He believed in nothing, except power. When he had power he did nothing with it, except talk and keep inflation down. The illegitimate are still not legitimate, the poor are still with us, unemployment has almost doubled, as has the national debt, farmers still don't pay any tax, the PAYE sector are still over-burdened, the people of the North are still divided. And that's only for starters. If only we had someone good, honest and decent who would "come into politics" and clean up all this mess.

In Dublin, February 1987.

(The telephone number in Montpelier Square is no longer in operation.)

A PARTY BANKRUPT
OF POLICY

The next Fianna Fail government fell in the summer of 1989 because of its policy on health cuts. This time, after the election, Haughey was forced to go into coalition with the Progressive Democrats.

It was the winter of discontent. It was that period between the signing of the Anglo-Irish Agreement in November 1985, and the rise of the Progressive Democrats in the opinion polls a few months later. Dessie O'Malley was already out of Fianna Fail for his stand on the contraception bill; Mary Harney was to follow shortly.

The strongmen of Fianna Fail were in Limerick that weekend to deal with O'Malley's followers, to make them decide one way or the other. If you confessed to Brian Lenihan and expressed true sorrow, it was said, then you would be let stay in the party, but those without a firm purpose of amendment would be expelled, put out into the cold. Des O'Malley's wife was involved in the organising committee of a writers' conference to honour Kate O'Brien, which I was attending and which was happening in the city that same weekend. O'Malley was lucky, then, he had somewhere to go on the Friday night while his former colleagues were downtown hearing confessions.

After the evening session, he came to the pub with us. If he had gone home the phone would have rung and journalists called. Here he was safe. He watched the door nervously, and a few times he tried to take a cigarette from a packet on the table, but was told to put it back. He was off smoking.

He listened at some length as someone explained to him the merits of several Irish writers. Listening seemed to keep his mind off what was going on in his political front-yard. For an hour or so he seemed passionately interested in literature.

The following day, in the lobby of the hotel, I bumped into one of the men who had been sent to Limerick to gut O'Malley, a senior and experienced Fianna Fail politician.

What would Fianna Fail do now about the Anglo-Irish Agreement? I asked him. It had expressed its deep opposition to the

Agreement which it promised to renegotiate, once in power. What now?

He looked at me in surprise. "That's that now," he said. "There'll be nothing more." Did he mean that the party's opposition to the Agreement had ended? In effect, if you listened carefully, that was what he did mean, and if you read further between the lines, you would discover that Fianna Fail policy and what Fianna Fail says in opposition are meaningless.

Fianna Fail is interested in pragmatism rather than policy. It is close to the Peronist party in Argentina in this respect; the recent Argentinian President-elect announced that he was not for anything, or against anything, he was a pragmatist.

For a voter it is impossible to know where Fianna Fail stands on any single issue. A week before the last election, while sitting in Rory O'Hanlon's livingroom, I asked him about health cuts and hospital closures. He assured me that there wouldn't be any; greater efficiency within the hospitals and the VHI would save a great deal of money, he said. He even looked at me as though he meant it.

The problem is not simply a voter's problem, however. The lack of serious policy formation in Fianna Fail does not simply serve to delude the voters, but it deludes the politicians as well, and it has caused, perhaps more than anything else, the mess which Fianna Fail has made of the country during its periods in office since the rise of Charles Haughey.

What, for example, is Fianna Fail's view on Anglo-Irish relations?

Haughey started by giving Margaret Thatcher a Georgian tea-pot and getting her to agree to the phrase about "the totality of the relationships" between these islands. It was a good beginning. She, too, is pragmatic. She is also prudent, and she would never have hyped the meeting to journalists later, or let her equivalent of Brian Lenihan on to the BBC World Service to say that anything, including unity was on the cards.

It was like the county councillor running out of the meeting saying that the bog would be drained after all. It bore no relationship with reality. Haughey became someone you couldn't do business with.

He went on to hype what was happening further in his subsequent Ard Fheis speech in which he almost promised Irish Unity to his followers. He was dreaming, as the Argentinians dream of the Falklands, and his dreams were doing nothing but damage to his country.

The end of his relationship with Margaret Thatcher came with his refusal to support her in the Falklands war. He gained short-term yelps from his most fanatical supporters; in the long term it would mean that the British would never treat with him again.

The sound of short-term yelps could be heard once more last year as the Irish Government sought to rub the noses of the British in the case of Father Patrick Ryan. Haughey's efforts to woo the British have come to nothing; because of Father Ryan even his willingness to deal with them pragmatically over extradition, will not help his case. The lack of clarity in his party's policy on the North and Britain has left it open to bursts of sudden pragmatism with equally sudden roars of Up the Republic. He cannot be trusted.

On economic matters, as well, he has dealt in expediency rather than strategy. His address to the nation in 1980 shortly after taking office about the nation's finances and the country living above its means showed him as sharp, tough-minded, determined.

And yet, until taking office more than two years ago, he never acted on his own advice. He did not cut back on public spending during his first term in office, nor did he significantly increase revenue. When a Coalition government tried to deal with the nation's financial problems and were brought down by a few Independent TDs, Haughey told us that there was no financial crisis facing the country.

"I am not here to be cross-examined," he told a press conference in February, 1982. Someone told him that he was there to be cross-examined; but he still had no strategy to reveal. Early in 1980 there had been a crisis. Now suddenly, there was no crisis, even though things were worse.

Fianna Fail talked of boom and bloom instead of Fine Gael's gloom and doom. Haughey bought Tony Gregory's support and on his way out of office produced a document, "The Way Forward", which said that there would have to be serious cuts in public expenditure, which Haughey had told us several years before, and then denied in the meantime.

He dismissed the value of economists; if you want a statistic you sent for an economist, but you never sought economic advice from an economist. Then, on taking power this time round, he changed his mind on this, too, and economists now wield power within his administration.

In November, 1982, he made the issue of the abortion referendum an important one in the campaign. He told a press conference that Garret FitzGerald couldn't be trusted to hold the referendum. More than anybody else, he is responsible for the deep divisions and bitterness of that campaign. It is unlikely that he has

155

strong views on abortion or, indeed, divorce. His sights are set, instead, on short-term political advantage. Winning office is everything; what you do with power doesn't matter.

Power has made him increasingly pompous, and his pomposity has been greatly helped by RTE. His grandiose tone during the Gorbachev visit was only a patch on his tone during his visit to Japan, proclaimed as a great triumph by himself among others.

Selling Ireland abroad is part of Fianna Fail's package. The heady rhetoric, the optimism and the lack of specifics are all part of the coinage in which the party has been dealing for some time.

In New York in March Albert Reynolds came to celebrate St. Patrick's Day. He came to the Puck Building in Soho where the new professional Irish in New York were holding a fund-raising ball.

There was a large jazz band, the food was good and drink flowed. Half the people there were more than one generation away from Ireland. Reynolds told us that Irish people did better abroad than they did at home, as though emigration was invented for this purpose.

He went on to ask the new Irish to tell their companies to invest in Ireland (even though people never do as well there as they do abroad), "so less of yiz will have to come over in the future". People cringed. Who is this guy?

Reynolds stayed on for a while at the ball as the new Irish danced the night away. Some of the people there could have got work in Ireland, but had left because of the narrowness of the society as shown in the abortion and divorce referenda, had left because of the lack of clear vision and the abundance of loose rhetoric in the public life of the country.

Albert Reynolds and his wife sat there alone at their table. After dinner, no one came near him. He had just spoken in praise of failure and complacency, like Patrick Pearse used to talk about blood sacrifice, and these things don't go down well in America. So he sat there alone, a man ideologically bankrupt from a small, bankrupt country and proud of it. And the band played on thousands of miles from home. Nothing seemed to bother Albert Reynolds.

The Sunday Independent, May 1989.

VI.
THE DISCREET RISE OF THE BOURGEOISIE

Spring 1990: By train through Eastern Europe from Bucharest to the Baltic.

Everywhere you went you sought images of change, you looked for telling moments. You learned to fill in the details. You kept notes of items displayed in shop windows; each ordinary scene could be made into something. A deserted main street at ten o'clock at night could thus become an image of the old regime or the present tension. The old Eastern Europe was being slowly unimagined, and a new place was appearing before our eyes.

So, out there in the night in Bucharest, Romanian Germans waited. I was summoned to the window: come and take a look. They arrived each afternoon, small groups of them. They collected wood and cardboard so they could light fires to keep warm when the night came down.

What a dramatic image! We stood gazing out, so aware, so conscious that we were watching history. In the morning these people, trapped in Romania for so long, would stand in line outside the German Embassy to get visas which would allow them to start a new life in the old country.

The crackling of the fire, the quiet vigil, the presence of the police were made all the more appealing as an image to take note of by that sense of destiny, of each person's life changing in a way which would have been unimaginable a few months ago.

Inside one of the buildings on the same square a few nights later another significant image was making an appearance. A group of men from one of the EC countries gathered, experts in the intricacies of credit export control. They wore suits and remained sober at the reception for them after their hard day's work assessing if the new Romania could be trusted, if there were people in charge with whom you could do business.

Quietly, in buildings like this, undramatically, a new world was being negotiated.

Elsewhere, you sought images of stark contrast, snapshots of moments when two worlds collide. In the city centre, the Writers'

157

Union building stood apart, untouched by Ceaucescu's terrible urge to re-make Bucharest in his own likeness. It was old-fashioned in every detail. I sat in the main office noting that each object, from the huge baroque tiled heating apparatus to the colour and texture of the paper, was new to me, strange, different.

Where were the old writers? And where were the new ones? Some of the better known collaborators with the old regime had fled, disappeared, didn't come here anymore. But most still did, the place was warm and comfortable, and food and drink were cheap. In the dimly lit dining room, among the fading fin de siecle splendour the two groups of writers sat apart, ignoring each other. The compromised older writers whose day was done sat on the right-hand side of the long room. The new writers sat on the left hand side.

Most of the new writers had not been dissidents. Most of them had made their work obscure ("allusive, intricate, semiotic and esoteric", as one of them put it), had not compromised and had been rewarded with badly-paid hackwork and literary obscurity.

Now they were ready to take their rightful place in the ruling class of the new Romania. Bogdan Ghiu, a poet in his early thirties, used to make his living typing out novels by members of the Writers' Union. He lived in a two-room flat with his wife and two children. He had to wait five years for his first book to appear.

Now, a few months after the revolution, he had his magazine "Contrapunct", funded by the state, with articles on American writers like Robert Bly and Donald Bartheleme, and work by the new generation of Romanian writers. Now he was going to move from his two-roomed flat into one twice the size in one of the new blocks which Ceaucescu had built before the Revolution. And he was also going to France to study for a while on a grant from the French government.

Some of the work by Romanians appearing in "Contrapunct" was not new: it was so hard, he smiled ironically as he said this, for poets to write poems in such times as they were living through here. Now in Romania everyone was busy. People who once had the long day to themselves to dream up new poems, to invent and imagine and play with words, now had meetings to attend, magazines to edit. The poets, he said, were all writing articles and polemics. When things were quiet again, they would return to the stillness of the empty room, and poetry.

I was enjoying the strange anxieties and divisions in the building, and came back for lunch a few days later to meet Bogdan Ghiu and a couple of his friends, all of them widely read in contemporary

French and American literature, all of them speaking French, but one of them speaking English and Italian as well. None of them had ever been out of the country. Yet they had read the same books, and been influenced by the same sources, as any intellectual in the west.

There was no sign that their lives under Ceaucescu had made any mark on them as they talked about Foucault, Derrida, and contemporary Romanian writers such as Mircea Dinescu and Marin Sorescu. But it came in odd moments, attitudes and beliefs which were disconcerting. It came first, I think, when we talked about abortion. One of them grinned when the recent legalisation of abortion was mentioned. It came just in time for him and his wife, he said: it cost just 30 lei (about 25p) and could be done in half an hour. His wife, it seemed, had availed of the new freedom, but he sounded blase about it, as though he had received an unexpected present, as though it hadn't taken a feather out of either of them. I didn't know what to make of this, but I knew that I had never heard anybody in the west talking about abortion like this.

It came up again in another discussion when I asked about prisons. Who was in prison now in Romania? They shrugged, they didn't know, and then one of them said that it had been a mistake to release the burglars and thieves with the political prisoners in the general amnesty. The others nodded in agreement. Surely, I thought, these followers of Foucault could not be serious? The more we talked the larger the gap appeared between their reading and their experience and opinions.

It arose again when I asked about homosexuality. A young official from the Writers' Union immediately butted in to say that it was illegal and would remain so, as it was unnatural. The young writers looked bored, this wasn't what we were here to talk about. It was easier, then, to discuss Faulkner and form in the modern novel.

One day, Bogdan Ghiu and myself were invited into the main office of the foreign section of the Writers' Union where we could drink tea and talk more quietly. Here it was simpler: here I could watch the last days of the old regime, and capture telling images of the old Europe now withered and dying.

Six people worked in the room, their job, as far as I could understand, involved organising trips abroad by Romanian writers, but during the time I spent in that room, none of them did anything. They wandered in and out of the room, they talked and gossiped and made tea. They looked out of the window. Their salaries were paid by the state. I wondered what they would do when the state rationalised its spending.

One man, older than the rest, disturbed us as often as he could.

Once, I was sure I heard him muttering as he passed by. He was the boss under the old regime, I was told, the one who decided which writers went abroad and which writers didn't. His days were numbered now. He would make no more decisions.

It was easier to take note of this than to make sense of another, young, liberal, well-read writer's response to my question about gypsies. Most of the contraband and currency speculation in Romania was caused by the gypsies, he said. I might have seen them selling flowers but they caused a great deal of damage, and would have to be integrated into the society. At the moment, he said, they didn't fit into "the moral patterns" of the society.

I wondered what these patterns might be, but there was no point in pursuing the matter. They weren't interested. The liberal politics of intellectuals in the west had not, as yet, taken root here. It was more fruitful to talk about the difficulty of producing a novel in Ceaucescu's Romania, and how it might be easier now: a novel, we agreed, gave the game away, politically and emotionally, you couldn't hide behind a novel, unlike poetry.

There was a life in Bucharest, a city I was slowly getting to know, there was a seedy underworld, which I presumed they would know and be interested in. I mentioned some of the low-life places I had been in, and they were puzzled and horrified even. They warned me to be careful. It suddenly struck me that day in the Writers' Union that something had survived in these people from long before the Ceaucescu era, some deep bourgeois sense of themselves, and that all of their reading, their involvement in literature, philosophy and discussion, their whole attitude towards the world arose from their vision of themselves as a class.

This was something which would preoccupy me in other cities in the coming weeks: this overwhelming sense that the old bourgeois world had held its breath when communism came, and simply waited, and had survived intact to take over power once more.

On the streets people walked aimlessly by, as though to walk with a purpose would be to give away a secret. People narrowed their eyes and looked towards the horizon, as though squinting. This, one of the features of Ceaucescu's physiogomy, was common among the faces you saw in the city, although none of the young writers had it. People seemed distracted, guarded. They could have been country people coming back slowly from a market.

Bucharest too, seemed only half there. Ceaucescu had removed whole streets, he had uprooted buildings and replaced them elsewhere, creating a strange emptiness in the city, but leaving signs of what the city had once been.

The Orthodox churches, for example, the ones he had not destroyed, studded Bucharest like small jewels. Squat and modest, but richly decorated buildings, their entrances were like small mouths, and the candle-lit atmosphere inside was dark and moist, like a cave.

An official from the Writers' Union brought me through the old quarter one evening, towards a bar called the Carru cu Bere, which resembled an enormous basilica, with arches and gilded columns. The tables were full, beer was brought in tankards by uniformed waiters, four men from the army at the table beside ours were enjoying a heavy meal. The decor was florid and perfectly preserved; the place was flourishing and intact like nothing else in Bucharest, like a small joke a dictator could play: leave one clue of former splendour.

Outside in the evening there was a great quietness in the city: few cars and even fewer people. The evening light was mellow and soft and southern. In one of the low-life bars down from the National Theatre, however, panic was setting in. At each table four or five disgruntled men sat with empty glass tankards in front of them, and more stood beside a door which led into a back room, waiting. The atmosphere was smoky.

Suddenly a man burst out of the back room with a large tray full of tankards of beer. Now there was chaos and shouting. Everybody demanded a tankard, and those who didn't get one roared at the man, who retreated, calmly, with his tray into his inner sanctum. Soon afterwards, he reappeared with another load of tankards, but still not enough to satisfy his clients.

In the underground station near the Intercontinental Hotel and the National Theatre the crowds assembled every evening, groups of four and five stood there shouting out their opinions, discussing the new order of things with passion and fire in their eyes. The tone all the time was heated and animated, as people stared at the speaker and listened carefully to what was being said, drinking in every word.

A man with a beard came by, looked at each group, listened to each intense debate, then stopped at one as though he had selected it as the most interesting, like you would choose a television programme in a multi-channel area. Soon he butted in, and then all eyes were on him.

Everybody paid attention. Although there seemed to be violent disagreement at times, there was never any sense that these people would come to blows. There was too much wonder in the raw way that they spoke and listened. I understood very little of what they

161

said - Romanian is a Latin language and thus it is easy to pick up individual words - but one word came up over and over - the name Illescu, another word was strangely absent - the name Ceaucescu. He was now history, and these people in the metro station were discussing something more urgent and important.

All around them, as they mouthed out their brand new visions of the world, newspapers were being sold. New ones were being launched every day, as new factions and groups declared themselves ready and willing to take power. Handwritten manifestos were pasted up on the walls of the metro stations. They were closely read and examined by most passers-by. Everything written and said took on a rare excitement in those early days after the fall of the dictatorship in Bucharest.

The government was now housed in one of Ceaucescu's dream buildings, modern and imposing, in a square where much had been razed to make way for it. The building was surrounded day and night by the army. Young recruits stood at five metre spaces around the outskirts of the grounds and talked and laughed and smoked and listened to radio and slouched and did everything except stand to attention and look serious. They grinned at you as you passed by, and then carried on with whatever story they were telling. A few times as I passed, during the time I stayed in the city, I noticed one recruit in each group talking and soldiers on either side of him listening in rapt attention, regularly breaking out into giggles or uproarious laughter, as he continued his tale, or whatever he was saying.

At the other side of the city Ceaucescu had built his new palace at the end of a long avenue dedicated to the Victory of Socialism. The avenue was full of modern shopfronts, but there was little inside the shops. Above them, for seven or eight storeys, were apartments built in a 1930s fascist Gothic style. The fountains on the avenue were not working. The street lamps mixed florid art nouveau shapes with completely functional modern, square lamps.

The avenue led up to a hill, and at the top of the hill was a huge new construction, like a hospital, or a government headquarters with a balcony on the first floor where the leading citizen could make speeches. If someone had told me that this imposing structure, built to impress, had nothing behind it, was merely a front, then that would have been easy to believe.

The palace, like the avenue, looked like a plan, with all a plan's symmetry, more than an actual building. It was certainly grandiose, but in some odd way, because of its sheer scale and size, it was grand as well and oddly impressive. The apartment buildings, in

162

particular, looked comfortable and habitable.

But the absurdity of the palace grew more apparent the closer you got. A note at a side gate said that it was open to visitors until one o'clock every day, this was the late afternoon, but people still seemed to be streaming in and out of the building, and I wandered up, passed by a soldier guarding the gate who glanced at me nonchalantly, and I approached the palace. No, I was assured, when I arrived, it had definitely closed, but after a while the woman in charge relented and let a group of us in. Once inside, we had to buy a ticket, which cost a few pence, and then we could go where we liked in the huge unfinished palace building.

The ceilings were high and the main staircase wide, like in a film set for some movie about the French court in one of its opulent phases, but the closer you looked the tackier the work seemed. Some of the detailed marble work on the floor had already loosened. Most of the decoration, even the marble, looked like an imitation. The chandeliers were too big, hung too low, which gave them a faintly comic air. On the first floor there was nothing but huge rooms. It was as though Ceaucescu and his wife had been planning enormous state receptions, as though they dreamed of guests wandering from room to room marvelling at the wealth of the new Romania.

Now, instead, ordinary people paid their money and went through in a mixture of bafflement and amazement. It wasn't finished; you could see the concrete where the marble had not been added and now probably never would be. If you made your way through this maze of bloated decoration and ersatz grandeur you came to the main room and you could walk across it and stand on the balcony as the dead dictator must have dreamed so many times of doing, of addressing his people from here rather than from University Square.

It was the people now who stood and surveyed the empty avenue, waving to phantom crowds in mocking gestures, or simply standing there watching, bewildered, uneasy about walking so freely in this temple to a dictator's power. As I went back down towards the main staircase, I watched two women examine the gilded wood, and understood the two words they said; "Sublime, superb". Like most of the visitors that day, they didn't see Ceaucescu's unfinished palace as vulgar, or mad, they seemed full of wonder at its size and the money spent on building it.

Should it be finished? A notebook rested on the table in the entrance hall; visitors were invited to comment. Opinion was divided on what should be done with the building (one wanted it to be turned into a discotheque; another wanted a university, another a museum), but most believed that it should be finished. A large number of people wrote at great length, filling up pages with their views on what should be done with Ceaucescu's last abortive dream.

I walked home every evening along a leafy boulevard and then turned into a warren of quiet streets, full of French style villas and large houses in their own grounds. Some of these were embassy buildings, but most were not. Most seemed to be in private hands. As you passed in the evening, you could see the globed lamps, the drapes, the old paintings, the walls lined with books. You could catch a glimpse of an old world of money and ease, that old bourgeois world which we thought had gone with the rise of Hitler, the war, and the rule of Stalin.

I had been reading Isaiah Berlin in *Granta* who wrote: "In the course of the last two years, I have discovered to my great surprise and delight that I was mistaken (about the death of the true Soviet intelligentsia). I have met Soviet citizens, comparatively young, and clearly representative of a large number of similar people, who seemed to have retained the moral character, the intellectual integrity, the sensitive imagination and immense human attractiveness of the old intelligentsia."

Berlin seemed to imply that such qualities ("moral character" for example) were "retained" rather than, say, acquired; that settled society with its old money and its deeply-ingrained sense of purpose instilled something in its children and grandchildren which the newly-educated could never possess.

They knew how to wait, the bourgeoisie. Their culture was based on waiting, on saving, collecting, and on educating their children. Their whole lives were spent consolidating the future. They held on to what they could when times were hard. More important, they held on to a sense of themselves, and this was what their children inherited, and this I thought was what Ceaucescu's regime and other regimes failed to take from them. The old intelligentsia were ready now, power was in their reach once more: the new rulers of Eastern Europe would not be those who had been educated from poverty by the communist regimes, who now sought freedom from communist tyranny. The new rulers in general would be those whose parents or grandparents had known wealth and power under the old regime. They had simply skipped a generation and waited.

It was easy to understand as you walked through the bourgeois quarters of Bucharest how somebody poor and ambitious, alone in one of these cities, could have built up such resentment against the owners of these houses, whose material comfort was combined with such an easy, proprietorial relationship with culture. Ceaucescu had set out to destroy this world, just as Hitler had. He knocked down most of the old bourgeois city, moving its residents to high-rise, unheated flats in order to build such monuments to the new as the Avenue of the Victory of Socialism. He worked with these people. It was, after all, this class, the leisured and thoughtful children of the bourgeoisie, which had helped propagate the ideas of Marxism, people such as Valeria in Saul Bellow's "The Dean's December".

In a book-lined room at a party in Bucharest a few days later sat another image of this old inheritance. A government minister, who until before Christmas was under house arrest, was moving with ease between his own language, French and English. His face was relaxed, and regularly lit up with laughter. He fitted his new role perfectly.

The entire country, he said, was looking for a job; a man from a circus, for example, had approached him, wanting to be made head of all the circuses in Romania. The minister was enjoying himself now, several people who had been talking among themselves were now listening. Well, the minister said, he had checked this man out, and discovered that the fellow had put on pornographic shows in his circus ring for party members, and clearly - the minister smiled ironically and shrugged, - he couldn't be given the job.

He talked as though he had held power all his life. No one asked him how he felt about having such easy access to the personal files on circus managers. Later, when I made enquiries about him, I discovered that he too came from one of those families who had held power in the days before the Second World War. He was now fulfilling his destiny.

Buying a train ticket from Bucharest to Budapest proved to be one of those classic Eastern European experiences we have been reading about for years. You queue for information, you queue at the cash desk to pay your twenty-one dollars for a first class ticket (the journey will take fifteen hours) and you queue once more to show your receipt and collect your ticket. It took more than an hour.

The train left on time. The weather was beautiful as we went out into the country; the cherry trees were in full bloom. It was a Sunday and we passed scene after scene of rural bliss and ease: people fishing, people lying out in the fields, people cycling along the roads. There were very few cars and no lorries or trucks to be seen, but a great number of freight wagons waited on the rails.

A woman wearing a knitted suit, aged about forty-five, sat in the compartment, and was soon to be joined by a stranger, a man a few years older. They established my nationality and that it was my first time in Romania, and they smiled at me regularly to make sure that I was happy. Then they talked non-stop to each other. After a while they moved out into the corridor to talk more. They concentrated on each other's words, without the slightest hint of sexual tension between them. The name Illescu again came to the fore.

We passed wooded hills, pasture land, some ploughed fields and dozens of old-fashioned sleepy villages.

The man got off a few stops before the woman. His town, she explained to me, was a Magyar town, inhabited by members of the two million Hungarian minority in Romania. Her companion had been a Magyar, she explained. Was she? I asked. No, she wrinkled her face in scorn, no she wasn't. The Romanians and the Hungarians were said to hate each other, but these two people had shown each other family snapshots, and behaved like old friends. Soon the woman came to her destination, and I went to investigate the restaurant, which I had been warned would be primitive.

There was an excellent lunch on offer which included chicken consomme, savoury meat, rice, potatoes, saurkraut, with ginger ale to drink, all for fifty cents. By the time I returned to my compartment two men were there, and I could tell from the words Ilescu and Petre Roman that they were talking politics too. When one man fell asleep his companion told me that they were both miners.

We had already passed a few towns with apartment blocks at the edges. One had chimney stacks close to the centre with sickly black smoke pouring out of it. As we neared the border with Hungary, more and more such stacks appeared side by side with fields of hay and houses with old traditional wells beside them. Most of the scenery was idyllic: we passed huge flocks of sheep and came to a wide plain, where the fields had no fences and tiny farmhouses lay in clusters. Still the cherry trees were in their full white bloom.

At the last town before the border the train began to fill up again. A Japanese tourist, and two other men, one large in his fifties and going all the way to Berlin, the other young and going to Budapest, came into my compartment. The Japanese had a time-table for trains all over Europe in both English and Japanese.

At the border there was a long stop. Groups of officials got on to the train. One man's job was to take a ladder into each compartment and check the roof space above the hatch with a torch. Because the train was crowded, this took a long time. The next group came to check passports. They were Romanian, and were now followed by another group, Hungarians, who also wanted to check passports. As

166

soon as they looked at mine, they asked me where my visa was. I said that I had no visa, as it was no longer necessary to have a visa to enter Hungary. Trouble, one of them said, and looked at me warily. Trouble. He handed me back my passport, but he did not stamp it, and I realised that he would be back.

Almost an hour later, after many other checks, he came back and motioned me to follow him. He left me with a senior colleague, who made it clear that I needed a visa and would have to travel back to the nearest town, wait the night and apply for a visa in the morning. I was looking forward to Budapest, and hated the idea of a night in some dull border town. I remonstrated with him until he let a roar at me in German. No one had ever shouted at me in German before, certainly not a man in a uniform. I stood back and looked at him for a moment.

He got off the train, my passport in his hand, and said that he would be back. He stood on the platform, laughing and joking with a colleague, aware that I was watching him from the train. I went back to my compartment and sat down. There were still checks being made on the train. Someone said that we would now not arrive in Budapest until almost midnight. My companions in the compartment knew that I was going to be thrown off the train, and I sat there feeling that I had committed a crime.

More time passed. Then the army man who had my passport came back down the train, handed me my document and a visa application form, told me that his colleague would collect the form and looked at me sternly. I could enter Hungary without a visa. I tried to sound grateful. By now we had been at the border for almost two hours and several times it seemed as though the train was about to start, but it was always a false alarm. Eventually, when it did start we were well and truly fed up. It wasn't long before a ticket collector came and moved the Japanese from first class to second class. The Japanese waved at us sadly as he was taken away.

We sat there in silence, until after about an hour, the man going all the way to Berlin went out and stood in the corridor. I asked the younger man in English what was the currency in Hungary, and he told me in fluent English that it was the forint. We began to talk: he was a doctor, living with his wife and child in a single room in Budapest. He had been born in Romania, and his family still lived in Transylvania.

As soon as the older man came back into our compartment, the doctor beckoned me to come out into the corridor. He didn't feel safe talking, he said. And there was something specific he wanted to talk about. Did I know what was happening now to the Hungarians in Romania? In the last decade of Ceaucescu's regime, things had become much worse. Ceaucescu had sent in Romanians to take over jobs from the Hungarians; the university had ceased to be an all-Hungarian institution; the regime had tried to dilute the Hungarian presence in Transylvania.

But now, the new government was going to be worse. There had already been violence against Hungarians in one town, Tirgu Morues, and this would be followed by further acts of discrimination. He tried to telephone his parents, who lived near Tirgu Morues, but the lines from Hungary had been cut off. He had no idea whether they were all right. He was still desperately worried.

I asked him, besides the language, was there much difference between Romanians and Hungarians? He stiffened in the corridor, and his tone became even more intense. He was still in his twenties, stocky, fair-skinned, sandy-haired. Words failed him. He searched my face for a moment, and then put his hands out and touched his own clothes and then his torso as if they spoke for themselves. Everything, he said, was different. Look at me, he said, do I look like a Romanian? For him, the word Romania stood for something primitive. Hungary, for him, was the Austro-Hungarian Empire, civilisation itself. My question had taken his breath away.

When he recovered, he talked about the changes in Hungary: even as a specialist his pay was meagre. Most of his colleagues were getting involved in business, opening shops for example, because the medical profession was so badly paid. Patients, also, were starting to pay their doctors, but it would still take years for a doctor in Hungary to have the same lifestyle and status as a doctor in Austria, for example.

His father was also a doctor. As soon as he mentioned his family he returned to the matter of Romania. He didn't know how he would contact them. He was in despair, not just about his family's present plight, but about the whole future of the Hungarians in Romania. It emerged, as we spoke, that his trip to Romania on this occasion was to see a relative, but more important, to buy some goods there and smuggle them over the border: women's make-up, he said somewhat sheepishly. It was much cheaper in Romania. He knew that I would think it really odd for a doctor - not just a doctor, but a specialist - to spend his Sunday smuggling make-up from Romania to Hungary, but what could you do, he said, you had to make a living.

He had been in the west a few times. He spoke about an occasion in Frankfurt railway station. An announcement came over the tannoy that a special fast train was going to come through the station without stopping. It would arrive in four minutes. He talked about standing there, watching this beautiful new modern train sweeping by on time. He talked with the same intensity as he had used when describing the difference between Romanians and Hungarians. This, for him, was the west encapsulated.

As we stood there in the corridor, I realised that I was going to need some forints, so I asked him to change money for me, and he did so, remarking later with frankness and satisfaction that he had done rather well out of the deal, although he hadn't ripped me off. I gave him what Romanian currency I had left for use when he next went smuggling. It would be no use to me. When we arrived at the station, he came with me to the street, and found me a taxi, giving the driver the name of the hotel. He was going, he said, in the opposite direction.

But the hotel was full. So, to my surprise, the driver radioed back to his base and asked them to telephone hotels until they found one which had vacancies. We had crossed the Danube at this stage, and driven up one of the hills above the city. Eventually, the radio told us of a nearby hotel and we drove there. The taxi fare was incredibly low.

In the morning I telephoned the Hungarian critic and translator Ferenc Takacs, and we agreed to meet that evening. Thus I had the whole day to explore Budapest. The city came as a shock that morning, not simply because I had just experienced the dismal atmosphere of Bucharest, but because for years I had imagined that every city in Eastern Europe was full of queues, empty shop windows and material desolation. Budapest, that Monday morning, was thriving.

I crossed the Danube and went around the market. The stalls were packed with fresh fruit and vegetables; the prices, if you still thought in dollars, were unbelievably low.

The electrical shops, too, were crammed with the most modern up-to-date equipment. There was even a shop in the city centre devoted exclusively to the sale of Lego. Package tours on the Riviera were advertised in shop windows. The only queue was outside an Adidas shop, and most of those in the queue were Austrian tourists. A thirty-six film Kodak roll cost just a few dollars; records, cassettes and CDs were cheap. How did this society run? How did it work?

Ferenc Takacs shrugged when I started asking him questions: such as when did Moulinex first come to Hungary? About the same time as it came to Ireland, he said laconically. It was important to remember, he said, that Hungary has always been different, that the prosperous city and well-stocked shops were not the result of any recent upheaval, that a mixed economy has been gradually emerging.

At the beginning of 1984, he said, he wrote an article for a state magazine; the article purported to be a publisher's reader's report on the novel "1984". He ended by saying that the book was excellent, publish it. The article was published, and not the book, and this was typical, in some way, of the mixture of liberalism and double-standards which existed in the last decade or so of communist power in Hungary.

Ferenc was spending a lot of time in his girlfriend's flat in the city centre, and his father was in hospital, thus his flat in a high-rise building in the suburbs was vacant, and I moved in there for a few days. I had been reading Juan Goytisolo's autobiography "Forbidden Territory" in which he writes about the strange freedom available to people living in such buildings on the unfinished edge of cities, a freedom which Goytisolo also associated with his homosexuality: a loosening of ties, a pure form of existence.

There was a strange comfort in living on the sixth floor in a building built in a hurry as people fled into the countryside, as economic and social systems collapsed and changed; the flat in a high-rise building offered a soothing calm anonymity. No tanks had rolled through the roads and passageways of this new complex; no mass-meetings had been held in the nearby square. The only history was the history of the Romans who had come as far as here and, daunted by the Danube, gone no further.

But the Roman remains all around were archaeological; there was no history here, only a vacancy swimming in the pure light which came into the windows of the sixth floor, a vacancy which each identity could inhabit, freed from the constraints which city streets or village life imposed. I asked Ferenc about this, if he felt different when he woke in the morning in Anna's flat in the nineteenth century city or in the new high-rise apartment on the outskirts. He felt it too, he said: you could shuffle to the shop across a piece of waste ground, and be a different person, than the one walking along the streets of the city.

The floors of Anna's flat had been sanded and varnished, and I wondered how, in a communist country, you could get such things done. She smiled: she had looked it up under services in the evening newspaper, just as I would in Dublin, and she had paid the people who came to do it.

The city was busy and beautiful, despite being, as Claudio

Magris says in "Danube", a copy of a copy, based on Vienna's version of Paris. Individual buildings such as the Parliament, the Cathedral and Gerbeaud's, the Art Nouveau cafe in Vorosmarty, stood out for their opulence and oddness. The turn of the river and span of the bridges added to the drama of the place. The Nazis had been here as well as the Romans, both forces haunted the Europe we lived in now. I came from outside that Europe, yet felt it as my heritage (much more than, say, the Celtic heritage), so these days here at the heart of things, crossing and re-crossing the Danube, were like catching for a moment through a window a glimpse of a long-imagined home, a world more real and complex than the place where I was ment to belong."

I wandered through the nineteenth century city. The grey, uniform apartment houses could have been in Paris, or Barcelona. Regularly at night you could see the rooms through uncurtained windows, the paintings lit by lamps, the sense once more of an undisturbed Europe. I stood at an intersection on my way to have dinner with Anna and Ferenc one evening and saw a huge, colourful Expressionist painting taking up the whole wall of a room; it looked like Max Beckmann, but it could have been one of his colleagues, or one of his imitators.

That night after dinner at Ferenc and Anna's I walked into the centre, stopping at bars along the way, all of which were doing a roaring trade, all of them full of young people. Loud Western music blared in the background. I wandered around Budapest until three in the morning, finding bar after bar open, there were taxis in the street, it could have been any European city.

One night we went to dinner at Gundel's, the best known restaurant in the city; the prices were high for Budapest and the service was elaborate. All around were the businessmen from Japan and Western Europe, ready to do deals with whatever new regime was slowly emerging. The food was good. A small number of musicians played rhapsodies to us, one of them a deeply melancholy, plaintive tune, which Ferenc told me was a reminder of the plight of the Hungarians trapped in Transylvania, and was, in fact, a nationalist hymn. It had all the slow, sad chords to bring tears to the eyes, but when it was played at a nearby table to a group of businessmen, the Hungarians among them remained stony-faced, unmoved. I watched one man's face maintain a mask of boredom, utter lack of interest as the tune reached its crescendo: there were more important things at stake in Hungary now than sentiment and badly-drawn borders. As the musicians moved away, the businessmen resumed their discussion.

Ferenc and I walked through the city in search of a bar. The streets, for me, were reminders of other streets, or were, at times, fascinating in their difference to anything I knew. For him these were the streets he knew as a child, which the tanks rolled through in 1956, streets which members of his family had known too. We were in two different cities as we walked along, I was still looking for telling moments, things to take note of.

Later, when we came out of a bar, we stood on the pavement watching what for me was a sign of the times, but for him was normal, something which had been there, he was sure, for some time: an all-night fresh fruit and vegetable stall, the goods beautifully packaged and displayed, the stall carefully lit, so that each object looked attractive. It was an Eastern Europe I had not expected to find.

Going in search of a railway ticket to Prague, however, had all the old comic routines attached to it which we associate with Eastern Europe. The queue, the single ticket seller disappearing regularly into a back room, the labyrinthine forms to be filled out and timetables to be consulted each time a prospective ticket-buyer arrived at the hatch. Foreigners paid in dollars, she made clear, as soon as she saw my passport. It sounded like a threat. I told her I wanted a first class ticket to Prague. Seven dollars, she said. I gave her ten dollars, and she gave me three singles in change. I wondered what the train would be like.

In the morning I took the tram and then the metro from my high-rise suburb to the station. The train was in good condition and left on time. I was sharing a compartment with a Yugoslav in his early twenties. He came from Sarajevo, and once we discovered that we had no language in common, we smiled at each other and settled down for a long sleepy journey. He was going as far as Bratislava. Almost as soon as the train left the station, a new comedy began, officials in all types of uniforms, officials of both sexes and of all shapes and sizes came to inspect us, our tickets, our passports, our visas, both entry and exit. One man checked the watermark on every page of the Yugoslav's passport while two colleagues of his looked on. Each time we were starting to snooze more came. The Yugoslav, as far as I could understand him, kept saying that this would never happen in Yugoslavia.

Soon, we were joined by another man, a chirpy looking fellow in his early forties with glasses. We were now passing lakes and wooded hills, and wooden three-storey houses. My Yugoslav friend went on into the corridor to have a cigarette; some of his cigarette smoke wafted into our compartment, causing the fellow with the glasses much obvious distress. Clearly, he was a member of the anti-smoke lobby, and as he protested, it became clear, too, that he was an American.

As he introduced himself, it emerged that he was no ordinary American. He was of Hungarian descent, and was obsessed with the greatness of the Hungarian past and the plight of the Hungarians in Transylvania. ("I fixed on this as my theme.") He talked about it as a great cause, how he had met people who were prepared to die for it. "This is no penny-ante place. This is the headquarters of the horsemen of Europe."

He hated Romania, and made a number of anti-semitic remarks about the new leadership. By this time the Yugoslav had fallen asleep, and I decided I wanted to sleep too. But the American continued, his voice becoming louder until he woke up the poor Yugoslav with his rantings about the greatness of the Magyar race. He had made his fortune, he said, in the manufacture and sale of lollipops, and now he wanted to do something for the world, so he was going to stay here and lend what support he could to Hungarian nationalism. He was desperate to publish articles in the international press.

There was now a low mist over the fields. We passed clusters of factories and then more pastureland and woodland. Despite the cherry trees which were abundant here as they had been in Romania, I was aware that we were moving slowly into a northern landscape.

The quiet Yugoslav and the fanatical American got out and were replaced in the compartment by three men, one of whom was blind. His two companions went off to the bar, and we sat there in silence, until he pressed a switch on his watch and a voice told him the time in English. He spoke good English and explained that he and his friends were chess masters and they had travelled all over the world: they were now on their way to a tournament.

We were nearing Prague now, the restaurant car was full of tourists. It was Friday, and soon it would be Holy Week and thus more tourists would be on the trail. I was meeting a friend in the Hotel Paris at four thirty, and I hoped that he had booked a room in what, the guide-book said, was a notoriously difficult city for a tourist to find accommodation.

There was a light drizzle in Prague and the Hotel Paris was much less majestic than the guide-book said. The streets around the hotel were quiet, as though there was a mass meeting elsewhere. This was, after all, the city in which the government was overthrown by the people simply gathering in the streets on cold winter nights and making their position clear.

I had been thinking more about the middle classes. In Budapest I had looked through an English edition of Marx's writings to see what his view was of the old European bourgeoisie: there seemed to be hardly anything, no awareness that while they would be instrumental in fomenting revolution as intellectuals and idealists, once the revolution had occurred, they would seek power, and idealists, power would slip away from them, they would educate their children and wait. Now, in Prague and elsewhere, their time had come. Dissidents were now former dissidents.

It was worth considering now who was going to benefit from these quiet, or in the case of Romania, not so quiet revolutions. Clearly, there would now be unemployment, two-tiered health services, fewer opportunities for at least half the society. But the professional classes would have their lot improved, and the old intelligentsia would return to their rightful place of power.

There was an interesting passage in Marx's "The Class Struggle in France 1848-1950", which went some way towards explaining - or more precisely, prophesysing - what had already happened over the previous few months in Eastern Europe and what it would mean: "All revolutions up to the present day have resulted in the displacement of one class rule by another," Marx wrote, "but all ruling classes up to now have been only small minorities in relation to the ruled mass of the people. One ruling minority was thus overthrown; another minority seized the helm of state in its stead and refashioned the state institutions to suit its own interests. This was on every occasion the minority group qualified and called to rule by the given degree of economic development; and just for that reason, and only for that reason, it happened that the ruled majority either participated in the revolution for the benefit of the former or else calmly acquiesced in it. But if we disregard the concrete content in each case, the common form of all these revolutions was that they were minority revolutions. Even when the majority took part, it did so - whether wittingly or not - only in the service of a minority; but because of this, or even simply because of the passive, unresisting attitude of the majority, this minority acquired the appearance of being the representative of the whole people."

On the day I came to Prague there was an article in the *Guardian* by the Hungarian former dissident writer Gyorgy Konrad about his recent visit to Prague. Previously, Konrad had made his position clear about the Iron Curtain and how it could be torn down: "It appears," he wrote, "that the intelligentsia - not the working class - is the special bearer of internationalism." He sought an "international intellectual aristocracy."

Now in Prague he admired the "certain old-fashioned dignity" about the waitresses and went on to say: "These people (the Czechs) cherished urban and middle-class traditions, still reflected in behaviours which neither German nor Russian domination was able to destroy." He went on: "The barmaid and the waitress (in another cafe) are pleasant, attractive ladies one would be glad to talk to in the company of friends," he wrote in a tone of old-fashioned and deeply-ingrained snobbery. He then went to meet Havel, the man whose photograph appeared in so many windows in the city. "A member of the Prague haute-bourgeoisie with a pedigree of 20 years resistance is in his proper place in this Castle." It is unclear whether Konrad believed that the Castle was Havel's proper place because of his resistance, or his class origins. The haute-bourgeoisie, in any case, had come back to haunt us.

The haute-bourgeoisie were not to be found that evening in the bars of Prague where the beer is twelve percent proof. These were men-only establishments, the clientele would not, perhaps, be the sort whom Gyorgy Konrad "would be glad to talk to in the company of friends". They were men on the way home from work; they talked in groups at long tables; the talk was animated, serious.

The city was quiet as darkness fell; that same strange absence I had noted in Bucharest was here too, not just of traffic or pedestrians, but of people using the streets as their own. Budapest, in comparison, was large, stately, remote, whereas Prague was intimate, accessible, gentle; a fairy-tale of a city rather than a epic. The area around the Old Town Square and the Charles Bridge was badly-lit at night which added to its medieval atmosphere; but even here there was something playful and open about the old quarter: the clock in the old square with its sense of harmony and symbol; the golden globes which adorned each pinnacle. There was a feeling, too, as you wandered around Prague in that spring of 1990 that all this was precious and could go, that a sudden burst of capitalism would produce traffic, more cars and lorries, and a need for offices. The city would become a set of square metres, each with its own value, and slowly, with no strategies to protect itself in an open market, Prague's fabric would be radically altered.

Kokoshka's wonderful painting of the city, done from the hill across the river, now hung in the National Gallery, close to where it was painted. It gathered together all the excitement of paint and colour, the joy of water and fluidity, with the semi-abstract, map-like city as viewed from a hill. Kokoshka's large painting depicted the city as it was, each district and contour was there, but it improved the view: Prague would look like this if somehow we learned to look at it in terms of colour and texture.

Everything new in the city, everything done since the time when Kokoshka flourished in Prague was over-designed: the light-fittings in the new hotels along the river, for example, came in grim, elaborate angular shapes. They were stern in their ugliness, and all around these new hotels there was not a single object which had any grace or beauty about it. A whole new school of design existed, whose main aim seemed to be to over-design, to provoke unease and discomfort.

You could eat in these new hotels, or indeed anywhere else you could find open in the city, for almost nothing. A large lunch served in an empty dining-room overlooking the river came to less than two dollars a head. Again, the service was impeccable. The waiters looked as though their uniforms and their manners had been acquired before the First World War - Gyorgy Konrad would have been pleased - and the food was heavy, filling and solidly cooked. As each day went by, it was hard not to think about how long this would last, how to wander in this city was to witness the last days of a whole system which could not continue under the weight of political change. How long would it be before these waiters would be working behind the counter in McDonalds. Or desperately looking for a job?

To find a hotel in Prague involved turning up early at the office opposite the Hotel Paris and joining the queue. Foolishly, we had booked a hotel, which cost as impossibly little as our meals, for only three nights. After that, the hotel could accommodate us no longer, and, on returning to the office opposite the Hotel Paris, we discovered that all hotels in Prague were booked out. In the street we were accosted by a very self-confident young man, who immediately offered to look after us. He could rent us a room in a house just off Wenceslaus Square, he said. It was privately owned, clean and cheap. Hesitantly, we followed him; his accent had an American edge to it as he offered to change money for us as well, the street rate being well above the official rate. We wondered if he wasn't some sort of crook.

He took us to the top of a nineteenth century house, showed us the room, which was fine, and introduced us to the owner who was surly. He showed us where the bathroom was and gave us the key. We could come and go as we pleased, he said, and took a wodge of notes from his pocket to change money for us. He had to go soon, he said, as he played tennis every day, and he had a match arranged, but before he went he stood back for a moment and looked at us. On the journey from the office to the house we had asked him about the changes in Czechoslovakia, and he seemed indifferent to them, although he seemed to dislike the communists more than the new regime. Now he stood there, more confident than ever, and asked us if we had any idea how much he had made on the exchange rate deal and the accommodation deal he had just made with us. We did not, we said. Enough, he said, to equal two weeks' normal wages. Anyone who worked was a fool. We had changed twenty dollars with him, and paid him less than fifty for the room for three nights: but the dollar in Czechoslovakia was so powerful that this small transaction, conducted so casually, would leave this fellow free to play tennis and generally doss instead of working.

One evening we went to the flat of an Irish friend who lived in the city. There were others present, Czechs who had been through the revolution. That night there was no talk about the old regime, and the revolution itself also seemed stale to them, a piece of over-recounted history. One of them had made heads of Stalin, Lenin and Gottweld, the Czech communist leader, from the wax from the candles lit where students were beaten up by police. And these were on display in various sizes, enormously comic, mad souvenirs, with tapers coming out of their heads.

When the talk turned to the present the tone changed. Too many people from the old regime were in positions of power, they agreed. Some of them had even more power now. Havel and some of his friends held power at the top and that was good, but, in every area of Czech life, it was agreed, this power was filtered through the ruling class of the old regime. Everywhere you went now, it was agreed around the table, you were told about the change, but no real change had happened, and no real change would happen until all these people, so willing to serve under the corrupt communist regime, were removed.

I remembered the same tone being used in Barcelona in 1976 and 1977 when the transition, as it is called, was taking place, when it seemed that only the names for things had changed and certain restrictions had been lifted, but the same people ran things. I remembered the same conversations in rooms late at night, the same feeling that real change would never come now. And I knew how deceptive those early days of a peaceful transition can be, how a whole generation was waiting in the wings in Spain then, as possibly in Czechoslovakia now, to take over the filtering of power and the managing of things.

On Sunday we passed the old Jewish cemetery which presented a most surreal image: thousands of gravestones crushed into each other, as though some accident had happened. All of them were at different levels and angles, all of the stones, with Hebrew inscriptions on them were different shapes, all of them had weathered in different ways. This strange variety of old tablets standing so chaotically above the clay, and above the bones of so many generations of Jews from Prague was beautiful and arresting. A young guide took us around it, showing us where the more famous members of the Jewish community were buried and explaining how, because the cemetery was part of the Jewish ghetto and thus could not expand, graves had to be stacked on each other. I asked him where the Jewish quarter had been, and he said here, all around here, all these houses for several blocks were Jewish before the war. It was hard not to stop and imagine it: how different it must have been fifty years ago, the tight, traditional community in these streets, now lost to us, for ever gone.

We went upstairs to the museum where the most heart-breaking exhibits were on show: drawings from Jewish children from a nearby concentration camp, recovered after the war. They had all the frail colouring and naive perspectives of other children's drawings; for a moment, if you didn't look at them too carefully, you mightn't notice that all of them dealt with the camp. So just as other children depict innocent scenes, these showed hangings, barbed wire, guards. There was no sense of fear in the work, no dark colours used to express horror. They drew what was around them and made it seem normal. A note explained that most of them were later transported to Poland and died at Auschwitz.

Down in the entrance hall there was a print for sale of a drawing of Franz Kafka, who came from here, with Felice Bauer. He must have known this cemetery, and this sense of impending doom for his whole world must have been there too for someone as sensitive and watchful and imaginative as he. In 1911 he wrote in his diaries: "I saw Western European Judaism before me in a transition whose end is clearly unpredictable and about which those most closely affected are not concerned, but, like all people truly in transition, bear what is imposed upon them."

His diaries are full of a sense of Prague: "The one pillar of the vault rising out of the Elizabeth Bridge, lit on the inside by an electric light, looked - a dark mass between light streaming from the sides - like a factory chimney, and the dark wedge of shadow stretching over it to the sky was like an ascending smoke." There are constant references, too, to his own childlessness. He imagined everything, the cold, slow, highly-technical systems the Nazis would use to murder the Jews are there in his story "In The Penal

178

Colony", and the sense of an irrational force operating against the guilt-ridden innocent is there in "The Trial". But nowhere in his diaries is there any sense that if he did have children, they would probably have ended making drawings of camps, treating the trappings of the system designed to wipe them out as ordinary, mundane, almost colourful objects. He was lucky he died so young; his three sisters and his friend Milena, as well as many others from his circle, died in concentration camps. One of his sisters died in Auschwitz.

Close to the graveyard, in the old Jewish quarter where there are no more Jews, there is a beautiful statue of Kafka on a corner building in the house where he lived and worked.

An hour before the train left there was an atmosphere of frenzy on the platform as Poles acquired large bags laden with bottles of beer from a shop, as well as various comestibles. Up to now the train stations had been sedate, calm, well-kept, but this was different, this train was crowded, and some carriages were full of men, all Poles, who could have been migrant workers, but were certainly excited at the prospect of going home. The train was going all the way to Warsaw. I was getting out at Katovice.

In my compartment there was a Polish family, two of whom were extremely fat. They seemed upset at a stranger joining them, but soon resumed an animated conversation. They were very cheerful; they talked, laughed and giggled almost without stop, and they told me that I would be arriving at five o'clock in the morning, so, they mimed, I had better not sleep too soundly. It was almost dark as we set out, and the usual round of inspections began: tickets, visas et cetera. My Polish companions laughed heartily each time an official left our compartment; they seemed to view authority with immense amusement.

The oldest of them went out into the corridor to have a smoke, and this was, for some reason, forbidden on our train. A Czech official walking down the corridor stopped and interviewed the smoker at some length, and then confiscated his ticket. He was somewhat shocked as he came back in, but soon he and his family all started to laugh again, rocking merrily at the pomposity of the official. But the Czech train authorities were taking the smoking in the corridor seriously, and between Prague and the Polish border my companion was interviewed a few times, and eventually fined the equivalent of one dollar, a great deal of money in Poland. He was handed back his ticket, and sat there silent, suitably chastened, before returning to his normal self, giggling at the good of it all in the company of his family. It seemed to me an extraordinary little episode, and I wondered, in my search for telling moments, if this wasn't a message from the Czechs to the Poles, if it didn't in some way typify the Czechs' view of their Polish neighbours: the sort of people who would smoke in the corridor against all the rules. But I wasn't sure that it meant anything at all, so I settled back and tried to sleep.

At the Polish border in the early hours a woman in uniform came and wanted to know how much money I had. This hadn't happened before. The Poles watched me carefully as I showed her my dollars and my travellers' cheques. For them, I knew, it would amount to a fortune, and I felt guilty then as she left and the Poles remained silent, as though taken aback by the sight of so much money.

Between four and five in the morning the train arrived in Katovice. The train station was busy with people going to work. I wandered through the dark city, which was bleak and cold in the hour before dawn, and found a hotel which changed dollars for me into zlotys and then I went back to the station where I found a Pole who spoke no English, but listened and understood where I wanted to go. The word in Polish is Oswiecim; in English we know it as Auschwitz. I showed it to him on the map. There were regular trains from here, because all of this area, and Oswiecim was less than an hour away, was heavily industrialised. I gave him the money and he bought me a ticket.

The train, just a few carriages, was old and moved slowly through a landscape dotted with chimney-stacks and sidings with wagons full of coal. Everything was untidy-looking, the machinery seemed old and in the dim light of the early morning the place seemed at the end of its tether. We passed large brick houses standing alone. These were the first brick houses in this style which I had seen, and they bore no relation to anything I had come across in Romania, Hungary or Czechoslovakia. This, then, was a new country.

The station, I knew, was some distance from where the camps had been, but these were the same train lines along which the condemned had been ferried. There were reports that locals had made signs to some of them, running their finger across their throats, and it was certainly true that locals continued as though nothing were going on at Auschwitz.

I got a taxi to the camp, noticing the brick buildings all along the way, the same brick buildings which made up the reception centre and small, modest hotel beside the museum at Auschwitz. I hadn't slept, and I hadn't understood what it would be like to arrive here just like that, I simply didn't feel now that I could tour the museum, have a look around and go again. I thought of leaving immediately without going inside, of going back to the station and catching a train to Warsaw. But I asked at the hotel if they had a room. The woman was quiet-spoken, and the atmosphere was like that of a convent, and it struck me that relatives of those who had been murdered here would perhaps wish to stay the night closeby, and this hotel was a facility for them. She said that she had a room. I paid her and took the key. At the top of the stairs there was a print of a famous Polish painting of a jester from the nineteenth century. It was an incongruous and deeply disturbing image, a mocking figure as I walked down the corridor.

The floors were covered in polished lino, and the room was small and bare with nothing except a bed and a table, and nothing on the walls. I slept for a while, awoken later by the sounds of a school tour visiting the site of the camp, the noise of young people's voices breaking the stillness. I got up and went downstairs, and into the building next door where I bought a ticket for the camp museum and another ticket to see a film on what Auschwitz was like when it was liberated.

Inside the camp it was difficult to know what to do as you walked along. Most people were subdued and quiet, and there was a note asking visitors to keep silence. I passed the office for receiving newcomers in the years when this was a death camp and walked up and down among buildings of the same brick as I had seen from the train where the prisoners had been housed. I saw the original gallows built for Rudolf Hoss, who had run the camp and was tried at Nuremberg. I looked at the map which explained which buildings were used for sterilisation, and which for extermination. I walked into one which housed a sort of expressionist exhibition about the horrors of what had happened, using black paint and light and photographs, but it was too distant, too artificial and I wandered out again, still wondering if it was right to be here, if the whole place should not be closed, fenced off in honour of those who died here, or had their lives destroyed.

As I walked down the path between the brick houses I found a tour-guide talking to his group in English and I followed them. "And now," he said, "we're going to go to gas chamber and crematorium number one, follow me." I walked away, back towards the gate, the words he used were so ironic - even poor Kafka could not have imagined such a thing. I decided to go to the film and leave. At least I had been silent as I walked around, but nothing you could do there would be right; being here in the first place had its ambiguities, its difficulties. It was probably wrong to be here.

The film did not help; the film, in fact, was a piece of propaganda made after the war by the Allied forces which concentrated more on the success of the Soviet Army than the plight of the inmates of Auschwitz. Some of the actual scenes were very affecting, but the old-fashioned newsreel voiceover was too full of the joys of victory. The film ended with Roosevelt, Churchill and Stalin joining together to talk about world peace.

I went back into the camp again, I don't know why. At least half the brick houses were closed up, but when I walked into one that was open there was another tour going on: six hundred people lived where we are now, a man was saying; it was a long, bare room. I went into the next house where in a long room a whole wall was made of glass, like you see in the zoo, and behind the glass were all the basins and pots the prisoners used, just lying there together at random. In the corridor there was another glass case, again from floor to ceiling, this time full of their shoes; another glass case showed wooden legs; another full of children's clothes; another full of hair; another full of gas cannisters.

A few daffodils were left at the door of the block where the standing cells had been built. The same guide was explaining how prisoners would be made work all day and then in the evening would be locked in here in a space where they could only stand, and left until the morning. Eventually, they would die, but it could take up to eleven days. Everyone who stood there watching these primitive systems of murder seemed cowed by the cruelty. Why didn't they just shoot them? Gas them? Instead they led them out to work every morning, and back in every evening, for the long night's half suffocation.

Of all the exhibits in old-fashioned glass cases on show in block after block the starkest were the suitcases, with the inmates' names and addresses carefully written on labels stuck to them, all of them now piled up. But worse, for me anyway, was the pile of discarded glasses and lenses, all mashed together. You stood there thinking of the books these people had read, of the things they had seen in their lives, of the light in their eyes, of the moment when their glasses were taken from them, when they wouldn't be any use anymore. Each lens carefully constructed to suit each person's sight now on display.

Along the corridors in rows were photographs of the prisoners, which were taken with that peculiar precision that interested the Nazis so much: each head shaved and in exactly the same position as the next. The photographer was clearly an artist and caught a peculiar direct beauty in each face. I walked along the corridors of several blocks looking at the faces, and there wasn't one which seemed disfigured or in any way diminished by the suffering they must have been going through. The way each head was tilted back and lit by the photographer gave each prisoner a gaunt fearless dignity. The photographs of the children, however, like the case of children's clothes, were almost unbearable to look at, but none of the children looked frightened, and all of them, like their parents, met the camera with equinimity. Below each photograph were details of the prisoners' date of birth and date of arrival and date of death.

At no time was the word Jew mentioned that day in Auschwitz, nor was it written anywhere. There was a large bunch of flowers in the place where Father Kolbe, the priest who allowed himself to be starved to death in place of another, had died. But there was no special Jewish commemoration.

I went into the restaurant and sat there for a while. When I looked up I saw the taxi driver who had brought me from the station in the morning sitting alone at another table. I joined him and we talked for a while. He told me that he could drive me to Krakow, less than a hundred kilometres away, for twenty dollars, and I decided to go. I got my bag from my room, and left the keys at reception. Outside the gates of Auschwitz there was a building, which was part of the general complex of the camp, but had now been taken over by Catholic nuns, who had erected a large cross in front of it. A nun was now walking up and down outside.

We drove to see the camp at Birkenau, just beside Auschwitz, which was now left as a shell rather than a museum. Four million people were killed during the war years in the two camps. It was a relief to talk to the driver and his wife when he went back to their house for tea before setting out to Krakow. He had gone to America to work for several years, he said, to raise the money to buy the house, one of those brick houses I had seen from the train, and start the taxi business. Prices had risen in Poland over the previous few months, he told me; before this, the rate for the dollar on the black market was high, but now it was more or less the same as the official rate. It was good to have the communists out, he said, but the real hardship would start now; the prices of some commodoties had gone up by as much as fifteen times.

The city of Krakow had been spared in the war, thus its medieval quarter was intact. At seven o'clock in the evening the streets were busy and the prices of such items as shirts or bags were for me incredibly low, despite the rise in prices. The second-hand bookshops were good. Away from Auschwitz anything was beautiful.

In the huge, wide, airy medieval square, big enough to house an old squat basilica, a nineteenth century cafe and a covered market in the centre, there were flower-sellers everywhere. In the cafe the trendy youth of Krakow had congregated wearing Western-style clothes and long hair and they sat there indulging in sexual play and general disrespect for their elders. One youth had a cigarette holder with the cigarette at right angles, and he puffed this to the delight and amusement of his colleagues. The Pope and Solidarity seemed light years away.

My hotel housed a casino, and after a dinner which cost two dollars, I wandered in there to find it full of Poles playing for dollars, some of them playing for a great deal of money indeed. In the outside world, the price of ham had risen ten fold, but here a young, blonde Polish woman was placing hundred dollar bills on the table as though they were zlotys. I couldn't understand it. Nor could I make sense of the long line of brand new taxis on the rank outside.

The city was dark and quiet at midnight, the vast, medieval square was like a city in itself. Suddenly, towards the edges of it, I caught a glimpse of a woman overburdened with bags and parcels as she flitted into the shadows of a side street. For a moment she seemed like a figure from the dark past, but soon I understood what she was: she was a baglady, a familiar sight on the streets of western Europe, but the first of her kind I had seen in Eastern Europe. She was the only figure still wandering the streets of Krakow in the small hours.

In the morning the city was beautiful, low and splendid in the raked light of spring; the flower-sellers were there again, and one of the old bookshops was selling modern etchings in the style of Durer depicting Biblical scenes; it seemed as though the methods used were the same as in the time of Durer. Outside, a real live trumpeter came to one of the openings in the spire of the cathedral and played as each hour came round.

I noticed a queue outside the church, and I thought perhaps there was a special tour, but when I went inside I realised what it was: it was a queue for confession. This was the Tuesday before Easter, and the priest was sitting in an open confession box in the church. The host was out of the tabernacle, it was dark inside the church and the priest could be heard whispering to the penitent. It was something I had forgotten about, the importance of confession in Easter week. Most of those in the queue were teenagers, or people in their early twenties, most of them had a devout and deeply serious look on their faces. The clothes, hair-styles and the lack of make-up made the women look like figures from old photographs of the 1940s or early 1950s. They stood there in the queue, preparing themselves for Easter, so different to the young people I had seen in the cafe last night. It was as though two different Polands were now growing up side by side.

The kiosks on the street corners were blaring out pop music from cheap cassettes: Simon & Garfunkel, The Police, The Rolling Stones. The shops were full of bread and fruit, vegetables and clothes. Only meat seemed to be in short supply, and there were queues for the shops which seemed to have bad cuts of meat on sale. Nobody, despite the recent rise in prices, seemed underfed, or hungry. One restaurant, overlooking the old square, seemed to be very popular, and there was a queue for lunch, but because I was alone, or spoke English, or because she liked the look of me, the haughty, impeccably-dressed woman in charge gave me a table at the window. The menu and the service once more were elaborate. I had beetroot soup, followed by duck and vegetables with beer, and dessert and coffee later. The decor was plush, the view magnificent, the waiter's self-importance beyond belief. The bill came to less than three dollars.

I caught a train to Warsaw the next day. The train was busy with people going home for the long Easter break. There was a sense of Easter in everything, not just in the queues for confession, but in the decorated eggs for sale and the traffic jam at the station. In the morning in Warsaw I walked along the wide, airy streets of the city, where there were long queues outside the cake shops, in search of the Jewish museum. The building was hard to find at first and when I walked into the hall the porter seemed surprised and immediately summoned a woman from a nearby room. What did I want? she asked. To see the museum, I said. She told me that I could go upstairs and look around and if I needed anything else, I could come back down and she would help me. There was hardly anything upstairs, a few blown up photographs of distressed people being led away, some momentoes, but nothing that could hold you for longer than five minutes. When I went back downstairs, the woman told me that she was busy, but if I waited, she said she would find me someone else. Eventually, a younger woman came and immediately asked if I wanted to speak in Hebrew. I said no, I simply wanted to know if this was the only museum, and if there were any monuments to the Jews in the city. I also wanted to know where the ghetto began and ended, and if it was marked now.

She smiled. There was one monument a good distance away, and there was one more room of the museum which she would open for me, but there was nothing exceptional in it. She didn't know why it was locked. No one came here much, she said. At one time there were half a million Jews in the Warsaw ghetto; now there were only three hundred religious Jews in the city; for a long time there had been no rabbi. Anti-semitism was still alive in Poland, she said; the communists had purged Jews from the government. But in general, there was little interest in the subject, and there was certainly no line marking where the ghetto began.

That evening I went in search of the monument, walking along the ground which was once the ground of the Jewish ghetto and now the site for a series of pleasant, leafy, suburban roads with low, well-kept blocks of flats on either side. No one I asked for help with directions looked even slightly afraid at being accosted in the dark by a stranger, and they all tried to help. Eventually, I came to the monument in a grassy square, the only sign now in the city of what happened to a crucial part of its heritage, which for many centuries must have added so much to Warsaw, and which thrived up to fifty years ago. Then in a few years it was wiped out, and wiped out too from the public memory.

So nothing is resolved, nothing redeemed. Poland still has not faced what happened on its soil with the collaboration of some of its people; so concerned is Poland with its own martyrdom that it is prepared to leave unresolved, unremembered what happened to the Jews. Europe, I thought, as I sat at the bar of the hotel, is entering a new phase in its irresolution: the problem of the Hungarians in Romania will be left unresolved, so too the plight of the Romanian gypsies, so too the relationship between the Czechs and Slovaks. And so too here in Warsaw they will have only this monument in the suburbs to the catastrophe which occured: the wiping out of a great culture.

It was easy to find ironies and good stories in the city, to visit the old Writers' Union to try and find the address of the new Writers' Union and be assured that it did not exist. (It did exist, but by the time I found it, it was Good Friday and being good Solidarity members, the new writers had closed for the day.) I went to the building which pays royalties to writers and asked if they could find me a writer who spoke English, and I sat there in the room examining each object - the drum-like filing system, the blinds, the lamps, the make of the desk and typewriters - and noting how different they were to anything I was used to.

There, I met a Polish woman in her twenties who had just returned from London; we walked through the city together for a

186

few hours. She explained that you didn't see the poor and the hungry because they hadn't the money to come into the centre. Even the price of a bus ticket now, she explained, had gone up to what was, for most Poles, an unbelievable sum. I told her about the queues for the cake-shops, and about the casino and the posh taxis in Krakow. There was, she explained, money moving, the prices going up meant that some people now had money, just like in the West, but in general, people's spending power had decreased enormously. As we walked along through the streets of Warsaw on that Holy Thursday, crowds were making their way to the many churches in the city centre. I was interested in this, and wanted to go and sit through at least part of one of the ceremonies, but my friend, who had recently come back from London, was having none of it. She refused even to look at the people going into the churches.

Poland, she said, was bad under the communists, but now under the Catholics it was much worse. Now, you turned on the television and instead of having to listen to party members extolling the party, you had Catholic priests telling people that if they had a dog, then get rid of the dog, and have another child. It took forty-five years to remove the communists and now it was going to take another half century to get rid of the church.

"Look," she said as we passed another bunch of churchgoers, "look at their *Solidarnosc* eyes." I thought that I understood what she meant, I couldn't be sure, but there was about each person who passed us, and indeed those in the queues for confession, a sort of mildness, a quietness, a sense of a guarded and cautious nature hidden behind each face.

I dined alone that night in my hotel; the service was as ceremonious as usual. A band came and played for a while, offering hits from the past sung in English; several waiters offered me Russian caviar in exchange for dollars. After dinner the waiter told me that there was a cabaret downstairs which guests in the hotel could attend free of charge. He seemed to think that I would enjoy it. I wandered down there some time after eleven o'clock and had a drink. The place was full, most of the clientele were Polish, but there were some tourists as well. Two men came on dressed as women and sang a song, then they did a cabaret act with vaguely sexual overtones, then a woman came on and did a half strip-tease, then the two men returned and the sexual overtones of their act became less than vague. It was nearing midnight now and soon it would be Good Friday. I had to remind myself that this was Poland, as the lady began to strip rather than tease, hanging around the place topless at first and then removing her underwear so that she was completely naked, and then doing a tour of the joint so that everybody could see her properly.

The old quarter of Warsaw had been restored after the war's destruction, but it still bore the marks of its reconstruction, as though it were built for tourists. There were a few bars, but they were uncomfortable and they closed early, and the only restaurants were in the hotels. There were a great number of priests and nuns on the streets. People walked as though they were busy, as though on the way somewhere. In these days around Easter people were usually on their way to a church. There was nowhere else to go in Warsaw, except home.

In the churches the ceremonies that day related, of course, to the martyrdom of Jesus, but the symbolism dealt, too, with the martyrdom of Poland. Not long before this, the Soviets had finally admitted the extermination of the Polish officer class at Katyn in 1940, and there were references to this in many of the churches. That night the host was on display in the churches, the side altars were lit up with graphics showing the resurrected Poland, the crowned eagle beside the monstrance with the host. Those who came to pray came to kneel in front of the martyred and risen Poland as much as the martyred and risen Christ.

That night after dinner a knock came to my hotel room door; it was a man in his seventies who had been contacted by the office which pays writers their royalties. He spoke good English; he was not a writer, but a translator, and his special field was the translation of technical terms. I asked him if he could tell me about himself, his background, and he seemed prepared to do this, prepared to help in any way he could. Although his father had Austrian nationality, he said, he felt himself to be Lithuanian, he had been brought up there, and was deeply involved at an emotional level with Lithuania's fate. He had also spent some of his teens in Siberia where his father was sent to work; everybody in those years, he said, was moved; hardly anyone ended up in the village where they were born. After the Second World War he had come to Poland, and he was a Polish citizen, he had also served as a junior diplomat in Yugoslavia.

This seemed normal to him, this disturbed life and disturbed allegiances, and I had to try and understand how much his story was part of a fabric: Central Europe over the previous seventy years. But it was still strange to me and fascinating. We turned on a lamp in the room and my friend kept talking. I tried to work out a few times by indirect questions to what extent he had been involved in the old regime, but his answers were evasive, not I think because he wished to hide anything but because involvement and non-involvement, especially in Poland, were complex matters. He seemed to feel that I would understand the nuances of his position, and at times I didn't.

Walesa, he felt, was finished; he would not win an election as President, and if he did he would not be a good President. He was successful, my friend believed, because of those with whom he surrounded himself, the intellectuals, the academics, the experts. Without them, he could not survive. My visitor had listened to Walesa just a few days previously when he was televised talking to ordinary people on the street. He had noted how rough and uneducated he sounded. He spoke no foreign languages. My friend did not think that Poles would elect such a man.

I asked him about the re-emergence of the bourgeoisie as a ruling class in Eastern Europe, but he pointed out that because of Solidarity and the Catholic church it was only partially true in Poland, but in Lithuania, he said, some of the emerging leaders were from the old families.

He was defensive about the Jewish question in Poland: a great number of Poles had helped the Jews in the war, he said. Also, the reason why there were so many Jews in Poland before the war was worth considering. They were appreciated and tolerated, he said, which is why their numbers grew to such an extent. But most of them had gone now, the ones who survived the war. After the purge of Jews from the communist party leadership in the late 1960s, they realised that there was no future for them in Poland, and most of them went to Israel.

He was tired now, he had talked a lot, he enjoyed talking English, he said, and he shook my hand, and went off, leaving me several pamphlets on the importance of developing an international language for technical terms, a matter to which I had not given much thought up to then.

In the morning the churches were full once more, this time of children having Easter eggs blessed, of members of the faithful who wished to visit the Blessed Sacrament, still on the side altars in the monstrance beside the paraphenalia of Polish nationalism, such as the flag and the crowned eagle. There were still long queues of penitents waiting for confession.

In the early afternoon of Easter Saturday I took a train to Gdansk, the old German port city of Danzig. The train was crowded and those who wished to find seats seemed to have no compunction about pushing, shoving, elbowing and, when in groups, stampeding their way into compartments. The rest of us were left sitting or standing in the corridors.

I was booked into a modern, high-rise hotel just beside the old city. From my window I could see the cranes and gantries of the great shipyards, stretching out for miles against the sky, beautiful now in the early evening. Gdansk, I discovered, is merely one third of a vast coastal conurbation; the other two parts are Sopot and Gydinia, and these contain a number of sea-side resorts. I went to Gydinia to buy a train ticket for Berlin, but suceeded only in leaving baggage at the left luggage, as the ticket office was closed. I walked down through the town, the shops were closed and there were few people around. The Baltic was calm against the pier and the sky was a billowy grey with patches of blue still visible. At the end of the pier there was a huge statue in stone to Joseph Conrad which had been erected in 1976; his customary signature had been carved into the stone.

I had been aware of his shadow in the great square at Krakow. ("The Square," he wrote, "immense in its solitude, was full to the brim of moonlight. The garland of lights at the foot of the houses seemed to burn at the bottom of a bluish pool.") His father died in Krakow when he was eleven: "In the moonlight-flooded silence of the old town of glorious tombs and tragic memories, I could see again the small boy of that day following a hearse; a space kept clear in which I walked alone." He was brought up in Krakow, remembered it and thought about it enough to re-visit it in early August 1914, the week when the war broke out when he was lucky to get out to safety.

Here now at the very edge of things on a huge plinth sat his shape in stone, his back to the mild green waters of the Baltic Sea, he was honoured in his own country, a place he had left in his own words "as a man gets into a dream".

Gdansk, too, was a sort of dream in which the beginnings of the modern world took shape: narrow streets of tall, severe-looking brick houses leading down towards gates to the waterfront. A world of merchant families, Protestant ethics, guilds. A dark Hanseatic city full of images of early wealth, the world which Thomas Mann described in "Buddenbrooks", reconstructed after the devastation of the war. Again, there were no bars and restaurants, merely the dark streets and the churches.

The churches here had photographs and exhibitions from Katyn, as though Katyn was part of the Eastern liturgy. Here was Poland once more, so insistent on its own martyrdom, so self-conscious about its status as victim that it could only contemplate Good Friday and Easter in terms of its own Passion and Resurrection. The nation and Christ were inseparable, and again here, on the side altars around the consecrated host were images not of Christ or of the church, but of Poland itself, the eagle, the flag and the resurrected nation. After mass, held at nine o'clock, people came to pray in the cathedral. At the side altar guarding the host and the paraphenalia of the nation stood two youths dressed in some sort of military uniform, they remained steadfast and serious for a long time, frightening in their military rigour.

There was nobody wandering in the old shadowy streets of the city once the churches closed, and there was no sound from any of the old merchant's houses. The city was dead, and in the morning there was nothing open either, no newspaper kiosks, or bread shops, no bars or cafes. Once more the only things open were the churches. I went to the main morning mass in the cathedral, the church was packed not by people who had what my friend in Warsaw had called "Solidarnosc eyes". All human life was here this morning, not just simply those with devout features and conservative clothes. It was impossible to generalise.

In the afternoon I went to Sopot where I had coffee in the Grand Hotel, built in the early years of the century and which backed onto the beach and the Baltic. To the side of the hotel was a long pier, and all afternoon families walked up and down the pier. There was no breeze from the sea, it was a calm day, the waves broke in a small curl without much energy. It could have been an Easter Sunday in any seaside town, and, indeed, the Grand Hotel could have been anywhere. There was nothing Polish about the scene except the dull, heavy Northern light.

But there was something else; there was nothing for sale. Outside the hotel, there was no bar or restaurant, there was even no stall selling drinks or ice-cream or sweets. The Poles seemed happy enough idling up and down the pier; most people in the west would have had an urge, a serious compulsion to buy something, however small, under such circumstances. It would be part of the day, but not here. Although the days of a market economy would be soon upon them, the spirit of enterprise - the corner shop, the market stall - had not yet broken out among the Poles of Sopot.

The cafe in the station at Gydinia was dreary and underlit; a number of badly dressed men were queueing for stew. I had bought a ticket for the night train to Berlin, but I had no sleeper. There was a real sense of misery in the cafe, as though it were a soup kitchen, and the stew looked as though it had been lying there for days. The men in the cafe had the glazed, watchful expression of people who live on charity, and it struck me that if you had no food at home, this was the only place you could come if you were poor and Polish, this was the only place outside the churches where there was a bit of heat and the possibility of company.

The ticket collector was a cheerful, tubby man, who sold me a sleeper for ten dollars, which he put into his pocket. He seemed pleased with the money, and made clear to me that I would have a compartment to myself all the way to Berlin where we would arrive at nine o'clock in the morning. For a few hours after the train started he sold Coca Cola for foreign currency, and made a vast profit, then he fell asleep in his own little compartment.

When we got to the border with East Germany it was discovered that I had stayed in Poland one day beyond my visa, but the official, having looked at me sternly, said it was all right, and handed me back my passport. We got out in East Berlin when the train arrived, and I caught a metro to the West. It was only then that it occurred to me that I could have stayed in East Berlin, but just then I didn't really understand how anxious I was to get to the West.

I found a hotel off the K'damm, and found, to my relief, that I was in a world I understood. I understood the vast shopping centre at the end of the street. I understood the crowds in the city, aimlessly window-shopping on a bank holiday Monday. The clothes, the manners, the public life of the street were all familiar and reassuring. I hadn't expected to feel like this. I had always considered Germany as alien in some fundamental way, and I didn't speak the language. But after more than three weeks in the East, I felt at ease here, back in my own world.

I rang a friend, the Irish painter John Noel Smith, and we agreed to meet in an Irish bar later in the evening to drink some Guinness. The Guinness was good, and the bar was open until very late. At one stage a fellow came in whom John Noel Smith had met before but couldn't remember where, and he sat beside us, and made the odd remark to us in German, but we were busy talking to each other and didn't pay much attention to him. Later, however, the waiter drew our attention to the fact that his drinks were being put on our bill, which we would pay at the end of the night. He had just ordered a cigar, a commodity which is widely available in East Berlin from which this fellow came, but he wanted a special one, one which he had seen advertised: he wanted a Schimmelpennick. The best Havana cigars could be bought cheaply in the East, but for him now what was advertised in the West was good; that was what he wanted. He was smoking it as though it were a new-found freedom.

I walked slowly through the city that night to clear my head after all the Guinness and cigar smoke. As I crossed a street I saw that a bar on the opposite side had disgorged its entire clientele, who were now standing on the streets, as many as fifty of them. All of them were men, and all of them were dressed from head to toe in leather. They seemed perfectly happy there at three in the morning. After the cities of the East, the silence of the night and the dullness of the streets after dark, this came as a bit of a shock, a big bevy of men dressed in leather gear, standing around.

The next day I went to the East, showed my passport to the guard, changed a small amount of money at the official rate which each visitor had to do, and a larger amount from a tout at the street rate. They were still selling bits of the wall along the street in West Berlin, but here you could walk down Unter den Linden and rent a hammer and chisel from a number of enterprising youths, paying, of course, in hard currency, and join in the destruction of the Berlin Wall. This wasn't as easy as it sounded: the wall was made of concrete and all you could chip away were tiny fragments, it would take real skill to get a big chunk. So most people contented themselves with having their photograph taken with the hammer and chisel at work against the wall.

The city had that same stillness and artificial air as Warsaw, as though it was pieced together according to some plan, but it was, in some ways, more attractive than West Berlin. I watched a group of men take sausages and beer from a cafe to an outside table and stand there casually studying people moving up and down. The table was old and rusty, and the cafe, too was run-down. Such a scene after twenty-four hours of air-conditioned West Berlin was oddly comforting. To be here, to stay here for a few days, would be to avoid the battle for space and status that was going on in West Berlin. I didn't know where I wanted to be. I went to a museum on Unter den Linden which had a huge exhibition of the recent revolution, already history. Tickets for the opera across the road were incredibly cheap. I bought a CD of Brahms' German Requiem for about a quarter of the price it would cost in the west.

Crossing back into the west meant you didn't have to be on your guard any more, on the look-out for telling moments. The bar where you ordered a beer had nothing strange about it, the currency was hard, the decor was international, the barman's manners were easy to understand. It was over; I was home.

I went out for dinner that night with John Noel Smith, his German girlfriend and her sister. Both women spoke English and were interested in fashions and trends. The business of German re-unification filled them with horror. The opening of the Wall had caused them to visit East Berlin and take a good look around; they were appalled by the grottiness of it all, by the way buildings damaged during the war had still not been repaired, by the fact that when you moved away from the main streets you were in a ghastly run-down city.

And the people. The people came to the West every Saturday and formed long queues in the supermarkets and made life very difficult. One of the women laughed: you always knew the East Germans, you could see them coming in the distance, they were the ones eating bananas. It seemed that they didn't have bananas in East Germany.

We went to Einstein, a fashionable bar away from the centre in an old house. Everyone there was carefully dressed; everything from hairstyle to facial expression was carefully chosen; it was all cool and sexual and watchful. Most people who live in Berlin work hard, it was explained, and don't go out much, but when they do go out they make a night of it, another aspect of the choices which people make, the freedom not just to say this, but to make it true, by discussing the possibilities now, what places are in vogue, what places are old-hat.

We checked out a few places. It was now after two. There was a feeling that if we didn't find exactly the right place, to match our mood, then we would leave it and go home. Eventually, we settled on a bar, ordered beer and the four of us stood in the centre talking, drinking and looking around. Two boys near the door were kissing each other, if not passionately then with a certain vigour. But, my companions explained, this wasn't a gay bar; it was, they said, mixed. Choosing this place was like reading a menu, or going into a supermarket, and knowing the score, knowing what you wanted in a world of infinite variety. Have another drink, someone said, this place is open late, and getting home won't be a problem. The taxis are running all night.

The Sunday Independent, May/June 1990

VII.
ENNISCORTHY
1992

What difference will the Single European Market make to Ireland when it is introduced in 1992? Opinion is divided on how it will affect us. But some of us know already, because there are places in Ireland which have already been through the process of 1992.

I come from one of those places, and I spent Christmas there. It is a beautiful town in the south east - a market town for its rich agricultural hinterland. It has a thriving mart, and ten years ago it had a thriving flour mill, a thriving maltings and a thriving bacon factory, all three of them were family owned and all three provided employment for all sections of the community. Two members of my family worked in the mill; in our housing estate a large number of families made their living from the mill or the maltings; so too, in my school a great number of my classmates' fathers worked in these industries.

The whole atmosphere of the town depended on these factories: on certain days you could hear the pigs squealing on their way into the factory. In summer there was a permanent smell of dust and grain in the vicinity of the mill and the maltings. In the 1960s when I was growing up, both industries were expanding; over the hump of the railway bridge the maltings added new iron lungs, the mill built new offices beside the silos.

And the owners seemed patrician figures: Old Mr Browne who owned the mill, when we saw him, was remote and exceptionally polite; there was a kind of steely innocence about him. It seemed natural that he should run a mill. The owners of the maltings had their own mystique, they had once lived in the Castle in the middle of the town. In the sixties, the owner of the bacon factory built a huge modern house outside the town. No one had ever seen so much glass.

These people had inherited the earth and we had inherited our place in the world they created. But there had been changes: all around stood old stone warehouses, derelict now because transport was easier and storage of grain and other materials not as important. There were also remnants of an old mill in the town, a sign that technology was improving, that a mill wheel was out of date now in an era of electrification.

But none of these monuments to times gone by had prepared us for the changes which were to come: at first they were small, just changes in name, the name of Mosse was added to Davis of the mill, Roche's maltings became Roche Gibney. No one thought too much about this, it was part of the inevitable process of modernization.

Now, ten years later the bacon factory is gone and the mill and maltings have been scaled down, and are as good as closed. They did not close because of falling profits, or shifts in the market. They closed because of take-overs, they closed because a larger conglomerate moved in seeking a larger monopoly; they closed because such small town industries are a thing of the past, pre-1992 Ireland. They will not open again; the processing of grain, which has been the basis of the town's economic life for hundreds of years, is finished.

In the meantime, the roads have improved beyond belief. People keep marvelling at the new stretches of road, all built with the aid of EC money, which is helping to prepare Ireland for 1992. At the moment they are building a new bridge in the town, it is badly needed, what with all the container trucks which trundle through. Suddenly, the town has become a place on the road to somewhere else. It's a blueprint for what will happen elsewhere in Ireland in the decade to come. It's already happened to us. We know what it's like. There's nothing more that 1992 can do to us now.

A Sense of the Eighties, RTE Radio, December 1989.

ACKNOWLEDGMENTS

In the ten years during which these pieces were written, truth was often stranger than fiction. The news report itself never seemed enough: the complexities and contradictions behind what the papers said cried out to be explored. In Ireland during this time a number of magazines flourished which encouraged its contributors to write five thousand words rather than five hundred, and spend a month on a piece rather than a few hours. I am grateful to the editors who gave me a start at this sort of work, in particular John Doyle and David McKenna at *In Dublin* and Vincent Browne at *Magill.* These pieces were written without the prompting of a daily deadline (except the account of the Ireland Italy match which was written in half an hour after the match while simultaneously trying to monitor Jack Charlton's press conference) and appear more or less as originally published (with the exception of the Eastern European piece which is printed here at more than five times its original length). I am grateful to the other editors who comissioned the pieces, in particular to Aengus Fanning and Anne Harris (*The Sunday Independent*), Fintan O'Toole (*Magill*) and Ferdia MacAnna and John Waters (*In Dublin*). There are others to whom I am also grateful for their help and encouragement and these include: John Boland, Stephen Dixon Marlene Lyng, Robert Armstrong, Aidan Dunne, Mary Raftery Gene Kerrigan, Derek Speirs, Eileen Pearson, Tony O'Shea, Rita Byrne, Mark Brennock, Richard Kearney, Ronan Farren, Edward Mulhall, Betty Purcell, Pat Kenny, Cathal Goan, Julian Vignoles, Mary Dowey, Mary Holland and Eamon Dunphy. I am grateful to Maureen Gillespie for locating some of the pieces and to Helen Rock for reading them. Dermot Bolger of Raven Arts Press deserves a medal for his kindness and patience.